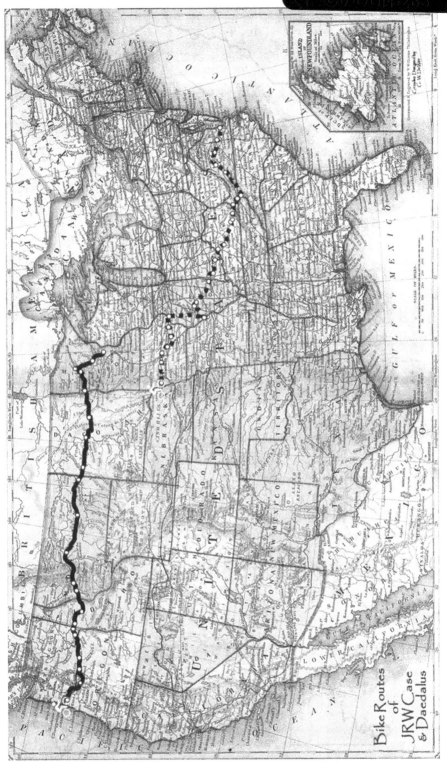

Bike Routes
of
JRW Case
& Daedalus

This is an important book, in turns powerful, funny, poignant, harrowing, and heartfelt. We meet a narrator who is processing through movement, community, and upon one of the biggest and most dramatic "ruptures" of his adult life; one that shifted not only his identity, but the identity of the community, and the country, as well. This is a fantastic premise for a book...one written in a propulsive, tightly controlled narrative.

I am deeply moved by the connection JRW Case felt with one particular victim of Columbine and his lacking a sense of belonging.... For the storyteller, of course, the perspective is unique because he was in direct contact with the events and personally invested. But the book tells an American story—of war, expansion, guns, "freedom," and people building new lives from the ashes of old ones. We are all invited by the strength of the narrative to reckon with this. The aftermath of Columbine is the aftermath for *all* of us.

In an early scene marked by indecision, the author wonders: "Is this the story of five guys who attempt to band together out of a shared interest in completing a bicycle tour across the continent, only to find that one by one the group grows smaller and smaller? Or is this the story of an aging parent who wants to reconnect with his prodigal child, an adult daughter and Iraq war veteran? Or is this the story of a solitary, self-sufficient cyclist who gets blown over by a ghost from his past, and has to come to grips with his long-avoided beliefs in a higher power?" *Cycling Through Columbine* is all of the above, and more.

—Emily Rapp Black, author of *Poster Child: A Memoir*

BOTTOM DOG PRESS

HURON, OHIO

# CYCLING
# THROUGH
# COLUMBINE

## JRW CASE

MEMOIR SERIES
BOTTOM DOG PRESS
HURON, OHIO

ISBN: 978-1-947504-31-8
Bottom Dog Press, Inc.
PO Box 425, Huron, OH 44839
Lsmithdog@aol.com
http://smithdocs.net

**CREDITS:**
General Editor: Larry Smith
Cover & Layout Design: Susanna Sharp-Schwacke
Photos: Author, Lee Case and Frosty Wooldridge

**ACKNOWLEDGMENTS:**

We thank all those who help support the publication of
this book through the GoFundMe program. Further Acknowledgments on page 253

**OTHER WORKS BY THIS AUTHOR**

*Are You Still Listening? 1969 Stories and Essays,* Brent Green &
Assoc., (2019) Contributing essayist.
*Icarus and the Wing Builder,* Kalliste Productions Ltd. (2014).
*Daedalus Rising,* Books to Believe In (2008).

# TABLE OF CONTENTS

## DEDICATION

*for Kyle Velasquez, the victims of Columbine,*
*everyone involved in the recovery,*
*and anyone still living in its*
*shadow.*

PROLOGUE

*April 20, 1999*
*Littleton, Colorado*

Once inside the library, they shot the fat, brown-skinned kid first. He was trying hard to be unobtrusive. It was a coping skill, a tried-and-true technique for staying out of trouble. Kyle knew that the world and the random people who crossed his path on any given day, were kinder and nicer when a smile showed on his face. But even with a smile as shield, his six-foot-three body betrayed him sometimes. Nature had a way of making him bigger and stronger every year. To counteract against this growing size problem, Kyle had a bag full of tricks, ways to make himself smaller, unheard, and unnoticed ("April 20, 1999").

That day fire alarms blared, invasive, and booming. The first one sounded at 11:44, activated by a homemade bomb exploding in the cafeteria. Cordite and smoke filled the air until the ensuing fireball activated the cafeteria sprinkler system. From then on, the entire building pulsated with the fierce energy of fire alarms and pressurized water (Erickson, 33). Anyone of us would have been scared. Kyle was too. He would have wanted to go home, back to his mother's house, or at least find a safe place. Outside the building, police sirens wailed. Helicopters *whaup, whaup, whauped.* The thought of leaving into the staccato sounds of gunfire and all that confusion must have filled Kyle with dread. Maybe it would be better to stay inside for a while longer. Find another favorite place. He walked to the sunshine and warmth of the second-floor library and hid there with his back to the door—in plain sight.

That's where Kyle was sitting, turned away from the door, when two classmates, one seventeen years old, the other eighteen years old, entered the room. They were young, white, and full of rage. Kyle must have heard them come in. Their armaments, absurd—neither boy had any kind of weapons training—were stupidly out of place inside the public high school of a suburban community in the first blush of spring.

Kyle probably kept his gaze on the indifferent screen of a computer terminal pretending not to notice the intruders. But his smile could not shield him that day and neither could any of the other techniques he used to try and disappear. All they could see was his broad back and shoulders—and that was where the younger one aimed his shotgun, its butt and barrel sawed off, and fired ("April 20, 1999").

Kyle Velasquez's plaque decorated for April 20, 2019 Memorial

# CHAPTER 1
## THE VIEW FROM THE BACK OF THE PACK

*July 1, 2017*
*Astoria, Oregon*

"Last call for beer before the campground!" the first cyclist barks, his left arm extended, index finger pointing toward a well-lit convenience store. It is a move and a statement with multiple layers; a turn signal for sure, for any cars following behind to notice that a line of five bicycles plans to make a left-hand turn; and it's an observation by the leader to the rest of us that a roadside attraction worthy of note is going by; and finally, to my ears, this is a suggestion that we are all due for some group bonding once we stop for the night.

*We must be close*, I think to myself, and watch the first two bicyclists make a sweeping left turn across the darkening highway, moving almost in tandem like the two old friends they are. Neither one even looks back. I'm last, the newbie, on my first visit to the grey skies and humidity of coastal Oregon, watching from the back of a pack where speeds top out at eleven or twelve miles per hour, and with no idea how far we've yet to go.

The eclectic cyclist from California goes next, the one with the Tibetan prayer flags extending from the flexible aluminum pole attached to the rear frame. He's been bike packing up and down this stretch of coastline for years, probably knows exactly where we're headed. *He's the logical choice for pulling into the parking lot and buying the beer.* But through the intersection he goes, a couple of long seconds behind the two leaders. That's right where he stays, pedaling on in their wake.

It's good to be cycling again. The world feels like a better place when I'm balanced on a bicycle seat, where the view is far different from the one I'm used to—inside the molded plastic and metal of a car. I can smell the trees and a distant ocean. I can hear the sounds of the earth through the rolling beat of the tires.

*Surely, Gerry will stop.* I've been following behind the Irish flag that flutters from the back of his bike ever since we left that big-box grocery store an hour ago. And there he goes, heading for the parking lot of the convenience store. *Thank you, Gerry, for your good judgment.* I let the bike coast, planning to slow down and stop, to follow him into the store, and then help out with the transport issue. *Oh shit. No! It's just a head fake. He's still pedaling, taking a shortcut through the parking lot. He's trying to close the gap, not make it bigger.*

What began as a simple left turn is happening so fast that there is no time to call out to anyone. No time to let Gerry know that I am already cruising into the parking lot, taking the hint, and about to make a contribution to the local economy. *Getting beer will make a good first impression, break the ice.* I lean my bike against the store's outer wall, not bothering with the lock. I decide to keep an eye on it through the store windows and walk inside. *Got to hurry. Choose something fast.* Behind the counter, a young clerk stands and watches like a silent sommelier. I ask him for a suggestion. He recommends an IPA from a local microbrewery. I take his advice, but the glass bottles turn out to be a rookie mistake. Oblivious, I carry the six-pack back to the bike and start opening panniers, stashing cold bottles one at a time, and somehow making room where before there was none. *It's Saturday night. There are places to go, things to do. I feel good.*

I throw my leg over the crossbar, snap my cleat into the pedal and push, harder than before, hopeful that the rest of the party is just a few minutes ahead. But the light is fading, replaced by shadows from the native spruce and hemlock that crowd in on both sides, close enough to feel like the road has become a darkening tunnel, the air inside humid and dense and tinged with salt, and with more than enough mystery to make the sweat-soaked hair on the back of my neck rise. I take a quick look off to the side. There could be any number of ghosts from my past lurking within and curious about this journey. I look into the depths of the shadows but see nothing, no sounds or movement, and no sign of my cyclist friends. Once again, my legs pick up the pace.

12

Sweat collects on the inside liner of my helmet. Sweat seeps into the vibrant colors of my shirt. I miss the cool elegance of Colorado's dry air. With affection, I think of the people I've left behind to come on this trip. High on that list is Lee, my daughter. While waiting around in a motel room one day before the other cyclists were expected to arrive, there was plenty of time for packing and repacking the panniers of the bike, and plenty of time to compose a compelling text, one that might tweak Lee's interest in the unusual circumstances in this undertaking. I wanted that first text to be the start of an ongoing dialogue between us, not unlike the emails we once exchanged during her first deployment to the Persian Gulf. It feels like we have been drifting apart ever since she was discharged. Lee rarely answers emails. Phone calls, forget it. With texts though, there's room for some hope. They don't require the same investment in time or interest. So, I reached out to her from the virtual keyboard of my cellphone: "I'm in Astoria, Oregon, meeting up with four other guys with a shared interest in riding our bikes across the USA. About to meet three of them for the first time."

\*   \*   \*   \*   \*

Long before Columbine, I wasn't sleeping all that well. My routine was to wake up early enough to make coffee, lounge for a while at our round kitchen table and read. A wood-burning fireplace and bookshelf filled one wall of the adjacent room, furnished with a grey corduroy couch, reading lamp, and a small TV. It was simple and ordinary and my favorite space in the house, this large area where we shared meals together. A small three-step kitchen filled the opposite corner, separated from a sturdy round table and chairs by cupboards and a countertop laminated in faux marble plastic. All of it with a view to our rectangular suburban backyard.

This open dining area was also the place where Lee and I often sparred, verbally, over which one of us would finish her math homework. Our habit, before Columbine, was to save up these confrontations until late in the day, for the times in which its lingering stresses were still accessible, but at least dinner was over. I had four or five dependable recipes that could be thrown together in thirty minutes or less. We ate pancakes when the budget was tight, and pizza when finances were better. But on the days when Lee signaled that she expected help with her algebra, she would linger at the maple table, stewing over the open math book. She was an excellent student who hated math. Smart, articulate, and sassy, she was an avid reader with a strong sense of social justice, the kind of student that English or history teachers encourage to stay in school and become a writer or journalist someday. But Lee did not like math. She also refused to eat meat. Not that the two were related in any way, only that Lee was ardent in her beliefs. And if there was going to be a struggle, it typically began with her returning to the kitchen table to stare at her math book with a long-suffering look, a blank piece of paper in front of her, and then allowing the silence to build. Suddenly, the book would close with a slap. And with a roll of her hazel eyes, she would ring me up like an old-fashioned cash register and declare, "I just don't get it."

So, it felt like a gift that Wednesday morning—one day after the entire community was rocked by a mass casualty event inside a public high school—when Lee came downstairs to join me at the same stout table just to talk without confrontation or strife, or algebra. She had worked late at a neighborhood bookstore the night before; could not have had more than a few hours of sleep, and, I have always been an early riser. Cody was spread out on the well-worn carpet, looking and smelling like an aging lab should, as Lee walked into the room with one of our two cats cradled in her arms. The dog's ears perked up. I put the kettle on to boil. The tail wagged, slightly. He did all the things a Labrador retriever can do to say hello without bothering to rise up and off his haunches. *Maybe I woke her up, rummaging around in the kitchen.* Lee pulled one of the four heavy chairs out from its resting place and sat down. "Want some tea, Lee?" I asked, mimicking the rhythm of the old Paul Simon song.

"Shore do," she replied, looking down at the table and towards the cover of the book I was trying to read.

"How was work last night?"

"Real busy," she answered, emphasis on the "real."

"Did you get any sleep?"

14

"Not so much. That's why I came down here to see what's going on...People just kept coming through the door. That store was packed, all night."

"Anybody famous in the crowd?" I asked, realizing that media personalities and reporters from all the major networks and newspapers were being drawn, irresistibly, to the unincorporated geography of south Jefferson County. All the available public parking near Clement Park was filled to overflowing with their vans and RVs. The reporters tasked with finding the right eyewitness account that would imbue their story with the right blend of fact and legend, to impart the magic required for it to rise like a helium balloon above all the others being written or broadcast that day. Far more than one thousand students and staff were inside the building when the first bullets were fired, all of them potential witnesses.

"Not yet," Lee answered, still stroking her peaceful cat. "But people are coming from all over. There was this big group of Christian ladies from Iowa, or maybe it was Missouri. They told me they were looking for Columbine, but they found this little shopping center with a Barnes and Noble bookstore instead...a little Starbucks sign out front. What are you gonna do except get in line? But what's really nice...nobody's in a hurry. And it was past midnight when the manager finally lit up the closed sign."

"Wow! That is late," I said, setting a steaming mug of tea in front of her. "When do you have to go back? Not tonight I hope."

Lee set Earl aside to warm her hands on the cup and gently blow across the hot surface. "We didn't see that many students last night. There are a couple of really big churches over in that part of town. They kept their doors open all night...The flyers were everywhere..." Seamlessly, she moved into a voice derivative of a television evangelist and continued, "Come on down...for 24-hour hot chocolate and cookies. Seriously, I had three different leaflets stacked under my windshield wipers after work. 'Free Hot Chocolate-Donuts-Coffee...Come In and Get Warm at Calvary Chapel.'"

"You're making me want to drive over there and check it out," I said, returning to the table with a personalized mug. "Maybe I'll have time to stop by the bookstore after work."

"Come if you must, Dad," Lee responded with candor. "But expect parking to be a bitch. And…you will definitely have to wait like everybody else."

"No problem," I said. "These are unusual times, and I don't want to hide from this. I want to see and hear and feel what's going on here! Experience it for myself."

Lee took a sip from her mug, looked up and nodded with approval. "Did you hear about the car in the parking lot?" she continued, switching topics with ease. "This is so cool."

"Which one?"

"Rachel Scott's…That girl had friends."

"Maybe a little. What about it?"

"They're only showing the video on every channel. Some of her friends found her burgundy Honda in one of the student parking lots, just sitting there where she left it when she got to school Tuesday morning. Like the car was still waiting for her to return. Her friends painted the windows with drawings and wrote messages to her to see from heaven. They piled up flowers, front to back. Candles on the bumper. Stuffed animals. The look keeps changing all the time."

"That's beautiful. They've made a shrine to their friend…"

"On one news program, they showed a mob of kids gathered around this well-aged car, singing and praying. You would have liked it."

"The press must be having a field day over there," I said, inserting some skepticism into my tone.

"Oh yeah," she agreed. "And one of the things they're reporting is how some of the school jocks have been taking it out on the gay kids ever since."

"And that's somehow different from any other day?" I wondered aloud. "Reporters love to speculate…"

"OK," Lee interrupted. "So, you're saying that jocks should be bullying the gays and the Goths."

"Of course not," I replied. "I just want to make a point about how we all love to speculate about patterns and motive, especially after a gruesome murder. But reporters use their microphones to lead people and witnesses around like sheep. They get paid to pack their stories with as much drama as one can hold, without taking any responsibility for objective…."

"Truth?" Lee interrupted, foreseeing one of my favorite themes.

"Yesterday, the story was all about two vengeful killers targeting jocks. But this morning, I look at the pictures of some of the victims and see a diverse bunch of faces. I'm saying that the shootings were probably more random than the press wants to acknowledge."

"Sounds like you might be drinking from the Kool-Aid, Da, over there at the county," Lee replied, referring to the Jonestown massacre of an earlier decade, a mass murder-suicide orchestrated by the leader of a religious cult who had transplanted his flock from San Francisco to Guyana in South America. Over nine hundred followers died at the scene, too many of them children.

"Yeah, you're right," I answered wistfully, "And I keep going back." Listening to my daughter talk about her evening near the epicenter of this massacre would turn out to be the high point of my day. But I left for work that morning able to tell myself how good it felt to feel confident and engaged, maybe even grateful. Grateful that my kids were alive and well—both of them—and that was enough. It was everything. It felt, at least for a while, like a good day lay ahead or at least a better one than the day before. My days as an overfed, introverted county employee were numbered.

\*    \*    \*    \*    \*

Almost twenty years later, I find myself standing in the parking lot of a rental car company in Astoria, Oregon, alone, and in charge of a fully-loaded bicycle and wondering, *How did I get here? My Denver home is over one thousand miles away. Auspicious or otherwise, this must be the beginning of a great geezer bicycle ride from the Pacific Coast of Oregon to Bar Harbor, Maine.* I was nervous. I look around for a store that might have coffee to go, but there's nothing like that anywhere in sight in this small town. Except for our leader, I have yet to meet any of the other guys, until another man in cycling gear and about my age walks over and asks, "You wouldn't be waiting for a couple of cyclists driving over from Portland, would you?"

"Sure am," I reply, relishing the wave of relief that comes with confirmation that this is the right place and time. "Robert. Good to meet you." From my reading of a few introductory emails, I remember that none of us are working at eight-to-fives anymore. But I don't consider myself retired and on the good days, I prefer to describe myself as an out of work writer. There was a brand-new journal in the front handlebar bag of the bike, a couple of pens, and a mechanical pencil. But this is more than the opportunity to write a bicycle travelogue. It's a journey, a personal quest to reclaim some lost health and vitality. I resigned from the career several years ago because of the emotional and psychological toll it was taking, and for the added benefit of opening up more time and opportunity to practice the art of writing. And like everyone else in this band of five cyclists, I bring a lifetime of memories, a personality and temperament.

"Frank," the fellow cyclist replies, "Just drove up from California."

We shake hands, exchange cellphone numbers, and look over each other's bicycles. Mine was boxed up and shipped from Colorado to an Astoria bike shop where it sat in a musty basement, waiting for reassembly and until I could arrive from Portland with the rest of the gear. I am confident with basic bicycle mechanics, adjusting the disc brakes and gears, and fixing the occasional flat. I even carry the tools for making these basic repairs on the road, as well as two spare inner tubes. One of them is buried deep down at the bottom of a front pannier. The other sits right inside the handlebar bag for easy access, along with an assortment of snacks, maps, and tools that I might want or need on any given day. It didn't take long for me to reassemble Daedalus at the shop, the gears shifting true, and the touring bike reborn for its inaugural cross-continental ride.

Today's gathering on the bank of the Columbia River is just prologue. Our leader, Forrest, is enough of a traditionalist to insist that any ride across the USA worthy of the name begins and ends on the shoreline of an ocean. Astoria is a quaint little town known for its sea lions and salmon fishing, but we are miles upriver from where its mouth drains into the Pacific. Two centuries before our arrival, Sacagawea, Meriwether Lewis, and William Clark wintered here before returning to St Louis, Missouri to complete their brand of long-distance travel and exploration. For us cyclists, the windy coast is still several hours away by bicycle.

This is not a commercial trip. There is no support vehicle. No prepared meals will wait for us at the end of the day. The trip's organizer, an ambitious cyclist who brought us all together, pulled me into the adventure with an email invitation six months ago, announcing that he wanted to celebrate his seventieth year by doing one last transcontinental ride across the USA. "Would you like to come along?" Forrest estimated that it would take at least two months to cover the four thousand miles across the nation's blue highways on bicycles. He has been doing this kind of thing for decades, a stringer in his younger days for several different outdoor or bicycling magazines. He looked the part. That was how we met, on a September bike packing trip through the high mountain valleys of Colorado, each of us waiting for the tourists to leave and the aspens to transform into their signature vibrant and shimmering yellow.

My bike was brand new when we met, still had the original tires on it—MSO foldable knobbies in 700- x40-mm—and I was a recent convert to the idea of using one for travel. But I hadn't ridden all that much since college. I was pleased with my choice, an "adventure bike" from REI, a Novara Mazama, stout enough to carry up to fifty pounds of additional weight on either asphalt roads or gravel trails. The frame was welded steel, made in Taiwan. The tires, in Thailand. This was not a fast bike, nor a particularly expensive one. But the bike had already proven itself to be an efficient and durable machine, fully capable of transporting me wherever I wanted to go, maybe even across a continent.

For a purist like Forrest, the international flavor of its parts was reason enough not to ride one. He rode a Surly Long-Haul Trucker, a "pure-bred drop bar touring bike suitable for traveling anywhere in the world," claims the Minnesota-based company that assembles and markets them in the USA. But I will take the flared handlebars on my Mazama, any day. They give it a profile and a look that grabs the eye, right from the start. Rather than drop straight down like the handlebars on the racing bike that it was never intended to be, these flare to the outside. And that means the brakes are easy to reach, which is a good thing on the twisting downhills of a two-lane mountain road. It is no fun taking your eyes off the pavement to look for brake levers, no fun squeezing them with a death grip in order to sense a feeling that resembles control. With the flared handlebars, the brakes are convenient and easy to operate and there are even several different options for resting my hands and wrists during a long day's ride. In those rare moments when I'm negotiating a narrow fence gate at a remote trailhead or the sewer grate of a city street, the wide handlebars promote a feeling of balance.

One of my favorite things about cycling is feeling a kind of kinship developing between me and this two-wheeled, mechanical device. It is easy and even tempting in the middle of a pleasing downhill run to imagine that I am actually in flight, with long graceful wings stretched out on either side. From this vision, it is an easy next step to start calling the bike Daedalus, after the renowned artisan and inventor of ancient Greece. I have rarely felt that kind of attachment with any of the automobiles I've owned or driven, not enough to give one a name. But then again, I have no clue how to service a car or truck, other than to pay someone else to do it.

\* \* \* \* \*

April 20th, 1999 began with blue sky and sunshine. But by early afternoon, puffy cumulus giants were taking over the sky. I had no interest in working late. All I could think about was getting out of the office and seeing the kids again. When I pulled into the garage late that afternoon, Ben and Lee were both at home, safe and sound, trying to be cool and playing down their parallel experiences of being in lockdown at a neighboring high school, like it was no big deal. But we were deep inside the zone of influence. None of us could have predicted, intuited, or even cared that much on the day of the massacre, about the changes that lay ahead.

Bright lights lit up the night, illuminating nearby Clement Park and inviting survivors, their families, and the curious to gather there. The crime scene was huge and complex, and harrowing.

Homemade unexploded bombs still littered the hallways of the school. Investigators from the FBI and ATF were on the scene, assisting with the Sisyphean challenge of collecting, sorting through, and analyzing the mountain of evidence inside the building, probably expecting to find evidence of a larger conspiracy, something more than just the bodies of the two killers finally located in the southwest corner of the library, their bodies facing each other, the murder weapons close by.

Countless decisions had to be made by the understaffed county coroner. Too many bodies had to be identified. The cause and manner of death determined. Despite the danger, early investigators were busy inside creating an unofficial list. Next of kin were being sent to Leawood Elementary to meet with the district attorney, the sheriff, or the coroner's chief deputy. Her office wanted more time to gather evidence before releasing the bodies of the victims. She wanted objectively verifiable facts to support the many findings and conclusions that had to be drawn, objective truths that would hold up in any court, civil or criminal. Jefferson County officials wanted another twenty-four hours to work the crime scene before officially notifying the surviving family members.

The police on the ground were assembling enough factual evidence about the identities of the killers and the circumstances of the case to go before a county judge with sworn affidavits seeking search warrants on the affluent homes of the parents of the two principal suspects. In doing this work the investigators operated under a higher standard or burden of proof than the press corps—personal knowledge of verifiable facts. With an army of journalists waiting in the wings, the police were able and willing to swear on the first day, that two killers, possibly students, had armed themselves, entered Columbine High School, and started picking off other students, indiscriminately, both inside the building and on the grounds. There were at least four dead, and many more wounded. That much the investigators could swear to, not that it told the whole story. The detectives wanted warrants to search the suburban estates that were the family homes of the killers, for evidence of planning or preparation. They sought evidence that might reveal the identities of co-conspirators or accomplices. And the judge agreed, entering orders authorizing searches of the designated properties and requiring that each set of parents vacate their homes. A complex crime scene grew larger.

And for the next five days, it rained.

*   *   *   *   *

Back in Oregon, pedaling through the highway's gentle curves on my way to the campground, a large sign comes into view with the words: Fort Stevens Campground, Turn Right. *Just in time. Daylight is fading fast. What a relief to be this close! There's no one else in sight.* I turn the handlebars into a hard right and pedal down the two-lane road into the gathering dusk, secure in the knowledge that a hero's welcome—or at the very least a cold beer—is waiting for me right down this road. Occasional signs assure me that I am still in the state park, pointing out additional parking lots and access points for fishing, enough to keep me going, all the while imagining that the band of bicyclists I'm following are not far ahead. So, I keep pedaling, looking hard into the fading light for a glimpse of the place where I can stop for the night.

Thirty minutes pass. I am still pedaling down the same dark coastal road. Daedalus is the only vehicle within sight or sound. And I am remembering how far I am from home, how elegant the air in Colorado compared to this damp seaborne mist, and wondering where it must have been that I made the wrong turn.

# Chapter 2
## We Begin

*July 2, 2017*
*Fort Stevens State Park, Oregon*

Lost, but on a road inside Fort Stevens State Park, the back pocket of my bicycle shirt comes to life, the vibrations cutting right through the croaks and chirps of the Oregon twilight. *"Buzzzz! Buzz!" Those noises are coming from my cellphone! Maybe it's a text from Lee!* My hands grab for the brake levers. Daedalus stops in its tracks. I'm confident that it's not my partner of thirteen years, Marceil. She would call me on the phone if she wanted to talk or had news to share.

By this time I have already turned the bike around and come back to the intersection with the tall streetlamp, the one with the large and imposing directional sign pointing the way to the campground, the place where I turned right one road too soon. The cellphone is quiet now. I reach for it anyway, not entirely sure which button to push to scan for incoming texts. I find one that looks like a Post-it note. The screen fills with messages, most of them appear to be ads. Ads I've never taken the time to read, respond to, or delete. At the top, is a recent text, but I'm disappointed. It's not from Lee. The good news is, the text is from Frank, one of my cycling buddies. "Are U OK?" he asks.

*Frank not only texts! He uses shortcut abbreviations!* I call him right back, relieved that I'm just a few minutes away. The lights that shine down from the parking lot of the campground office have come on since the last time I passed through. I can see the light poles from here. "Yeah, thanks for calling. I am OK and just a few minutes away. I stopped to get some beer for you guys back at that last convenience store. Catching up took longer than I thought it would."

"Where are you?" he asks. I can hear the impatience in his voice.

"I'm down on the highway…at the big sign by the campground entrance. I'll be there in a few minutes."

"Cool. Gerry and I are sitting at a picnic table right behind the office. You can't miss us."

$*$   $*$   $*$   $*$   $*$

When the shooting started, I was about fifteen miles away in Golden, Colorado, the home of Coors beer and Colorado School of Mines. But I worked at the courthouse. That's where I was when I heard the news, eating lunch in the basement cafeteria with some friends and colleagues. That was different, too. My typical lunch hour, especially in spring, was spent in running shoes and a T-shirt and going for a jog on the concrete walking paths that extended to Golden and beyond. A typical lunch consisted of leftovers from home, reheated in a microwave, whenever time allowed.

"There are active shooters at Columbine High School," said the voice of a sheriff's dispatcher trying hard not to choke with emotion. Silence swept through the room as if on wings, every face turning towards the small television screen that hung suspended in the corner of the room, nothing but grey static on the screen. But I walked towards it anyway, watching as the video feed of a local broadcast news program returned, the faces of the commentators still locked in smiles and enthusiastic banter. *No! I want to hear more about Columbine. That's too close to home!*

"Deputies are being dispatched," said the voice and there was a timber in its tone, a frequency that struck a warning chord hardwired into something primitive yet universal in my brainstem, overriding and penetrating right down to the core. Our house was less than five miles away. *Thank God the kids don't go to Columbine.* Eyes still fixed on the television screen, the insistent voice inside my head said, *Do something!*

I was a child protection attorney and most of my workday was spent managing a dependency or neglect docket at the Jefferson County courthouse. My days and weeks were devoted to the ongoing task of adjusting to the shifting balance of career and family. Our office represented the sheriff's department, the coroner's office, the Department of Social Services, and every other county department and elected official, whenever and wherever the county had legal issues involved. In this way I would soon learn of Kyle Velasquez' murder.

"The sheriff's department is requesting mutual aid from all metro jurisdictions," said the dispatcher's voice, but this time it cracked. Many who worked for the county had children who attended Columbine High School or loved ones who worked there or knew people that did. We were all worried that day, not about our jobs, but our families and friends. And we did our jobs that day.

In a complex blend of relief and dismay, I called home. I could not just sit there and watch the virtual faces of a pleasant television news team broadcasting from the secure comfort of their studio. Nor could I return to a conversation over lunch with my stomach gripped in fear. I left the commotion of the lunchroom for the privacy of my office and to leave a message for my two latchkey children. We had just celebrated Ben's fifteenth birthday. Older sister Lee was a sophomore. Both went to Heritage High School. They were supposed to be at school, and school was supposed to be a safe place to send your kids. Trying to sound calm against a rising tide of emotion, I said, "Hey! It's me, Dad. Something terrible is happening over at Columbine today. No matter what you've heard, don't go over there, not today…I love you." And it felt comforting to have done that much. I could feel the effort taking the edge off my anger, as if words alone would prove helpful or make a difference somehow. At least it would show that I was thinking about them.

We had an answering machine attached to our landline, but the only ones around at midday to listen to the words were Cody, the aging Labrador Retriever, and two cats: Fatima and Earl. I left the message anyway. We tried hard to be fair in our home and so each one of us had a designated pet: Cody and I were a matching set, Fatima and Ben another. And then, there was Lee and Earl, both with androgynous first names and bonded at a soul level. "Earl the

Gray" was born in the top drawer of her bedroom dresser when Lee was only a first or second grader. They grew up together. So, naturally, they spoke to each other in a language of their own, kept each other warm at night, and when Lee was home, were inseparable. But Lee was aging out of the routine. She was sixteen, had a driver's license and a well-used car. She kept herself as busy as possible and, to Earl's dismay, even had a job that took her out of the home. Lee was a barista at a Barnes & Noble bookstore, the one on Bowles Avenue right across the street from Clement Park, that large shady place with the baseball fields and playground equipment right next to Columbine High School. Lee could have been on her way over there to start her shift for all I knew. In my bones, I was frustrated and angry in my helplessness to stop her. *Thank God they don't go to Columbine,* I repeated to myself, and immediately remembered a few parents with children who did. *How would they survive the same news?*

*  *  *  *  *

Back at the campground, registering is easy as well as economical. Oregon has created hike or bike campgrounds in many of its state parks. If you can get there, self-propelled or just walking under your own power, you have a place to stay for a reasonable fee, without a reservation, and limited to a fixed number of days. Some of the campsites are primitive. Fort Stevens offers not just running water, but warm showers and well-appointed bathrooms. A five-star affair, as campgrounds go.

Frank and Gerry show me the area where all the tents are set up—everyone's except mine. I find a space close to one of the picnic tables and start unloading the bike, quickly pulling the IPAs out of the panniers. Neither one speaks. Frank puts his hands on his hips and watches as I unroll my one-person backpacking tent onto the flat and inviting rectangle of earth. He's shaking his head. Gerry walks over to the picnic table and finds a seat. Into the silence, I grab three bottles and set them on the table. "No thanks," says Frank. "If I drink one of those now, I'll be pissing it out all night long. Give me a rain check though, OK?"

"You got it, Frank," I reply. "Thanks for reaching out with that text."

"That's what these cell phones are for. Goodnight, you guys."

"See you tomorrow, Frank," I answer, reaching into my pocket for the utility knife with its bottle opener, and then get at least two bottle caps off. I hand Gerry a beer.

"Good night, Frank," says Gerry, reaching for the sweaty glass. "Thanks, Robert. Can I give you a hand with that tent?"

"You can help a lot more by telling me a story or two about where you're from and what brought you here," I answer. "I've never been to Ireland. Always wanted to go."

After his first swig, Gerry says, "And I'd like to show it to you someday." He lifts his bottle in the sign of a toast.

I raise mine back, take a swallow, and return to the task of unfolding tent poles into the flexible aluminum frame that will soon hold up the tent.

Meanwhile, Gerry is explaining that he has already crossed the USA on a bicycle once before, but that was at least a decade ago, maybe more. He did it with a friend from his hometown in Ireland, a small village near the northern border. That's how and when he first met Forrest, the cycling patriarch who invited each of us to come along on this journey. Gerry made his first tour as a needed catharsis after splitting up with his wife. They were raising an adopted daughter together, a young girl from Romania. Gerry has only been back in the USA for a few weeks, long enough to fly into Portland, Oregon, purchase a new touring bike and gear from a local bike shop, and pedal solo to Astoria to meet up with the rest of us. This time, he's grieving over his wife's death after a long illness. "It was my first and only marriage. I'm back on the bicycle for reflection, filling the empty spaces with good company, and making some music."

"What kind of music do you have in mind?" I ask, opening two more bottles. But before he can respond, my back pocket starts buzzing again. I reach for the cellphone and sit down across from him at the picnic table, thinking that this time: *It's got to be from Lee.* "I've got a daughter too," I explain, "a very independent one. And I think this might be from her." I open the screen to her single-word text and break into a smile from the pleasing mix of happiness and connection, the same feelings that accompanied a memorable early morning conversation the day after Columbine and when she was only sixteen. "Success, Gerry! Lee says that our bike trip is cool."

"Indeed, it is," he says, raising his beer again. "Aren't daughters grand?" he asks, taking out his cellphone to show me a picture of a beautiful young woman with long dark hair and a captivating smile.

"Grand," I say, keeping pace with the enthusiasm in his voice, and lifting the bottle in a toast.

Gerry nods earnestly. "'Cause who else is gonna care about ya when you're far from home?" The bottles clink. We each take a drink, celebrating our commonality as fathers, the fortunes—both good and sad—that brought us together, and making a toast for a safe and restorative journey. Gerry is traveling with a smartphone. But his is set up to stay connected with family and friends back in Ireland. It won't take calls originating from inside the USA without a hefty service fee. We exchange cellphone numbers anyway, just in case that changes. "And about the music," he continues, picking up a distant thread of the conversation. "I bought a little something back in Astoria to help pass the time in the evenings. I can't tell you what it is. That would spoil the surprise. I just hope you're not shy about joinin' into a singalong now and then."

"I'm guessing we've got some favorites in common," I respond, not the least bit intimidated by the prospect of singing together somewhere down the road, and glad, that after a substantial delay this first day on the bike is ending on a high note in a major key.

Fort Stevens State Park is part of a narrow peninsula that forms Oregon's northwestern corner. On a map, this strip of land progressively narrows until it disappears into the roiling mix of formidable crosscurrents, created by the constant surge of freshwater from the Columbia River into the vast saltwater depths of the Pacific. I am amazed by the inestimable numbers of mature salmon drawn into this underwater web from all over the Pacific every spring and summer. Eagles, ospreys, and a host of other flying predators, sea lions, river otters, beavers and bears, are all attracted, like iron to magnet, in this annual migration. They pursue the salmon upstream to the city of Portland and from there, into the Columbia River's extensive tributaries. But these are only the visible predators growing stronger every summer by feeding on the spawning fish. Entire ecosystems are dependent on the annual run, including the small riverfront restaurant made from an old fishing trawler, a tourist destination that served me one delicious lunch of deep-fried salmon chunks and French fries on my first day in Astoria. And if you've ever enjoyed salmon in your sushi, then you're on the list of dependent predators too, maybe a little further down.

On this first morning, I do not want to be the last one up and out of my sleeping bag. Before sunrise, I unzip the tent into grey skies and humidity, have breakfast going and the rest of my gear packed up while everyone else is still deciding whether it's time yet to get up. Well, almost everyone. Frank is way ahead of me. He's a lean and healthy-looking Californian, with the latest in equipment and gear. His tent is already on the ground, his stuff spread out into organized piles. Add to that profile a quick smile and a quirky string of Tibetan prayer flags that hang from the flexible pole on the back of his bicycle. They are both a prayer and a warning to approaching motorists, that a crazy guy on a bike is up ahead. Frank too, has one prior. He's ridden across the USA already, an unsupported ride with another cyclist friend on the US 76 bicycle route.

*That confirms it. I am the newbie!* Had I continued down that road last night instead of turning around, it would have led me into boat ramps and fishing access points along the Columbia River. These roads and the land they occupy were all part of a US military base created during the Civil War. The US government under President Lincoln was worried about attacks on the West Coast from either Britain or Japan. The US Army was tasked with building a fort to defend against one. Earthworks were constructed. Artillery pieces moved in and Fort Stevens became an operational army base for the next one hundred years, long enough to acquire the bragging rights of becoming the only site in the lower forty-eight states where live rounds of Japanese artillery bombarded the US mainland during World War II.

Had I been camped on this open ground seventy-five years ago, my life and this story could have come to an abrupt and unexpected end. It would have been difficult back then for any of us cyclists to pick out a grey Japanese submarine surfacing into the pre-dawn sunlight of early summer. The ship was too small, only about 354 feet in length, too low on the water, and the distance too great, about ten miles, for visual detection. But our tents were out in the open and a few of them colorful, easy to spot through field binoculars. The commander of the submarine had orders to take the war to the American mainland. What a difference seventy-five years can make! The captain had to settle for other targets to shoot at, backlit by the sun, like the flagpole or the backstop to a baseball diamond. His seasoned crew had been waiting a long time for this moment. No doubt they were feeling dauntless, eager to open fire. Their ship had come away unscathed from participation in the attack on Pearl Harbor just six months before. A few days before the attack on Fort Stevens, the I-25 went into battle against an unarmed Canadian freighter, the *SS Fort Camosun*. The submarine disabled the ship with a torpedo, then surfaced and fired eighteen rounds into the stricken ship with its deck gun. They were on a harass and destroy mission. The Army Base at Fort Stevens was next, well within range of the 10-cm deck gun. Standing on the deck just above the waterline—years before global positioning satellites and even radar—the captain and crew would have had enough of a visual to take aim and hit whatever stood out on the landscape. ("Japanese Submarine I-25") The gunners on the submarine had time to make adjustments and hone in on their targets, time to rain seventeen artillery rounds down upon the peninsula where we would camp seventy-five years later. I can speculate that the gunners from the summer of 1942 hit their targets with everything they had. It was more than enough to activate the blaring alarms inside the fort and drive its defenders from their sleep. But a counter-attacking light bomber, an airborne defender responding to a radio call to arms from inside the army post, would drive the I-25 back into the depths long before any of the soldiers inside would fire a single round. In its wake, the I-25 left behind a pockmarked baseball diamond, a twisted backstop, and some powerline damage.

The US and Japan were at war then. It ended in 1945 and with it, the need for weapons of war in civilian use or within our communities. It feels like that conclusion should be obvious. But the two boys who killed Kyle Velasquez in the library at Columbine High School over fifty years later were able to arm themselves with: "...dozens of explosive devices of varying potency, seven knives, two illegal sawed-off shotguns, a 9-mm semiautomatic assault pistol, and a 9-mm semiautomatic carbine rifle, as well as a substantial supply of ammunition..." (Erickson, 23 & 24).

Forget about the knives. All the rest of that should have been inaccessible to civilians, and especially juveniles. If instead of firing its deck gun, the Japanese submarine had dispatched a team of only two invaders, armed with these same assault rifles, extended ammunition clips, and shotguns, then the attack on Fort Stevens in 1942 would have been a much bloodier affair. And yet, the fellow student who acted as a conduit for three of those four Columbine guns described above would testify before the Colorado legislature in 2000, that she did not know that the guns were illegal, implying that had she known, she might not have purchased them for her two friends, Eric Harris and Dylan Klebold (Cullen). Her testimony and the unbridled fanaticism of her two friends highlight the monumental and critical need for federal laws to clarify in all the various regions of this immense country the essential difference between rifles that are designed for hunting (to kill with one shot with minimal damage to the muscles and meat), and the weapons of war recovered from inside bullet-riddled Columbine High School. Because semiautomatics like the AR-15 and the TEC-9 are designed for firing lots of long-range bullets into an intended target within a short interval of time, and, once inside the victim, to kill by tearing apart as much bone, tendon, and muscle as possible. That's why they're called assault weapons.

If the mission of the I-25 was to strike a blow on the US mainland, then the attack was a resounding success for Japan. In its wake, shock waves of rage and fear rippled out in all directions as if from the epicenter of an earthquake, down the California coast, east into the heartland, and north into Canada and Alaska—where another attack was coming across the Aleutian Islands before the end of summer—inciting fires of fear and anger across the country. The rage burned hot enough to convince President Roosevelt of the need for an Executive Order creating the War Relocation Center. There were ten camps, almost all in the western states, where tens of thousands of second-generation American families of Japanese descent spent the duration of the war, after first being separated from their homes and property. The War Relocation Centers should not be confused with Alien Detention Centers. The former housed American citizens and families, albeit of Japanese descent. The latter detained men only of military age and citizens of countries the USA had declared war against.

One of these Alien Detention Centers was constructed in Missoula, Montana, 600 miles to the east of Fort Stevens and directly in our path. My friends and I would reach it during the third week of the journey. But during the war years, it was home to handfuls of Germans and Japanese resident aliens, and several thousand Italian citizens, crew members of a cruise ship still on its way through the Panama Canal when war was declared. All those men spent the war years detained behind the chain-link walls of the Fort Missoula Alien Detention Center, raising their own food on the prison farm ("Historical Museum at Fort Missoula").

In recognition of this rich history, I feel compelled to recognize the utility and legitimacy of the machine guns, semiautomatic rifles, and artillery pieces carried into battle by the soldiers and sailors of World War II. But after Columbine and the steady stream of massacres in public places that have followed in its wake, we are long past the time for drawing the line that makes a clear distinction between the unequivocal lethality of these weapons of war—the ones designed to fire a multitude of small-caliber, high-velocity rounds within a short burst of time—and the bolt action rifles and shotguns commonly used for target shooting and hunting.

I believe that comedian Chris Rock was showing all of us that one good way to limit juvenile access to the large quantities of ammunition utilized by assault rifles, when he quipped:

> You don't need no gun control, you know
> what you need? We need some bullet control. Man,

we need to control the bullets, that's right. I think all bullets should cost five thousand dollars... five thousand dollars per bullet...You know why? Cause if a bullet cost five thousand dollars, there would be no more innocent bystanders.

\*　　\*　　\*　　\*　　\*

Southern Jefferson County is known for its proximity to both Chatfield Reservoir and Red Rocks amphitheater, and for the size of its evangelical community. Columbine High School is located near its politically and culturally conservative heart. Once old enough, most students had a car or access to one, including the son of a good friend I had known since law school. I called him on the day after the shooting to find out if his son was uninjured. Josh was a junior at Columbine. He had escaped from the building early on, just about the same time I was sitting down to lunch in Golden, part of a large wave of students that made their way into the fresh clean air, only to find injured classmates on the lawn outside and first responders tending to their wounds. He would later describe how good it felt to be free from the building, but how quickly that changed to shock and disbelief when he saw other students lying on the ground, bleeding and hurt. On the way to his car, Josh was intercepted by a man with a badge crammed into the pocket of his sport coat, asking three simple questions: Who are you? Where were you inside the school? What did you see there?

The anonymous man was one of the scores of police already responding to the scene from jurisdictions all over the metro area, meeting with hundreds of students and faculty as they poured out of the building, each one a survivor. The investigators would comb the grounds of the school, Clement Park, and Leawood Elementary throughout the long day in search of more witnesses, starting with these essential questions and on a mission to piece together the events of the day.

Witnesses to the bloodshed were quickly identified and marked for further, more in-depth interviews. Most described the shootings as "random." Quite a few had seen at least one of the shooters and recognized them as students. Friends of the gunmen emerged too. Some described one or both as wearing a long dark leather duster much like the one worn by Keanu Reeves in *The Matrix*, released across the USA only three short weeks before the massacre. Other witnesses called them trench coats. Those who recognized the murderers kept repeating two names over and over, Eric and Dylan, and the search for these principal suspects was underway. The well-known stereotype of the school shooter as loner/outcast did not fit either one of the suspects well. They were old friends. Both went to the senior prom. They were part of a select clique of friends and acquaintances, both at school and at the Blackjack pizza shop where they worked.

Josh knew nothing about their identities, but a senior girl named Robyn Anderson did (Erickson, 23). The last Saturday night was the prom, and she'd been Dylan Klebold's date. They went to the dance together as part of a group of five couples, brainy kids that gravitated towards each other. When interviewed outside the school by law enforcement, Robyn did not mention Dylan, the prom, guns, or anything else to make herself stand out. All she offered was her location inside the school and what she saw there. Hers was a lie of omission, also known as duplicity or deception (Cullen).

Josh said he made it to a student parking lot and the safety of his car and sat there for a long time wondering what to do next—until a friend banged on the window and asked for a ride. They were on their way home, moving west on Bowles towards the mountains and the main intersection at Wadsworth Blvd. where they sat at the traffic light waiting for the green arrow, while an endless stream of emergency response vehicles and sirens from all over the metro area, turned left directly in front of them, heading to the crime scene.

Back at the office, everywhere I looked there was another reason for going home. I was full to overflowing with a complex blend of relief and anger, dismay and unrest; not unlike the frustrations portrayed by Bill Murray's character in the movie *Groundhog's Day*. Although my entire adult life has been lived in the Intermountain West, part of me remains "just another kid from Akron, Ohio." In 1969, I was a senior in high school, eighteen, and about to emancipate—or at least graduate—into a larger world that included an expanding, costly, but undeclared war in Vietnam. Just four weeks before my high school graduation, thirteen students were shot, four of them fatally, by Troop G of the Ohio National Guard on a university campus just a few miles from my front door. And I would remain in Ohio no longer than it took to emancipate.

Three decades later, another massacre was casting its shadow over my community, again only a few miles away, but this time my children were the teenagers. All of us were about to become third-party witnesses to the aftermath of another public massacre, the witnesses close enough to the scene of a newsworthy event to form an opinion about what happened—who did what to whom—but without having a personal stake in the outcome. This community was being tasked with the massive chore of cleaning up and rebuilding. I believed even then, that this was going to change our lives.

*Don't we already have enough to deal with inside our Littleton home?* Both Lee and Ben were full to overflowing with the energies of spreading their wings to leave both me and the city they called "Littlefun," behind. I already knew that at sixteen, Lee's angry defiance was growing. There's always more to any story, different perspectives to uncover, words and scenes to edit to move the plot forward and improve the telling. The impulse to judge others is always tempting. But in those early days of Columbine, I did not yet know about the hole in Ben's wall.

*     *     *     *     *

Back in Oregon, it is a beautiful morning for beginning a quest, a bicycle journey across the continent; because the vista is so clear and unobstructed, almost impossible on a day like this to imagine that seventy-five years ago, uniformed men with artillery pieces and bombers were fighting over this same piece of real estate. Not far from the campground lies a long curving stretch of Pacific coastline. The tide is out, rendering a dramatic view of the beach. Strand lines mark the retreating surf. We plan to cross the wide-open beach with our bicycles and set our collective rear tires into the surf for a group selfie.

With our gear packed and ready, the five of us ride together along the short stretch of roadway that turns into the tarmac

35

of a small parking lot. Asphalt transitions into sand mixed with pebbles, and then sand and more sand. The air is cool. The breeze is constant. But I'm not lifting my head to look at the scenery. My eyes are fixated on the front fire and the irregular surface it's rolling across. I'm working hard to stay upright. *This can't be good for my chain.* Great swaths of open beach extend on both sides, almost empty of people. I can pedal only as far as the first strandline. There, the tires sink straight down into unconsolidated sand. Forward motion ceases.

Forrest is waiting right there, at the break into loose sand. "It will get better once we get across this. Look over there. The sand gets wetter again," he assures us, pointing with his finger. He's the adventure writer with a story to document. He's after a picture with fully loaded bikes, which means pushing and pulling our tires through loose sand, picking up one foot and setting it down, and repeating the process again and again. It's arduous and slow going. The finish line appears to be two distant wooden pilings sticking straight up out of the sand. I look toward them and imagine that at some point in their history, the same two poles once supported a horizontal sign. But wind and time have already rendered their opinion on whatever information the sign once announced.

Don and his bicycle are just reaching the first of the two well-weathered posts. Frank is right behind him. The surf is barely reaching them. This spot is ideal and these two posts, the perfect props for our Kodak moment, the group selfie. Long before I can reach them, several beach walkers have already stopped to watch our early morning enterprise. "What are you guys up to?" a woman asks as I walk Daedalus across the final stretch of sand and catch up with the rest of the group. I prop my bicycle against another at one end of the neat row that extends from both sides of the pilings. "Want your pictures taken?"

Further down the beach and within walking distance, stand the steel ribbed bones of an English cargo ship; placed there by an October gale in 1906. The Oregon Historical Society has a black and white photograph on its website of local tourists driving by after the storm has passed, who had driven their horse-drawn carriage right up next to the wreck of the ship. It's tilted to one side and half-buried in the sand, three of the four masts broken and twisted, a gentle reminder that even the best-laid plans of mice and men can often go awry.

Of course, we want our pictures taken. It's what we're here for, to record the time and place of our passing, our marks upon the relentless Pacific so that we can remember its blessings upon our tires and shoes as we pedal our way through the journey ahead. I want a picture, almost as much as I want to start pedaling down the road, making more memories, better memories, even as my footprints and tread marks are erased by the next slow-moving waves: which reminds me that I haven't yet responded to Lee's text. As soon as I drag Daedalus out of the sand and onto a surface where the bike can stand upright, I find her recent message and type the words, "The journey begins on a windy Oregon beach."

Three hours after the photo opportunity on the Oregon coast, we are riding together back through Astoria, ready for a late lunch. Gerry points out the pawnshop where he bought the musical instrument that's tucked away inside the black weatherproof case lashed to the rear frame of his Salsa Journeyman with bungee cord. He's told no one yet exactly what kind it is.

"How do we even know there's a musical instrument inside that case?" I ask.

"You'll just have to have a bit a faith, my son."

"There could be a giant sausage inside that case, or even a machine gun," I suggest, sounding like a comedian searching for the punch line. "You could be a cold-blooded killer like those boys at Columbine." But Gerry doesn't answer, and my attempt at humor falls flat on the tarmac of US 30 between Astoria and Portland.

## CHAPTER 3
## WHERE DO YOU SLEEP?

*July 4, 2017*
*Troutdale, Oregon*

"No Overnight Camping!" The highway sign warns. So does the next one, and the one after that. Pickups with camper shells, vans, and RVs are everywhere.

We are eating dinner, five hungry, happy, and tired cyclists, taking up an entire alcove table inside a large family-style restaurant. We eat with gusto and zest, full of the pleasure and satisfaction that comes from having pedaled about forty-five miles that day, from St Helens, Oregon in the valley of the Columbia River, into and through the commercial districts of Portland, a large cosmopolitan city that prides itself on its bicycle friendliness. The streets were practically deserted. Then we rode the rest of the way to Troutdale where every single motel room and commercial campground has been booked in advance for months.

The City of Troutdale stands at the western gate of the Historic Columbia River Highway and near the confluence of the Sandy and Columbia Rivers. Without all the traffic, it might feel peaceful or serene. But the city bears the look and feel of a location that has made a sustainable industry out of tourism. The quaint streets are lined with motels, restaurants, and gaily decorated tourist shops. The sidewalks are full of tourists in motion. Outside the restaurant, our bicycles adorn the parking lot, colorful accessories to the lamp posts and benches they lean against. The restaurant is just a stone's throw from the Lewis & Clark State Recreation Area and beyond that our day's destination, the western entrance to the scenic highway, which is where the warning signs are posted, the ones banning overnight camping on both sides of the road for many miles.

Today, we have ridden through several small-town celebrations. In one we joined in the festivities by purchasing, slicing, and consuming an entire watermelon, all five of us, in a grocery store parking lot. We aped for the passersby, grey-bearded men in bicycle attire laughing together and allowing the sweet sticky juice to run down our cheeks and chins. A few last-minute shoppers would even let their natural curiosity detain them long enough to connect with perfect strangers and ask the easiest of questions, "Where are you going? Where'd ya come from?"

These spectators were willing to take time away from their holiday afternoons to momentarily engage with an interesting but harmless bunch of self-propelled tourists, who are smiling, laughing and unwilling to move with the haste of an automobile or pickup truck, one with a flag on the back of his bike that looks either Irish or Italian or possibly Mexican, but without the eagle in the middle. Until Gerry looks up and gesturing toward his bicycle, opens up in his beguiling accent and declares that, "Anyone with eyes in their head for the colors of the world can see that this flag is green and white and or'nge: green, on the hoist side thank you very much. Not a speck a red anywhere on 'er." Gerry makes the rest of us sound boring.

Actually, the 4th falls on Tuesday, providing a long weekend for everyone who has traveled from all over the country to visit the world-class destination known as the Columbia River Gorge. It was here that federal dollars were accessed over a century ago to construct a two-lane highway around, above, and through the broad peaks and native forests of the Cascade Range and render its scenic splendor accessible to the automobile-buying, city-dwelling public in Portland, Seattle, and even distant San Francisco. One of the first national highway projects, the Historic Columbia River Highway opened for automobiles in 1922.

Oregon encourages bicycle and backpacking travel throughout the state. The legislature has enacted laws to fund and maintain hiker/biker campsites inside the state parks. Reservations are not accepted or needed for self-propelled travelers without support vehicles. Cyclists can set their tents anywhere within the designated area and have access to bathrooms and sometimes even hot showers. The state-owned land around the mouth of the Sandy River, with its sprawling and inviting sand bars sparkling in the warm July sunshine, is not one of them. This land is a public recreation area and a popular one at that. It closes at sundown. Open camping for cyclists—or anyone for that matter—does not exist. By the time we arrive, the riverbanks and sandbars and the parking lots that abut them are thoroughly packed with holiday revelers, sunbathers and frisbee throwers, dogs, kids, and their parents, some of them already packing up to leave to get an early start on the traffic out of there.

We eat full dinners and watch the sun go down outside. It has been a fun day, and towards the end of the meal, Forrest lays out his plans for the rest of the evening. It begins with glowing descriptions of the best stealth campsites he has found in multiple countries over the years, warming each of us to the idea. His good friend, Don, can attest to some of them. It's the 4th of July and the fourth night of our journey, with all of those nights spent sleeping on the ground in a one-person backpacking tent inside a comfortable sleeping bag on the grounds of one campground or another. This night, we have reached a destination that is so heavily impacted by tourists and RV's that tent camping is not an option. "We have to improvise," he tells us, "and that includes the possibility of stealth camping tonight." Forrest has no better or more specific idea to suggest, at least not yet. But this is his idea of the worst possible case scenario. "We could just wait here for a lot of the traffic to die down, then pedal up the long incline of the highway, past the "No Camping" signs, and separate one by one into the trees of the drainages that intersect the highway." Forrest proposes. "Then, with each bicycle and reflective gear out of sight, we get as comfortable as possible for the night. The end game would be to meet up safe and sound in the town of Corbett for breakfast in the morning."

In his next breath, he insists that there's still time for something better to come along. Forrest is the one who sold me on the idea of coming along on this adventure, the instigator who created our group, and the glue that holds it together. He takes pride in his old school, Surley Long Haul Trucker, one of the early models. Its mudguards are covered with decals of all the places he has toured with it. "Still too early to leave the restaurant," he advises. "Let's be open to all the possibilities and concentrate on dessert." I want another round of coffee with my cherry pie and ice cream. From the sound of it, there could be miles to go before we sleep. I want some caffeine on board just in case.

When we finally leave the restaurant, the sun is down and the sky is dark enough to get out my headlamp. We mount the bicycles and ride through the streets of Troutdale to the park entrance and onto the historic two-lane blacktop highway. Ahead of us, a steady stream of cars and trucks is escaping from the packed parking lots, many of them headed for Interstate 84 which runs through the gorge on the Oregon side of the river. We don't ride far, only to the gravel entrance of the main parking lot. Cars, pickup trucks, and RVs are backed up in long lines behind the stop sign. They slow down without stopping and quickly accelerate onto the highway, each one turning in one direction or another. Few stop, until Don in the lead gestures toward one of the cars indicating that he wants to cross the road with his bicycle. The driver scowls, but lets him pass.

I'm standing on the narrow shoulder of the incline straddling the crossbar, packed in between Gerry and Frank, watching and waiting like a duckling in the middle of the pack and with nowhere to go. But I can watch Don insert his bike into the opposing flow and reach the far side of the intersection. He turns it around as if waiting for the rest of us, silent and indifferent to the noise, engine exhaust, and confusion. Our leader hasn't moved. The two of them just stand there on opposite sides of the intersection, like sentinels looking inside the windshields of the cars and trucks that pass them by, each one with its own urgency to arrive at a next destination for another round of holiday celebration.

And in the solitude of the moment, I find myself wondering if this adventure is more than just a travelogue about five guys who band together out of a shared interest in completing a bicycle tour across the USA. Or is it a coming-of-age story told by an aging parent trying to reconnect with a prodigal child, who is an adult daughter and Iraq war veteran? Or, maybe, the real story is the quest of a self-sufficient cyclist and former child protection attorney, who gets blown over by a ghost from Columbine, and has to come to grips with his long-avoided beliefs in a higher power? Once again, I remember the cellphone nestled inside my handlebar bag and the last text sent to Lee from the beach at Fort Stevens. Once again, there's nothing, not from Lee anyway. So, I type the words, "Rode through Portland today en route to scenic highway through the Cascades. How about you? Doing anything for the 4th?"

It surprises me how much concentration it takes to write a text. Looking up from the screen, it feels like I'm returning from another world. While the eyes readjust, I can watch the grey outlines of people still walking away from the riverbank and heading for their cars. Directly ahead, Forrest twists around from astride his Long Haul Trucker to look right at me with a half-smile and a nod. Then, we wait some more.

*     *     *     *     *

On the morning after the second day of the Columbine Massacre, my office phone was ringing even before I pushed open the door, a morning newspaper in the other hand. The color-coordinated phone was a tawny desktop model with a long flexible cord attached to the handset. I knew from the ring tone that the caller was someone from within the network of county employees. One glance at the name on the caller ID and I knew that whatever was on her mind, it would be important. I picked up the handset and asked, "How are you holding up over there?"

"Not good," Dottie replied. It was the voice of a dependable and experienced caseworker, one who after years of working together had become a good friend. "Things are bad over here right now, Bob. We just heard it from the sheriff's office. One of our foster kids was in the library."

"Oh no," I said, startled by the disturbing news; sad news that made me stand up and walk away from the desk, as far as the phone cord would allow and look toward the distant crime scene. "Was our kid hurt?"

"Oh yeah," she answered in a thickening voice. Dottie worked with the neediest kids in the system, the ones on the

Children's Habilitation Residential Program (CHRP) waiver because of developmental delays. It was a small but essential piece of the huge Medicaid program and an essential source of funding for children and youth who lived with intellectual or developmental disabilities.

"What happened?" I asked, wanting details as much as conversation.

"He didn't make it out," she answered with finality. "The parents were officially notified by the Coroner and the DA last night over at Leawood Elementary."

I spread out the front page of the newspaper on the desktop, scanning the faces of the victims on the front page, looking for a name or face to stand out. "What was one of our CHRP kids doing at Columbine?"

"We placed him there!" she snapped back in reply, letting the irritation show. "The same way all our kids get mainstreamed into…" but then stopped in midsentence as if stifling a sob. Dottie only worked with young children. A teenager would be on someone else's caseload.

"Was it Kyle? Kyle Velasquez?" I asked.

"So, you remember him?" She asks.

"I've got today's newspaper on my desk," unwilling to pretend, especially with Dottie, that I had a working memory of the case. In Jefferson County, the county attorney's office filed between three and four hundred petitions in dependency or neglect (D&N's) every year. And every year about three million children across the USA are reported as victims of child abuse or neglect. One million of the reports are serious enough and credible enough to compel local child protective services to take legal action. The numbers don't lie: war is not the only calamity that leaves human lives in ruin (van der Kolk).

"Someone from youth services would have handled the placement," she continued, finishing her thought and starting to sob. "Someone from your office would have been there too." Every time a child or youth went into foster care, the department of social services assigned a caseworker to work with the family to provide recommendations and support, always toward the pre-

43

sumptive goal of returning the child to the home as soon as it was safe. A Guardian ad Litem (GAL) was appointed by the court to provide a third-party perspective on the progress and status of the case. Next came a treatment plan, developed with the parent(s) and then adopted by the court, designed to address over the weeks and months of the case the conditions that gave rise to the placement—like drugs or alcohol abuse or the need for mental health diagnosis and treatment. "But without the file, I can't tell who it was."

"This is so sad," I replied. Sometimes, there were CASA workers (Court Appointed Special Advocates) involved as well. In Colorado, every out-of-home placement had to be reviewed by the court on at least a six-month basis for as long as the placement continued. Most of our cases closed successfully within a year. But a significant number go on and on, so long as the need for placement continues, or until the child turns eighteen and ages out of the system. And I could feel the knot taking hold of my stomach, along with the dread that came with asking, "So when was it, the placement?"

"That's the real question, isn't it?" she said, resuming a conversational tone. "The one that's making everybody over here feel so numb."

"Ouch," I said, holding the phone closer to my ear. "I'm sorry this is happening."

"Me too," she agreed. "Everybody over here is just sick about it. Such a nice kid. Everyone who worked with him liked him. And he'd still be alive, if we'd kept him in foster care."

"God, I wish Nelson was still running the department," I said, venting an old frustration. Social Services had a new director, someone from outside the department, and appointed for his experience with accounting rather than in protecting vulnerable populations of children or at-risk adults. "Nelson would have been out in front of this with a press release and just the right words to let the public know that this wasn't just another kid in foster care." The new director was not a popular appointment with staff. But if anyone at the department needed to be notified, it was him.

"Is it too soon to talk to the caseworker?"

"Give it some time. We're on our third box of Kleenex already."

*     *     *     *     *

In 1922, the original Columbia River Highway wove and twisted its way across, over, and through the majestic Cascade Range for seventy-seven miles between the cities of Troutdale and The Dalles, Oregon. It began and ended at established river towns on the Columbia, both locations easily accessible to the fledgling Model T automobile. The government surveyors and engineers who mapped the region and created the designs and plans were tasked with finding locations of significant natural beauty intrinsic to the region and "along the line where they might be seen in the best advantage, and, if possible, locate the road in such a way as to reach them." The two-lane road was the first scenic highway built in America. Its "first business" was to make these locations accessible to American automobiles, according to Samuel Lancaster, the project's chief engineer. The highway would take ten years to build, during a decade in which the automobile industry was still competing with the horse and buggy for supremacy on the nation's roads. The highway was named US Route 30. And if the hordes of cars and trucks and drivers who continue to visit every summer are any measure of success, then the government road builders deserve high marks for delivering the scenic highway they set out to build.

By the time our tour of five cyclists arrives, only a twenty-two-mile stretch of the historic highway remains intact. What is left retains its original alignment including drainage systems, guardrails, and a comfort stop constructed from native stone that looks like a medieval castle perched on top of a pinnacle to guard against unspecified invaders from the surrounding countryside. And we will ride this remnant on the day after the July 4th national holiday, realizing that the other fifty miles lie buried underneath the concrete and traffic of Interstate 84. We'll rediscover the beautiful curves of the remaining two-lane road, twisting and turning its way through deep forest to reach once secluded waterfalls and majestic overlooks, each one a compelling example of nature's artistry. And in front of each one, the road will morph into a parking lot full to overflowing with cars, RVs, and their exhaust fumes. It won't be difficult to pedal our way around and through the traffic jams.

*    *    *    *    *

By midday at the county attorney's office in Golden, I was feeling completely numb, like a shell of a person. Many others were much closer to the crime scene. The stress there had to be rampant, like a viral contagion sweeping through the community, but instead of carrying illness or disease, this one desensitized the nerves in anyone it touched. It was that insidious, taking away the ability to feel, but leaving the ability to function, a numbness that would return on 9/11. We went on with our lives, but wondering all too often, if they were still our own.

After leaving work, I stopped at a grocery store to buy a small bouquet, guessing that the closer I got to the high school, the scarcer flowers would be. On the way home I detoured past the library and Clement Park planning to add them to the growing memorial but changed my mind after slowing down to a crawl while driving past one parking lot after another filled to the brim with media trucks and RVs, camera crews and lights. The bookstore where Lee would soon be working was right over there on the other side of the street, helping out as only a barista can with both curiosity seekers and survivors. It was right next to the epicenter of an earthquake that two days before, had rocked her hometown. Lee had a gift for blending verbal acuity with the innate enthusiasm of being sixteen. And I believed her when she said that she was willing to work as many hours as needed.

After arriving at home, I went straight to the storage closet with the large cardboard box dedicated to wrapping paper and gift bags. I found the green ribbon, added some white, and tied a simple bow around the stems of the bouquet. On the card, I wrote, "In Memory of Kyle," and left the flowers laying out in the open while I fed Cody and made dinner for us. It wasn't long before Ben noticed the flowers. He was younger than Lee by eighteen months. Outside, it was dark, rainy, and cold. I tried to sound enthusiastic about taking a drive over to Clement Park to add another bouquet to a makeshift memorial emerging from the ground. Mostly,

I didn't want to go alone. "Come with me, Ben," I said. "This is worth remembering! You can place the flowers anywhere you want."

"What for?" Ben wondered, "I'd rather stay home and study."

"This isn't just another school day. Something historic is happening right now over at Columbine. Before it was scary and ominous, but the memorial is different. This is cultural history in the making."

He picked up the bouquet and read the card. "Who's Kyle?"

"One of the kids that didn't make it out of the library."

"Why Kyle?"

"'Cause there wasn't room on the card for all thirteen victims," I replied, wondering if we would talk more about this particular victim. "Grab your coat. We can stop for some ice cream on the way back home."

My bribe worked, but traffic was intense. Thousands of people had been arriving at the northeast corner of Clement Park all day, most of them carrying something to add to the growing mountains of rain-soaked flowers. Crime scene lights blazed into the night sky. Verdant spring grass had turned to mud. Workers from the Parks and Rec District were responding with truckloads of hay bales, scattering the hay in thick layers to create sinuous walking paths around the rows of flowers. On the other side of Bowles Avenue, we could see the storefront where Lee was already working. We might have joined the line of raincoats and umbrellas, but there were faster ways to enjoy a hot beverage. Instead, we inched our way into the slow line of cars making its way past the park. When we were close, Ben jumped out with the bouquet in his hand. I watched him walk alongside the car for a few steps, but then he jogged away into the labyrinth of green. I lost sight of him in the crowds of people, but traffic was hardly moving. There was time for him to make a memory of the place. Then the car door opened, and he climbed back in, his shoes wet and muddy. "It's like a maze in there."

"What did you do with the flowers?"

"I found a nook with some candles and pictures, and only a few people standing around. I set the bouquet where it wouldn't get crushed."

"Thanks, Ben, for coming…and for doing that."

The makeshift memorials at Clement Park would grow from large to enormous. Poems, drawings, and teddy bears, wind-chimes, jewelry, and letter jackets, all of them decorating thousands of bushels of flowers that piled up in mountainous rows. The school district would be renting warehouse space soon to store the nonperishable pieces and parts. And tens of thousands more were coming from all over the region and country. In their wake the wet and colorful mountains of flowers would grow even larger; the footpaths surrounding them would shift. A huge public memorial service was scheduled for Sunday afternoon. Funeral plans were being made. The twelve dead students were all about the same age and stage as the two growing up in my home, and that was more than I wanted to think about during the daylight hours. Kyle would be buried on Tuesday. All we could do was get through the weeks ahead one day at a time.

*　　*　　*　　*　　*

Near the entrance to the Historic Columbia River Highway, the driver of a shiny new pickup and his young family stops to look Forrest over. His friend, Don, still hasn't moved, the stoic look remains fixed on his face. "Where you headed?" Asks the driver as he rolls down his window.

"Bar Harbor, Maine," Forrest answers.

"That is a long way."

"It is," the lead cyclist agrees. "You wouldn't know of a place along this highway where we could camp tonight, would you?"

"There isn't a campground for thirty miles," replies the driver of the truck, an earnest young man in his twenties. His blonde-haired wife nods from the other side of the cab. There appears to be a child's car seat in between.

"The one at Cascade Locks," says Forrest.

"Yeah," the man agrees, looking towards his wife as if

checking to see if she is engaged with the conversation. But she seems more interested in the young child sitting between them in the car seat.

"Wonderful family," Forrest starts up again. "Anyplace up ahead where we might just set up our gear and get out quick in the morning? What's Corbett like?"

"You don't want to do that, not tonight. The highway patrol and the forest service will be all over this road. I know. I work with those guys a lot. There's a big fine. And they'll run you off for sure."

"Uh-huh..." Forrest nodes in response. "What kind of work do you do?"

"Volunteer fireman," the young father answers and turns toward his wife again. They exchange a few more words. She laughs at something, shakes her long straight hair, and makes a call from her cellphone. "You know," he says in a voice that I can barely hear. "We're having a little party with some friends tonight to celebrate the 4th. Actually, it's my parents' house...and she's on the phone with them right now."

"And we've got a talented musician with us, a real troubadour. Back home in Ireland, he's the man of six-thousand songs," Forrest says, bragging about Gerry. "Carries his own guitar. And loves to lead singalongs around campfires."

"We'll have a campfire for sure, and fireworks, and beer. The backyard is huge. Plenty of room for you guys to set up your tents," the young father explains, excitement creeping into his voice. But on the other side of the cab, his wife still talks into the cellphone. The blonde hair starts nodding up and down. "My dad's a cyclist too," says the driver. "He'll be up for this."

She hands him the cell phone and says something like, "Your turn, Brian."

A brief discussion ensues, the driver nodding his head throughout. Forrest turns around with an intense grin on his face. He gives the three of us a thumbs up and says, "You got yourself a gig, Gerry. Better warm up those fingers."

The truck with the young family on board pulls out of the gravel driveway and onto the historic highway. It pulls off the road

49

and onto the shoulder, easing the tensions emanating from the line of traffic still waiting behind. Forrest follows, walking his bike. Through the rear window, I can see Brian scribbling something onto a piece of paper. Frank sees it too because he's already pushing his way through the line of waiting cars and trucks to insert himself into the exchange of information. Gerry and I exchange grins, still standing in the same spot on the shoulder of a crowded highway, not quite believing what just happened. Forrest hands the address and a cell phone number to Frank who enters the data into the MapQuest App on his cellphone. Google knows the way from here.

*     *     *     *     *

At the Jeffco Department of Human Services, there was a veteran's affairs office inside Jefferson County Social Services. Kyle's caseworker would be contacting his distraught family to help with the funeral arrangements. Kyle was known for saying that he wanted to be a firefighter when he grew up; or that he wanted to join the Navy like his dad; which meant that because Kyle was the minor child of a veteran, he was eligible for a military burial benefit. Plans were made to bury him underneath one of the familiar white headstones of the Fort Logan Military Cemetery. It was what the family wanted.

Once the funeral services were complete, I would file a motion in the Juvenile Court to close his dependency or neglect case for good cause, certain that no objection would be filed by his parents or the GAL. The motion would be granted summarily. A few days later a paper copy of the signed order would show up in my inbox, with a note showing that another copy was already on its way to the caseworker. I would flip through the file and remember and wish once more that Kyle was still alive somewhere, and then move on to the next case in a tall stack of manilla folders.

*     *     *     *     *

Back in Corbett, it is my first encounter with trail angels. A young man, out for a holiday with his family goes for a splash in the river and to play in the park near his home on the 4th of July, probably mirroring an event he still remembers from his own childhood. They could have looked the other way and rushed straight home. But that's not what happened. He and his extended family decide to make a gift of kindness to a group of five interesting strangers; an unexpected development that Forrest had hinted at over dinner, and then engendered out of a traffic jam. And I would learn, or perhaps remember, that trail angels have a way of appearing when a genuine and substantial need arises.

Inside Columbine High School that is exactly what happened as soon as the shooting started. There were many acts of heroism that day, kindness too. One of the standouts was by business teacher and basketball coach, Dave Sanders. Knowing that armed intruders were inside the school and firing live rounds at students and staff, instead of fleeing for safety, he ran towards the areas where students and teachers would tend to congregate, to warn and urge them to flee, to save their own lives.

Another hero that day was the principal. Frank DeAngelis was sitting in his office at one end of the main corridor, waiting for a prospective teacher to arrive for an interview when the first shots were fired at victims sitting on the grass outside the building, students eating lunch in the warm sunshine. Eric Harris was there too, standing by one set of main doors, armed with a 9-mm assault rifle and exchanging fire with Deputy Neil Gardner, the school resource officer, and the first emergency responder to arrive on the scene. Dylan Klebold stood nearby, armed with an assault pistol of the same caliber. But Dylan had yet to fire. The two senior boys retreated from Gardner's show of force. They took their weapons inside the building, just as a PE class full of young women entered the main corridor from another direction. From behind his office windows, Frank DeAngelis was witnessing a terrible tragedy about to unfold, more ominous than anything he had encountered in all his years of school administration. Although they could not see each other yet, the paths of the women softball players and the two heavily-armed young males were about to intersect. There were just too many students moving through the same corridor. DeAngelis went flying out of the office doors at a dead run. Harris and Klebold saw or perhaps heard the commotion and fired.

Bullets from both guns sprayed into a glass display case but missed the running principal. Frank reached the softball players without being hit and herded the class down a side hallway that dead-ended at a locked door into the gym. He had a keyring full of possibilities and was able to figure out which one fit in time for all of them to enter the gym ahead of the guns. From there, he and the gym class all reached safety outside the building (Cullen).

But Stephanie Munson was in the same corridor, talking with a friend when a shouting man ran past them, crying out words she did not understand. She never saw the bullet that hit her in the lower leg, just above the ankle; never saw the senior boy who fired the round. But both girls responded to the moment and a sudden urge to flee for the nearest exit. Her friend, Melissa Walker, was unhurt. Together, they were able to reach the safety of Leawood Park, where a bystander with a cellphone called 911 (Erickson).

Teacher, Dave Sanders, was not so fortunate. He chose to stay inside the building after the shooting started and the pipe bombs began exploding. Security footage from a video camera showed him in action, running through the cafeteria and warning others to get out of the building. But he didn't stop there. He went on to the second-floor library to continue to warn of the approaching danger. There, he encountered Eric Harris and Dylan Klebold coming down the same hallway. The dedicated teacher tried to turn and run, but two bullets struck him down, one in the back and another in the neck. Dave Sanders would die inside the school he loved, with students and other teachers trying hard to save him (Erickson).

*    *    *    *    *

In Corbett, the campfire is blazing in the backyard when we arrive. The extended family comes out to meet and greet us and show us where to put up our tents. It's true—the lawn is huge— but there's more than just beer, there are hamburgers and hotdogs, delicious potato salad and deserts, all the ingredients of a tradition- al 4th of July celebration. Gerry brings out his guitar. I am about to learn that when the maestro says that he knows a few Beatles songs, he isn't talking about the basic chords. He has a working memory from beginning to end of all their hits, and many other cover songs from the sixties, seventies, and eighties. The campfire becomes a stage from which he quickly reveals his talents as a musician, experienced in public performances and, with a manly talent for accompanying and encouraging unsteady vocalists.

The music doesn't stop until fireworks rumble in the distance. It's a low familiar sound that causes me to turn my chair and look into the cool darkness of the night sky. Showering fountains of red, white, and blue appear, taking over my field of vision. Waves of yellow, green, and orange are next, followed by the deep thumps of whistling charges being propelled into the air. The showering embers seem to fill the sky overhead in a thunderous roar. Radiant white and yellow sparkles drift earthward as if reaching for our campfire.

It takes me back to the memory of a similar display, enjoyed from the verge of a reservoir near our first home in Colorado. Lee and Ben were not even in school and Ben, so small that he still fit quite comfortably inside his mom's lap, which is exactly where he wanted to be when the lights, colors, and fading embers began descending toward the earth, and explosive charges thundered in midair. "Benny kaado." I could hear him say.

But his mother and sisters were rocking from side to side and watching the show, saying in unison, "Oouu. Aaah."

"Benny kaado," he repeated, a little louder this time.

"Honey," I said. "He's afraid. Benny's telling you that he's scared."

"Oooo, Benny," she said, wrapping him in her arms. She held him against her chest and rocked him back and forth until the show ended, and he was fast asleep.

But when this show ends, Gerry picks up his guitar and starts to strum again, highlighting different rhythms and reminding everyone that the evening is young. He asks for another request, insisting that he is there to play for as long as anyone cares to sing. I look toward the house and see that we have separated into two distinct groups, one ringing the fire on folding chairs and another one laying back on more comfortable loungers on the patio, some of them already rising up out of those cushions and looking

53

around for empty cans or dirty plates to carry away. It sounds like half of the group is preparing to depart. Forrest is there with our hosts, Brian's parents, and a few of their friends, all of them shaking hands or offering hugs, commenting on the excellence of the party, and all of them saying goodnight.

Meanwhile, over at the campfire, Gerry passes his guitar to Brian who wants to take a turn at leading a song. I look into the embers of the fire, still enjoying its warmth and an unmistakable sense of community. When that song ends, the guitar gets passed again to a third player, but it's followed by a lull in the singing. I look around the yard, expecting to see an empty patio. Instead, there's one remaining guest, leaning against the wall of the house, a tall man in a baseball cap starring off into the smokey residue or perhaps some distant corner of the galaxy. Behind the haze of the beer, it occurs to me that he should come over and join us. That's when he looks right at me, and waves, and I realize that he's the one asking me to come over to join him. This is the first time I've seen him among the guests. No one in the circle by the fire seems to notice when I stand up and leave my chair. But I take my eyes away from the new guy for just a few seconds to navigate the patio steps. When I look up again, there's no one there, nothing but a few long-handled garden tools leaning against the shadows on the wall.

# Chapter 4
## Wind for Breakfast

*July 7, 2017*
*The Dalles, Oregon*

We have wind for breakfast this morning. It is high in the tree limbs rustling the leaves when we break camp. Out on the highway, the wind becomes a roaring beast, howling in my ears. We mass together near the side of the road, standing close and shouting to make ourselves heard. The wind envelopes us and steals our words away. It flows like a deep river out of the north, which happens to be our direction of travel, toward a high cliff of volcanic rock about two miles away. Perhaps the wind will abate there, near the base of the cliffs. It's something to hope for at least, and this Lewis and Clark Bicycle Trail is directing us there, to the base of the cliffs and then eastward, until we run out of road. We talk it over.

No one wants to retrace our steps over the rusting highway bridge back to the town named The Dalles to look for a comfortable restaurant with bright lights and soft chairs and dine in comfort on eggs and pancakes and coffee. Nor does anyone want to wait it out on the small patch of green where we camped last night by a once quiet pond nestled under tall cottonwoods. It was our first night on the Washington side of the Columbia River. Only in memory is it a restful spot. We decide to push on, against the wind.

We have been on the road together for one week, and this group of five has become an entity unto itself. To anyone who asks, any one of us would respond with a smile and identify ourselves as severely retired. More important are the common threads of health, vitality, and the pursuit of happiness from the seat of a moving bicycle for as long as any one of us can. So far, it's working well. The reactions from friends and family on social media lend support to this growing satisfaction.

The trip organizer is the glue that holds us together, but long before its beginning, Forrest crossed paths with each one of us and cultivated a shared interest in bicycle touring. He brought us together by sending out a group email invitation during the short days and long nights of last winter. With the same stroke, he demonstrated his mastery of personal computers and email. He proposed that we all come together and join him on this next fair-weather, cross-country adventure. He thought it would be a great premise for his next book. However, his embrace of digital technology ended there. Wild horses could not drag Forrest into the world of smartphone technology. On this journey, he swears by his flip phone, but seldom answers it. So, the only reliable way to communicate with the trip leader is face to face. We proceed along our shared path based on experience, paper maps, memory, guesswork, and the kindness of strangers.

It's a top-down communication style I recognize with regret, the same one that worked so well during the world war that my parents and their generation fought. But in peacetime, within the bosom of the family and community, that top-down style of communication engendered a home life that was all too often like walking through a minefield, especially during my teenage years. I grew up in the heartland of Ohio during the 1960s while an undeclared and escalating war raged in Vietnam. Inside our home and from the top of the pyramid, my parents and oldest brother controlled of every decision, taking their infallibility for granted. Those of us in the lower tiers got to see, hear, and smell what was going on around us, but it was just easier to suppress any emotional reaction or meaningful verbal response. The higher-ups did not want to hear about it. Any talking in the lower ranks could only mean that the eyes weren't focused on school, or the carrot at the end of the stick. But I would only live that way until a better opportunity arose.

On the road, Frank is the earliest riser. I'm not far behind. There is no better way for me to start the day than watching the sun come up with a cup of real coffee close by and my hardback journal close at hand. Inside a pannier that's full of items that don't need to stay dry, I carry a small stainless-steel percolator and an easily replenished bag of ground coffee. I'm fine with carrying the extra weight. And now that we are into the second week, there's a happiness to it, a rare choice that favors personal comfort over practicality and one that contributes—when faced with the prospect of pedaling the bike another day and another fifty miles—a sense of satisfaction and accomplishment with the daily aggregation of marginal gains. There's solace in the rising total of miles traveled, even nourishment. I've only to look at the map to see it.

We are crossing the border into Washington and the semi-arid reaches of the journey. Headwinds fill the wide-open plains that separate us from the high adobe-colored escarpment and the next turning point in the road. It looks from a distance like the long wall of an ancient fortress. A geologist would recognize a remnant of the flood of basaltic lavas that poured out from deep within the earth and covering everything in its path. Today, I can dream of making it to the road that runs along its base and resting in whatever windbreak lies in its shadow. The wind provides us with the unity of a common foe and a goal to reach.

Don leads the way, breaking the trail. The bikes crawl down the road. I am in the lowest of the granny gears. It is the only way forward, and, every turn of the pedals is a massive effort. It's a struggle to keep moving, a struggle to stay balanced. No one gets far without stopping to rest. When my turn comes to break the trail, my bike, Daedalus, stays upright only with continuous motion. Even with sunglasses on, I cannot look ahead for long. I can see the slight curves in the road ahead, enough to make each one its own goal, one more piece of the puzzle. Then I drop back and pass the chore on to another, resting awhile to catch my breath. So it goes, until the fork in the road appears, a junction where two blue highways meet and one turns east along the base of the cliffs. One by one we stagger there and rest, our bikes turned in a new direction, a fierce wind on our shoulders.

It has taken over an hour to ride two miles, and I am exhausted. Everyone stops to rest together. We replenish our bodies with energy bars, trail mix, and water. But no one wants to stop.

The day is still young and there is hope for a better campsite ahead. My mid-morning fatigue is nothing compared to the hopeless res-ignation that once deadened my senses and stooped my shoulders when I came through the door after work on that first Friday eve-ning, three days after the massacre. Hope makes all the difference.

*　　*　　*　　*　　*

Sunday morning dawned wet and cold, perfect weather I suppose…for a funeral. There were so many of them that week-end. Rachel Scott was buried on Saturday. Thousands attended her service, while tens of thousands more watched on live TV. Kelly Fleming and Daniel Mauser would be buried later that day. Mourn-ers were expected in similar numbers. Kyle Velasquez would be buried on Tuesday the following week, and another thousand mourners would attend (Shepard).

I woke up Sunday morning aware and remembering that this was the day of the community memorial service. Inside, there was no doubt that I wanted to take part; however confusing or painful or difficult to reach it was, I needed to be, had to be there. This was the community mourning, our reckoning, and a time for showing up and being part of a genuine and unified search for that infinitesimal glimmer of hope, during this time of what could only be described as unimaginable, untenable loss.

Kyle's funeral would be held at St. James Presbyterian, a sprawling unpretentious suburban church. I knew it well. The salm-on-colored building with its sloping suburban lawn, sat on a hillside a short walk from the 1950s style, rambling ranch home where we all used to live together, before the divorce. My relationship with St. James and its congregation was short-lived, once inside and partic-ipating in the Sunday morning services, nothing on the inside of me seemed to change. I began attending not long after my first wife moved out, and I tended to leave the church building just as con-fused and alone as when I entered, adding disillusionment to the mix of emotions that kept me awake at night; back when the job at the county was just beginning and the children were still in grade school. It wasn't long before attendance took more effort than I could mus-ter, singing praises and praying to a god I didn't believe in.

The divorce was final in 1993. In its wake, I filled the months and years with raising kids, having a career, and having a string of serially monogamous relationships, while keenly aware of the passage of time. It was embedded in the blue, red, and black lines of magic marker ink on the doorjamb of our kitchen, displaying for anyone who cared to look how fast the children were growing into their own lives. Multitasking was my norm, every day a balancing act of competing priorities. My long-term goals seemed simple enough: to live one day at a time, keep moving, and get the kids through college. If there was a path, I sure couldn't see it, or at least struggled to find lasting joy and value as I followed it.

During this same interval, I decided to test the waters of an evangelical church. I went looking for faith, for something to believe in, but it wasn't the promise of a better life waiting in the beyond that drew me in. The appeal lay in the dynamic vocals of the choir and the skilled performances from the podium and pulpit. At least that was what got me through the doors and inside the large and impressive auditorium. Once inside, I could feel it, the allure of community and the promise, of a sense of belonging. It even felt like security. But the longer I stayed, the more I encountered a community held together by fear and the mistrust of a common enemy. The leadership stood united against evil, but their definition cut a wide swath, starting with the devil and sin, but including in no particular order: Communists, Democrats, drugs (except for prescription opioids), extramarital sex, minorities, socialists, and gays. And I wanted more from religion than the belief that even though surrounded by enemies, I was not alone. Within my small corner of the world, I wanted character strengths and virtue, integrity, and a pragmatic design for living and improving my life right here on earth. I opted to continue the search for a faith that shines from within, for a light that burns brighter and brighter over the years from deep attention and practice.

But in the here and now of the aftermath of a massacre, all I could feel was an absence of faith anywhere in my life. *Of course, going to the memorial service is the right thing to do.* It also meant having somewhere to go and something to do that didn't involve kids or work as the motivator. I might even weave myself into the grieving and curious crowds that would inevitably attend. All too often at night, my brain wouldn't shut itself down. Maybe I could let go of some of that edginess and find some release from this growing unease. And then when it was over, come back home, maybe even build a fire in the fireplace, and see if anyone other than Cody wanted to come and sit by its warmth and light.

Meanwhile, I asked Ben and then Lee if they knew about the service and if either of them wanted to come along. They knew. But the last part was a negative. It was already wet and cold, with more rain was forecast. They had better things to do than spend a few hours one on one with Dad—at a memorial, no less. They seemed surprised that I even wanted to go.

Since I was on my own for the service, I had the freedom to make individual plans for getting there. I could put on my running shoes and jog over. There were definite advantages in not having to make everyday decisions by committee. But the most difficult part of jogging involved getting out the front door. I knew from long habit that once I got the engine of my body started and the legs moving, the worries fell away. Jogging at work during the noon hour was getting me through the aftershocks of Columbine. The endorphins provided a boost that helped me get through the rest of the day. Denver was filled with accessible and safe running trails. I knew the ones close to home well. I could follow the Platte River Trail halfway to the vast shopping center parking lot where the service would take place, just across the wide boulevard from Clement Park and its majestic impromptu memorial. There would be no traffic on the trail, nothing but an occasional jogger, cyclist, or walker. Then, I would have to jog west along Bowles Avenue, for the last few miles, carrying my water and some raingear in the Camelbak Classic that Ben gave me for my last birthday.

I wasn't opposed to driving. We had a dark blue Dodge minivan, just like so many others in the neighborhood. Inside, it would be warm and dry, but I was opposed to cruising around for however long it took to find a parking space, and then, having to walk through the same inclement weather for another mile or so, before reaching the security gate. Jogging there instead of driving would make a decent training workout, and maybe untangle some of my conflicting emotions. I cobbled together all of these reasons, put on my running shoes, and headed out the door. And if the clouds broke open, the rain would fall on me and everybody else, the makeshift memorials at Clement Park, the empty high school building surrounded by crime scene tape, and on the crowds of people already gathering for the Memorial Service. Maybe, I thought, it might wash away some of our collective grief, as well.

*   *   *   *   *

After leaving behind the hospitality of the trail angels in Corbett, Oregon—but not without a mouthwatering and generous breakfast—the great geezer cyclists spent the next two days riding sections of highway and trail being incorporated into a new and improved version of the Historic Columbia River Highway. It is another massive engineering project and for cyclists and pedestrians, artistry in progress. The Oregon Department of Transportation has been hard at it for decades working to reclaim and redevelop the original road, one project at a time. During the summer of 2017, ODOT's efforts are apparent between the towns of Cascade Locks and The Dalles. Here, isolated sections of the original Historic State Route 30 remain intact or have been rebuilt. These choice miles alternate between tranquil shady forests of fir and sun-filled open terrain, and they are dedicated to bicycle and pedestrian use.

Self-propelled and surrounded by incredible natural beauty, today's route leads past majestic, hard rock cliffs and scenic vistas with no cars or trucks to contend with. *This day couldn't get any better.* I became so enthralled with the beauty of the ride that I feel like telling someone about it. At the next overlook, I check my phone for messages. There's a new one from Lee. "Sounds like a nice trip you got going there," she writes.

The winds on that day in eastern Washington drain us of energy and motivation. We ride for less than thirty miles, far enough to reach Maryhill State Park on the Columbia River. I bathe in the river and bask on the long sandy stretch of riverfront sand. Lying beside it, I can catch up on the journal, and recover from the day's effort. We've been on the road together for more than a week, bound together with the mutual respect for the bicycle as the most efficient, non-polluting, and inexpensive form of self-propulsion ever devised. My lungs and legs and shoulders have acclimated to the routine of balancing on one for five or six hours every day, to pedal through a vibrant countryside caught up in the full bloom of summer, with regular breaks for eating heartily and checking out interesting places. Meanwhile, my body gets lean and healthy.

Todays ride along the bike trail is high above the concrete of Interstate 84 and the railroad lines that fill most of the level ground in the Columbia River Valley. I take delight in imagining future generations of earth scientists, thousands of years in the future, digging down through layers of earth to uncover a bicycle and pedestrian pathway reclaimed by ODOT during the 21st century and superimposed over an interstate highway from the late 1900s. Todays' geologists can ponder two different layers of rock and because one is on top, assume that the upper one is younger in relative age, unless some massive tectonic forces have been at work. It's called the principle of superposition. Futuristic scientists would logically conclude that the civilization that built the bicycle trail was the more recent and advanced culture.

*What can I say to Lee that might interest her in riding this trail someday? "Today's ride is a joy to the senses! Well worth a return visit."*

My optimistic prediction—bicycle trails will abound in utopia. These efficient, two-wheeled machines are survivors, deeply rooted in our history; but two days ago, otherworldly as I pedaled mine through a herd of RVs, cars, and pickups jamming the accessible miles of the Historic Columbia River Highway, turning it into an elongated parking lot anywhere near the elegant waterfalls that have made this highway a world-class destination. Pedaling my self-sufficient bicycle, I felt exposed and out of place, a stranger trapped in an orgy of waste and extravagance. A one-hour bike trip burns up about 350 calories. By comparison, a one-hour trip in the car burns up about 18,600 calories in energy (Lamb). So I have to ask: Does the USA's brand of freedom really reward self-sufficiency and individual effort? Then, the bicycle should be the obvious choice for anyone healthy enough to ride one. And a long tour like this one is my personal choice for metabolizing the chaos of memories like those from Columbine.

While we rest and recover on the riverbank state park, a young car traveler in the next campground goes for a beer run and gives us a twelve-pack. When that's gone, a different set of neighbors shares a growler of their own microbrew and delectable blueberry cobbler, homemade inside a Dutch oven using the red coals of a campfire. It makes for a delightful end to a memorable day, these spontaneous and serial acts of generosity between groups of young campers that wish to give, and a group of older cyclists, surprised and happy to receive. It makes the day feel so complete, that even if I had to power to look back and alter a portion of it, I would change nothing, not even the winds. But a day of high heat is coming.

*   *   *   *   *

The Sunday afternoon memorial service had a 1:00 p.m. start. The cynic in me assumed it would not begin on time. Organizers had planned for a crowd of thirty thousand. Seventy thousand showed up and many of them came prepared to wait. They were passing through the security gate and finding seats long before I arrived. They had already filled the thousands of folding chairs that stood in well-defined rows before the black and imposing stage at the far end of a movie theater parking lot. An expansive blue and silver ribbon festooned the top of the stage. It did not seem to matter that all the chairs were taken. Unobstructed views were available from all along the outer perimeter. Hearing was not an issue, because audio speakers were set up on tripod stands spreading out from the stage like the web of a vast spider. The whole parking lot was set up to resonate with the words and music emanating from the microphone.

All the broadcast news networks were there, the cameras rolling, recording every second. This intense scrutiny by the press had been constant ever since that first day when I heard the news in the lunchroom at work. Kids murdering kids. In less than one week's time, their coverage was transforming the word columbine from the name of a hardy mountain flower, into a Colorado public high school where gun violence by students had created an enormous and unwarranted amount of bloodshed, death, and destruction.

The stage was sprinkled with national dignitaries, including retired General Colin Powell, Vice-President Al Gore, and most of Colorado's congressional delegation ("Columbine High School Memorial Service | C-SPAN.org"). To my surprise, it would be the students and local dignitaries sprinkled throughout the program that left me with things to consider on the way home. They were the ones on that grey and dreary afternoon who were able to project an irrepressible message of hope. And I felt comfort in the words of one of the last to speak, Rabbi Fred Greenspan, who called upon all of us to remember:

> Healing does not come in days or weeks.
> Our pain is just beginning to emerge.
> Our world has been forever changed.
> We have learned that we are not the community we thought we were;
> That safety is not achieved by living in a particular neighborhood, or among certain kinds of people...
> May we learn from this horrific experience, how better to live our lives.
> May we find within ourselves, the resources to repair our own small corner of the world.

Two student troubadours started the program, taking the stage without introduction. Jonathan & Stephen Cohen had written a song about their experiences inside the school on Tuesday last. They were young survivors and their audience was immense and emotionally charged. It had to be intimidating for them up there on the stage, but the two brothers found their voices and quieted the crowd, grabbing our attention and keeping it with their zeal and passion. They were singing to the hometown crowd. Surviving family members of the victims, those that chose to attend, were in a dedicated section right up front and center stage. Surrounding them in support was the Columbine high school student body, teachers and administrators, and their families. I was part of the tens of thousands that ringed them in the back, a third band of curious onlookers and third-party witnesses to the manmade tragedy, offering our presence and the possibility of contributing to the sense of community. And more people kept coming.

Meanwhile, at the podium, the Cohens harmonized their way into the up-tempo chorus of their original piece. They sang out, asking the audience and in particular their classmates: "Do you still hear raging guns,/ Ending dreams of precious ones?"

Two young brothers had the temerity to open the program with the "g" word. And it repeated every time the chorus came around. These two Columbine students were the first of only three presenters that day with the courage to mention the "gun" word. All the other speakers were there to provide assurance, to invoke comfortable ideas in words already familiar to the audience, words they had been listening to throughout their lives. But having raised their provocative question, the Cohens persisted, providing their answer in another line of the chorus:

"In God's son, hope will come."

From my place in the standing-room-only section, I felt the discomfort of hearing young songwriters linking the two concepts together, god and guns, right from the start. But it was their song to sing. These were Columbine students, two surviving brothers, who also happened to be part of the evangelical community. Here, in unincorporated south Jefferson County, it was the predominant religious faith. Even if that made me an outsider, I could still pay tribute to Kyle and other victims of the massacre.

But I was not yet willing to submerge the knowledge that Kyle's murderer and the weapon that killed him came from this same community; the shotgun part of a private arsenal assembled within the basement workshop of one of their family homes. So too, the homemade bombs exploded by the murderers inside the school building (Erickson). I was not ready or willing to let go or compromise any of those objective facts. *How can I bury my head in the sand? My family lives just a short jog away. How many more basements are filled with these arsenals? And what are you, my neighbors, willing to do to prevent this kind of tragedy from happening again next year, and the year after that?*

Like the leaves of a sprouting plant, the dichotomy between guns and God would play out all afternoon long. Following a prayer by the Catholic Archbishop of Denver, dressed in fine and traditional robes, Governor Bill Owens opened the program. Owens was followed at the podium by three elected officials, all of whom represented local governments in some capacity. Of these three local dignitaries, only Jane Hammond, the superintendent of schools, had the presence of mind and moral fortitude to include a call to action at the end of her three minutes: "Enough is enough!" she declared. Then, she called on "community leaders to come together to do all that we can do to make sure nothing like this can ever happen again" ("Columbine High School Memorial Service | C-SPAN.org").

But the pragmatists were few and far between at the podium. Between Superintendent Hammond and the next pragmatist to speak came twenty minutes of evangelical culture from the podium. I wasn't about to leave. Instead, I passed the time walking through the crowd, mindful of the words and music coming through the audio system. The mournful sounds of a popular country-western singer filled up a few minutes. She was followed by a local preacher, and then another performer from the same faith-based community, who went on for over ten minutes about his personal relationship with the son of God ("Columbine High School Memorial Service | C-SPAN.org"). Except for Amy Grant, the last two performers had me wondering, *When do we start paying tribute to the victims?* Meanwhile, the clouds opened up. But most of the audience opened the umbrellas and buttoned up their ski jackets. I got out my anorak and lifted the hood. I wasn't going anywhere. This wasn't over yet.

Colin Power was introduced by Governor Owens about sixty minutes into the program, but he was not among the speakers. Instead, Vice-President Gore was next to take the microphone. He was the keynoter, with thirteen minutes to fill. The other heavy hitter that day was Franklin Graham, a preacher with a national reputation and ten minutes of program. He would be one of the closers.

The stage was filled with clerical authority. Al Gore had a chance to stand out and distinguish himself as the spokesperson for scientific inquiry and the power of reason. He chose to blend into the background, instead, bookending his speech with quotes from scripture. Sprinkled throughout the speech were ten more. That's almost one Biblical quote per minute of speaking time, and this from a politician with presidential aspirations? The content was like a cascade of unrelated ideas, spewing from a firehose at the podium. But Gore did manage to get and keep my attention after he finally got to a point where he started talking about the here and now, and the heroism displayed by several people whose names were well known within the high school community. He drew applause by invoking the memories of two widely known victims, Cassie Bernal, and the dedicated teacher/coach, Dave Sanders. Then, he called on the country to "Change our lives to honor these children" ("Online Speech Bank: Al Gore—Speech at the Columbine Memorial Service").

The Vice-President went so far as to ask rhetorically, "What say we into the open muzzle of this tragedy, cocked and aimed at our hearts?" It had the ring of an emotional climax, but little of the fury, because he backed away from his essential question by following it with another line from scripture. It was a moment in this speech when I might have identified with Al Gore as a father and human being. But he never stepped into it. I wanted to know what it was like to be Vice-President and part of the administration in which the assault weapons ban was enacted into federal law, if only for ten years (Lichtman). Or even what it felt to him, as a father and grandparent, to have loved ones in the public school system. But his words never addressed my questions. He never left the professorial, third-person perspective behind.

He did go into a prolonged discourse about parental responsibility, including a repeating line that went like this:

> We have seen enough of violence in our schools. We must replace a culture of violence and mayhem with one of values and meaning. *It is too*

*easy for a young child to get a gun*; and everywhere we look, there are too many lessons in how to use one.

*We can do something about that.*

We need more discipline and character in our schools, and more alternatives to drugs and crimes.

*We can do something about that.*

We need to recognize the earliest signs of trouble, and teach our children to resolve their differences with reason and conscience.

*We can do something about.*

("Online Speech Bank: Al Gore—Speech at the Columbine Memorial Service")

The repetition of a line like that within a presentation is called a callback. Comedians use them to cue the audience that they are supposed to start laughing when they hear these words. Speechwriters use them to give an audience something to remember from the presentation, a takeaway. But the repetition has to be memorable. The man at the podium was a former governor of Tennessee, the Vice President of the USA, and a presidential hopeful for 2000. The podium at Columbine was a golden opportunity to demonstrate leadership by breathing some life into the nascent movement for gun safety, the one that swept across the nation in the wake of the assassination attempt on President Ronald Reagan, and before that in 1964 after the successful assassination of President John F Kennedy. Gore's callback had no teeth, nothing to take home from his words.

The memorial service lasted for an hour under a slow, steady shower of rain. But not many people left. I had come looking for closure, but I wasn't feeling it, not yet anyway. Three times I listened to the Vice-President invoke his tedious catchphrase. Only once in his entire thirteen minutes did he say the word *gun*. I wanted to hear him stand up for the common-sense prohibitions of the assault weapons ban. Instead, he quoted another line from scripture and sat down, leaving the audience with a confusing line with a double negative that has been used millions of times in millions of funerals, "The Earth has no sorrow that heaven cannot heal." He read the words without emotion or impact. I heard them without realizing that the Vice-President was finished until I observed him returning to his seat. He never mentioned the gun show loophole. No one did.

Popstar Amy Grant sang twice. Governor Bill Owens repeated the full names of each of the victims, pausing after each one for the release of a solitary white dove ("Columbine High School Memorial Service C-SPAN.org"). Thirteen doves rose into low-hanging clouds to wheel around and gather their bearings, searching for a way to return, not to heaven, but toward the safety and security of their nests. Kyle's dove was one of them, circling and mingling, searching for something.

But the single bird could not contain his spirit. And how could his soul advance into the next world with so much ambiguity and unfinished business right here at home? After today's service and his funeral next Tuesday, his spirit might decide to remain restless and unfettered. Then, he could linger in the hearts of those who loved him and wanted more time with him. Or it might appear as a ghost in the minds and hearts of those who had wronged him, rattling around in their heads at night and keeping them awake. And for someone like me who had just wanted to help, but couldn't or didn't, or at least not enough, Kyle's spirit could have a piece of my heart and mind for as long as it wanted.

Even though few of the presenters at the memorial service were comfortable using the "g" word, the NRA was not so squeamish. By a coincidence of such magnitude that only the Fates of Greek myth could have conceived it, the National Rifle Association was coming to Denver within one week for its annual convention. Fresh earth would still mark the graves of the victims. The wounds of the survivors, still raw and gaping. A long hot weekend lay ahead.

## Chapter 5

### Heat for Lunch

*July 9, 2017*
*Roosevelt, Washington*

We are in central Washington, the dry part. Wind is the constant companion, steady and strong and coming from the north, defying anything that even looks like a small-grained particle of sand or dirt from staying around long enough to become soil. This road follows the Columbia River. Along the edge, verdant strips of green show off their vitality, their fortitude, and the rare places on this landscape where soil has accumulated deep enough to support their roots. Dark cliffs of basaltic rock line the highway's other side, occasionally broken by a valley with a dry creek bed. When the road does offer a panoramic view, it's well worth stopping to admire the huge swaths of barren bedrock and strange rock formations, as well as the hundreds of wind turbines. This is a place for lizards and reptiles to call home and take comfort on rock faces heated by the sun. A rattlesnake or two along the highway would not have been unexpected. But I would not see any along this roadside, not until we reach Idaho. Three of the cyclists are behind me. Frank is up ahead somewhere.

The color contrasts are so dramatic this morning that I have to take a few pictures. Once the cellphone is out of its pocket, the rest break expands into checking for messages from the apple of my eye. *How about that? There's one from Lee waiting to be opened!* She asks, "What were you doing in that last text?"

"Beautiful scenery. No cars. A fast downhill. It's called Historic State Route 30. Amazing day!" I answer back. It was calm when we left the campground early, wanting to put some miles in before the wind came up again and dominated the ride. Two days ago, it blew like the blast from a jet engine. I had to stand on the pedals in the lowest granny gear to keep the bike upright and moving forward. Today we are heading east along a highway that bends and curves around obstacles, but faithfully returns to the course of the river. There isn't much traffic. In some of these stretches, I can feel the wind like a caress across the shoulders, pushing me down the road as if I were riding on a motorcycle.

It is a peaceful Sunday morning. The road more traveled is on the Oregon side of the river. A constant flow of interstate car and truck traffic, and the small communities they support all across the river. Here, on the Washington side, it's just me and the bike, the pavement, and the occasional jagged rock formations carved out by the relentless beat of the wind. I haven't seen any of my friends since leaving camp this morning.

I crank the pedals through a bend in the road that leads me into a roadcut blasted right through the solidified lava. I come out the other side and there's Frank up ahead. *What a welcome sight*. He's stopped and waiting in the coolness of a shadow from the same rock, a rare spot that the sun won't reach until much later in the day. *Probably munching on an energy bar*. His bike is turned around and he's leaning forward over his handlebars. I coast right up to him and stop, say hello, and reach for my water bottle. We talk about how few towns there are on this side of the river and watch the traffic go by on the other side. Frank tells me that we're not even close yet to the next town. I've gone through about a liter of water so far, and the next stop is at a convenience store in a place called Roosevelt, about thirty miles away.

"It should be good and hot by then," Frank jokes.

In this shared moment, we have found a shady spot on the side of a two-lane highway to talk about topics of imminence to the ride, and of minor significance anywhere else. I take a break from pedaling, munch on a fruit and energy bar, and enjoy the coolness of the immense shadow we share. But in the background comes a sound that will soon take me out of this reverie. There is a car approaching the same roadcut. My back is towards it, but I can hear the engine accelerating towards us. Frank turns his bearded face towards the car. He nods. As the car rolls past I can see by the light bar and markings that it's driven by a deputy sheriff. *Nothing unusual about that. In my career at Jefferson County I worked with lots of deputies inside the courthouse and out.* Frank and I return to our conversation, and the car travels out of sight.

*　　*　　*　　*　　*

On the Thursday after the Columbine memorial service, Isaiah Shoels, eighteen years old, was buried. His service was held at a nondenominational megachurch on Denver's east side called the Heritage Christian Center. Over 5,000 mourners attended. Many rose to their feet to speak on Isaiah's behalf including Martin Luther King III. More than one of the speakers waxed optimistic in declaring that now, with this last burial, the healing could begin (Guy).

But on the subject of healing, the National Rifle Association had its own agenda. By some quirk of divine (or otherwise) timing, the NRA's annual convention was scheduled to commence in Denver on a Saturday morning, two days after the burial of Isaiah Shoels. The community's wounds, both physical and emotional, were still open, raw, and exposed. Healing would have to wait.

Only ten days had passed since the massacre and in the interim, angry barbs flew back and forth in the form of press releases between the gun rights organization and the mayor's office for the City and County of Denver. A three-day event had been on the books of the major Denver hotels for months, maybe even years. But all the planning and the signing of contracts had taken place during the period when most Coloradans still believed that columbines were bell-shaped mountain flowers, ones that came in a pleasing variety of colors and patterns. Now the word "columbine" was taking on a new meaning, becoming synonymous with mass murder, and the failure of existing gun legislation to keep anyone safe.

At first, Denver's mayor began by wringing his hands and pleading with the leadership of the NRA not to bring their national conference to Denver. He begged them to take their annual gathering to another city; he even offered to compensate the organization for their expenses in moving to another venue (Cullen). Mayor Wellington Webb did all the things that effective elected officials do to manage the metaphorical train wreck that was about to collide in his city. He wanted to renegotiate. But the leadership of the gun rights organization answered with an unequivocal, "No. We are coming anyway."

So, the mayor's office issued a press release that read, "We don't want you here" (Cullen). And no one in Colorado had to ask who Mayor Webb was referring to. Next, he canceled the NRA's lease for the Colorado Convention Center. The mayor could not guarantee the safety of the 4,000 conventioneers; his city could not afford the increased costs of providing security; and the Front Range community in which Denver belonged was still in shock, reeling from the destruction of one of our public high schools and the massacre of its students, by two boys with unmitigated access to weapons of war from within the community. Other performers or promoters had agreed and stepped aside, complying with similar requests due to the horrific and incontrovertible change in circumstances: the local NBC affiliate had opted not to broadcast a movie which featured trench coat-wearing killers brandishing sawed-off shotguns; United Artists Theaters removed the teen horror spoof from all its Colorado theaters; apocalyptic rock star, Marilyn Manson, canceled the final five shows of his tour, including a concert at Denver's premier summertime performance venue, Red Rocks Amphitheater (Tapper).

At one point in the negotiations, Mayor Webb turned his attention to the flagship hotel for the NRA conclave, demanding that management cancel the reservation. I learned of these discussions years later after the general manager of the Adam's Mark Hotel, Andre van Hall, joined a Toastmasters Club in which I was already a member. Andre was an immigrant from Argentina, a polyglot with a green card, and a man who grew up under the struggling economies of a series of military oligarchs.

It was a privilege to talk with him and learn his perspective about what it was like to be inside the Adam's Mark in the days leading up to the event. "Every day, there was another huge stack of hate mail—this was before email had ascended into common usage—filled with death threats and bomb threats," Andre remembered, "both toward me and the hotel. Uniformed guards were opening all my mail before I could see any of it. For two blocks all around the hotel, there were concrete barricades for traffic control, erected and maintained by the city. Police and private security were in control of all vehicular traffic coming into and leaving the building."

Every time the native Argentinian spoke about his discussions with Mayor Webb, a black man, Andre insisted that his focus was always on the First Amendment to the US constitution, and never the second. "It was freedom of speech and the right to assemble that guided my decision to honor the NRA's reservation to hold their annual meeting in my hotel. My answer would have been the same had it been the NAACP."

Ten miles away in my Littleton home, Saturday morning was cloudy and cold, the weather matching my moody depression. I was angry. It felt to me like the city where we lived, my family and I, was being invaded by a hostile force. Any other weekend, it would have been a good morning to get out of the house and go for a long run. But no amount of running could make me forget or ignore the fact that the NRA leadership was meeting downtown, with opening ceremonies about to start. In the final days leading up to the weekend, the NRA leadership did make the concession to reduce their meeting from three days down to one, but only after losing the lease to the convention center. At my office, everyone at work seemed frustrated and upset that the annual meeting was still being held at all. And it wasn't just the people I worked with. The same tension filled the air inside the coffee shops, in the streets, and in the grocery store; essentially everywhere. I had never before experienced this kind of community outrage, so palpable that a broad coalition of students and teachers, concerned parents, and local politicians came together to create a countervailing force, calling itself Sane Alternatives to the Firearms Epidemic or SAFE. This was a diverse and growing voice of reason, making a public demand for responsible gun ownership. Its leaders were making headlines, and I was drawn to the common-sense approach to the message. It had to be wrong that the murderers could purchase that kind of firepower, as juveniles, and then store it for months undetected in a basement of one of their suburban homes.

I grew up with one foot in the city and the other in the country and was no stranger to the National Rifle Association.

But the NRA of my youth was all about gun safety and marks-manship. During those same years when Charlton Heston was a fledgling young actor, my grandfather was still running his dairy farm with a few tired cows and chickens on 200 acres in Pennsyl-vania. I have fond memories of bucolic days and weeks there every summer, including going to the county fair where there would be an NRA-sponsored shooting competition for the adults. During autumn, I have memories of the damp, musky smell of decay-ing leaves underfoot, the sounds of squirrels chattering from tree limbs and the single-shot .22 caliber rifle that I was allowed to car-ry, with adult supervision, during hunting season. It was Grandpa's varmint gun. I loved that rifle and learned to shoot well with its open sights. But Grandpa also taught me what it meant to be a good hunter, to be sure of the target, and to only need one shot. Besides, ammunition cost money. Grandpa never had that much.

Today in the basement corner of my Colorado home, the old .22 rifle sits leaning against the cinder block wall. Right next to it is Grandpa's single barrel shotgun, and his deer rifle, a .32 caliber, lever action Remington, all of them covered in an ample supply of dust. I like to think that the shotgun still provides some measure of home security, but the deeper truths are that I've kept each gun be-cause of the memories they instill. I have tried to give them away. But neither Ben nor Lee has any interest. Apparently, old guns like mine do not elevate into the category of family heirlooms. So I am in a position to recommend that the state of Colorado or the county in which we live impose a hefty annual property tax and license fee on each gun—in the same way that I have to pay a tax to license my car each year—because that kind of tax on gun owner-ship would not just raise revenue for the state, in my case it would provide the motivation to either find a new home for the guns or haul them over to the county sheriff's office to find out if they can be destroyed in lieu of paying said tax. No one needs to wonder or worry about having to pry one from my dead hands.

\*    \*    \*    \*    \*

Back in central Washington and twenty years later, it would be easy to fall into a habit of describing the dry landscape as austere. The early settlers had a different word for it. They called it the scablands because it wasn't good for farming. Geologists call the rocks that created this landscape flood basalts; all around us for hundreds of miles in every direction, the region was covered by a great slow-moving flood of lava, frozen in place millions of years ago (Frisk).

This is a different kind of lava from the dramatic flows that blurp out from mountainsides in Hawaii and hiss into the sea. The flows in Hawaii harden into a kind of igneous rock that contains vesicles filled with tiny pockets of air. Those rocks are porous like a sponge, so that falling rain doesn't linger on the surface. On those habitable islands, the abundant rains drain down into the earth and collect in widespread aquifers and water tables that support the varied lifeforms that grow and thrive there. But, here in central Washington, the scant rains tend to collect on the surface of these hard rocks and then evaporate away.

The ground basalts of central Washington have little or no natural porosity or permeability. The entire landscape was formed by a fountain of magma making its way to the surface from deep within the mantle of the earth in a slow-moving current. On the surface the flows cooled slowly. Any gases that might have collected inside of them to form vesicles escaped into the atmosphere. The lava that created these immense flows took its time, cooling into enormous sheets of homogeneous rock, including the cliffs that line the highway we pedal down on our bicycles.

Frank and I are still standing together in the cool shadow of a massive basaltic escarpment, talking, when the car returns, coming from the opposite direction. This time, I smile and wave as it slows down, guessing that the deputy might be bored on a quiet Sunday morning and looking for someone to talk with. He brings the car to a stop directly across from us. The window rolls down. From the framework of my social conditioning, I am expecting: *Where are you guys from? How far are you going?*

Instead, a young man in a sheriff's uniform looks at me and asks, "Are you trying to give me a hard time?" The eyes behind the sunglasses are focusing on the black mustache and skin-tones of my face, reflecting the Greek side of my ancestry.

This is no greeting, and I am stunned into silence. The hostile tone takes me right back to the kid from Akron and his days on the playgrounds. To that smart-ass young kid this is a challenge, a line in the sand, and a small part of me wants to push right back with the twenty-first century equivalent of, "Oh yeah, well my Dad carried a tommy gun."

But I am a stranger in Washington and a long way from home, with nothing to gain by pushing back and engaging in the battle of wills he's trying to provoke. If I say nothing, however, he will probably keep right on pushing, upping the ante, until I feel coerced into showing my irritation. (At least, that's what happened back in the playground days.) I don't know this man, but instinct tells me that it's time to find my voice. The words, "not at all," roll out of my mouth. The tone is as flat and plain and vanilla as I can muster.

"Then *what* is your foot doing all over the white line of that highway!" the deputy demands, pressing his point verbally and, by leaning his arm out the window far enough to display the strips on his sleeve.

*       *       *       *       *

As a young boy, I watched Charlton Heston talk to God, win chariot races against teams of faster horses, and part the Red Sea, all from the back seat of the family 1956 Dodge station wagon, parked at a drive-in movie theater. I was in awe of his powers, impressionable, and too young for school. I would also be fast asleep in the back long before the credits rolled for early movie epics like *The Ten Commandments* and *Ben Hur*. But my idolization did not stop there. As I grew into a young teen, I watched Heston battle overwhelming numbers of intelligent apes to a standstill, a lone American astronaut on an earthlike planet. The early *Planet of the Apes* movies became cult classics. I was a huge fan. And the train kept on rolling. In my early twenties, Heston starred in another movie destined to become a cult classic, *Soylent Green*, once again cast as the lone heroic figure struggling against a different set of incredible odds. Heston was always cast as one man against the evils of the world, which, from the perspective of the seat of this moving bicycle, seems to align with the worldview of the evangelical church that briefly lured me in, not long after the divorce.

Outside the Adam's Mark hotel, no vehicle can enter the parking garage without a bomb-sniffing dog first confirming the absence of danger. Cars trying to get into underground parking first had to have handheld magnetometers swept underneath. But even with all of their numbers and state of the art technology, the security detail was unable to stop one solitary individual who slipped inside the hotel in the early Saturday morning and made his way undetected into the same basement ballroom where the business meeting and luncheon would be held later that day. According to Andre, the general manager, the intruder lay down on the carpet and hid underneath one of the tables with a long drop-down tablecloth, a homeless man more interested in food than sabotage, and fell asleep.

Inside the hotel ballroom, the idol from my childhood was trash-talking the city where my children and I lived, where Kyle Velasquez died, where far too many teenage students were shot down by two of their peers in possession of weapons with high-capacity magazines used to fatal effect, all the while relaxing behind the thick walls and air-conditioned comfort of a downtown hotel. *Somebody should take a stand against this guy.* Except for his glaringly fake hairpiece, Heston at seventy-six still bore the same craggy good looks, and still spoke with the same pregnant pauses that were part of his signature. But no longer was he playing the disenfranchised loner struggling against the forces of evil. Charlton Heston had morphed into an insider with exclusive membership in a private world, something that his lone hero counterpart might have once sought to dismantle. The little boy inside me felt betrayed. Heston was a powerbroker, an elderly superstar ensconced in the comfort of vast accumulated wealth from a long portfolio of successful box office movies. He has come to Denver wearing his true colors as the spokesman for the well-funded political machine that was, and is, the National Rifle Association.

For all those reasons I found myself on the grounds of the capitol building early Saturday morning among the thousands of protesters gathered beside its golden dome, preparing to take a stand for the enactment of laws designed to prohibit juveniles from acquiring weapons of war, and to protest against gun violence in our public schools. Taking the lead at the head of the growing body of outraged parents, students, and teachers was an unassuming man named Tom Mauser. He lost his son at Columbine. He was the day's true hero, the one struggling against overwhelming odds, about to lead this freshly minted Colorado Coalition Against Gun Violence to the doorways of the Adam's Mark Hotel (Tapper).

Earlier that week, the NRA had made public accusations against Tom Mauser, accusing him of "profiting" from his son's murder, or of being a "dupe" of gun control activists. Both statements were unsupported lies, but issuing from the mouth of an aging superstar, they had a smooth and easy listening way about them; words intended to dissemble and deceive, and above all to conceal the NRA's true motives or beliefs. The diatribes of the NRA elite always overlooked or ignored the incontrovertible, that Tom Mauser's son Daniel died in the library at Columbine, not long after Kyle.

But the NRA that Heston welcomed in the opening ceremonies at the Adam's Mark Hotel was nothing like the one I knew as a youth in rural Pennsylvania. Under Wayne LaPierre, who elevated Heston into the roles of president and spokesperson, the organization has morphed into a multifaceted, tax-dodging chameleon, corrupted beyond all recognition by the demands and wealth of its corporate donors (Lichtman). The original NRA has been split apart and reassembled into multiple legal entities, including both charitable foundations and political action committees; one limb of the resulting Hydra solicits donations from individual members, another from gun manufacturers and retailers, while a third arm funnels donations into the election campaigns of malleable candidates who aspired to hold public office including George W Bush. Once in office, NRA money would continue to flow into their campaigns, for as long as the newly elected officials showed their willingness to march in step with the NRA's drum. The same public officials could demonstrate this allegiance by following the recommendations of the lobbyists and lawyers who worked in yet another tax-exempt arm of the National Rifle Association. In 1999, the NRA was a well-oiled juggernaut, a lobbying force that two years later, following the election of George W Bush to the White House, would be recognized by *Fortune Magazine* as "the top political lobbying organization in the United States" (Sarasohn).

LaPierre couldn't have done it alone. He needed the charisma and voice of the aging superstar, Charlton Heston, to explain to their loyal members why it was better for American gun markets to remain untaxed and unregulated, than to prevent troubled teens from possessing weapons of war like the 9-mm semiautomatics that killed Daniel Mauser and fatally wounded a beloved teacher, David Sanders. Charlton Heston had a way of making us feel good about owning a gun.

*    *    *    *    *

Back in central Washington, there is no need for me to see the eyes behind the sunglasses to catch the meaning in the stripes. I have seen the look of feigned indifference before. The man in the uniform, a deputy sheriff, is showing me without words that on a Sunday in this remote Washington county, he is the law: that should this conversation go into any direction except for the one he's proposing, he might have to choose whether to transport me and the bike to the opposite end of the county for a long ride back across a hot and inhospitable landscape, or to the county jail where I'll sit until the courthouse opens, maybe Monday morning, when the county judge will inform me of the charges against me and set bail.

The young face is like a mask of stone staring down at me from a few feet away, and I respond by making myself smaller and smaller in appearance, collapsing my shoulders and looking down at the shoes on my feet, backing up my bicycle, and turning the handlebar enough so I easily guide the wheels closer to the inside edge of the painted width of shoulder. Slowly, I walk it back towards the spot where Frank still waits. "How's that?" I ask in the plain vanilla voice.

"You know," the young deputy declares in reply, "we're just trying to keep you cyclists safe out here." The harshness in his voice becomes conversational.

*My children are older than this dweeb*, thinks an angry piece of my brain. But I say nothing. Frank speaks up and says, "That's what we're about, too," interjecting himself into the scene.

"Are you with those other three guys?" the bully in uniform inquires, turning his head so that the sunglasses focus only on Frank.

"Yeah," Frank responds, nodding his head in agreement.

"There're back a couple of miles, taking some pretty pictures and admiring the scenery."

"They'll catch up when we get close to food," Frank answers with smooth assurance.

"That's gonna be a while."

"We know. Any place out here you can recommend?" Frank asks.

"There's a good place to eat up ahead in Roosevelt. Don't let the gas pumps fool you. The food is real good," the deputy responds, sounding like he's taking Frank into his confidence. "You'll see the restaurant just before the turnoff that takes you up to the big landfill on top of the cliffs. You can't go wrong there with anything from their grill."

"You talkin' about the landfill or the restaurant?" Frank jokes in response, showing that he's alert and paying attention.

"No worries," the deputy says. "The landfill's closed today," making a quip of his own. "Seriously, the burgers and fries, are not to be missed."

"Guess we'll be taking off then," Frank says, turning his bike around on the otherwise empty highway.

"It's gonna be a hot one. You guys take it easy in the heat." The deputy says goodbye by lifting his stripes back inside the car, closing the tinted window to his airconditioned SUV, and taking the last word, all in one smooth motion.

"Let's get out of here," I say, only to Frank, but remembering a different outcome when I was a young protective father, face to face with the feigned indifference of men, and women, in sunglasses and riot gear, when they lined the sidewalks outside the Adam's Mark Hotel.

Frank gives me a thumbs up and pushes down on the pedals. I wait by the side of the road, watching his Tibetan prayer flags grow smaller and smaller—nothing but a couple of hose clamps on a flexible aluminum pole holds them in place—feeling numb and wanting to stay that way, so I can think back to that long ago protest against the NRA. I don't want to talk about or relive today's interchange. Don't want the distraction. All I want is to push the pedals and keep Frank within sight.

*     *     *     *     *

Eight thousand people assembled on the capitol grounds that Saturday morning to expose the lies. I should have been tired, far too much of last week's time and energy had been dedicated to cleaning up after the NRA-inspired massacre. I could have let myself be distracted by work or family, but I wasn't. I reached the capitol building and found myself within a swelling sea of like-minded people and felt my energy and confidence returning; as if there was a deep reservoir of energy that would keep not just me going, but the entire SAFE community, all of us poised to march against unmitigated gun violence and the repressive politics of the NRA. A few signs read, "Shame on You NRA" and "Guns Do Kill People." Tom Mauser wandered through the gathering crowd of supporters with a grim, tired face and large buttons clipped to the sides of his taupe, all-weather jacket; each button had a picture of his son's smiling face. Behind him, a volunteer carried another sign that read, "My son Daniel died at Columbine. He'd expect me to be here today" (Cullen).

At 10 a.m., the crowd went silent as a nearby church bell began to ring. It rang not thirteen, but fifteen times, one for each of the Columbine dead. As silence returned, a local clergyman spoke to the crowd, and then another. Then, it was Tom Mauser's turn at the podium. "There are reasonable gun owners, many," he said. "But the time has come to understand that a TEC-9 semiautomatic weapon like the one that killed my son is not used to kill deer. When a child can grab a gun so easily and shoot a bullet into the middle of a child's face, as my son experienced, something is wrong," Mauser said, struggling to maintain his composure. "It is time for change," he said, raising his hands in the American Sign Language gesture for love before collapsing in sobs (RIDDER/ TRIBUNE).

When Charlton Heston took the podium in the basement ballroom of the hotel, he first paused and stood with the gravitas of the biblical Goliath himself, a posture practiced in his long movie star career. In his opening comments, he referred to the city's repeated requests that the NRA stay away from Denver as "offensive" and "absurd." Heston went on to explain, "I guess what saddens me most is how it suggests complicity. It implies that you and I and eighty million honest gun owners are somehow to blame, that we don't care as much as they" ("National Rifle Association Convention | C-SPAN.org").

Did you see it? The opening lie? It's the first of many layers of subterfuge to come. Charlton Heston is assuring the crowd that he alone is the voice of eighty-million gun owners. He's claiming that not only does he speak for eighty million other people, he's also vouching for their honesty. Right from the start, I have to ask whether or not Heston is including me in his calculation? Because no one from the NRA ever called to ask what I thought about reasonable limits on gun ownership, or about taxing and regulating the industry, even though I own a couple of hunting rifles and a shotgun. I would have answered that I support universal background checks before anyone can buy a gun. I would have mentioned my belief that when bullets cost as much as a car, there will be a lot fewer of them in the hands of juveniles with no weapons training.

Back on the capitol grounds someone took up the song "We Shall Overcome". It spread through the crowd and the march began, moving away from the higher ground of the capitol building, across Broadway Boulevard and toward the Adam's Mark, standing tall near the end of the 16th Street Mall, and ringed with parallel rows of low concrete barricades. Behind them, the sidewalks overflowed with Denver police, state patrol, and plainclothes security. They wore Kevlar vests and impassive faces, and sunglasses on a cloudy day. They had the building surrounded. All that separated thousands of protestors from Denver's largest hotel was about six-hundred yards of asphalt and concrete. Even within this crowd of people, the first steps were tenuous. Alone, I would never have found the will to do this, to walk in protest and find myself within speaking distance of a wall of police. When we reached the barricades we stopped, more than enough to ring the hotel and face off symbolically with the Goliath inside, a near-sighted monster that refused to see any point of view other than its own. When my knees felt weak, I reminded myself of Lee and Ben and Kyle, remembering that our cause was just, and that history was on our side.

Under existing federal law, it is illegal for surviving family members to sue the companies that made or sold the weapons that killed or maimed their children in all the public places where mass murders have taken place since Columbine: because Columbine was the tipping point for this particular brand of tragedy. And up until leaving home to go on this bicycle tour, the numbers of dead and wounded Americans from mass casualty events have been steadily rising (Canipe and Hartman).

Here, on the Front Range of Colorado, it feels like we are having to bear far more than our share. The Aurora Theater massacre took place in an eastern suburb of Denver during the summer of 2012. Twelve more innocents were killed inside a movie theater, and seventy more injured. Colorado's third massacre with victims in the double digits, was the grocery store shooting in Boulder, Colorado on March 22, 2021. Ten were murdered that day, including a police officer.

Of course, it's not just in Colorado. Las Vegas, Nevada, endured a terrible massacre at an outdoor country western concert in 2017; sixty-one innocent victims were killed and four hundred eleven wounded by gunfire. Sadly, large scale public massacres have spread into eastern states as well. During December of 2012 in Newtown, Connecticut, another angry, young, white male with an AR-15 shot down twenty-six innocent victims at Sandy Hook Elementary School. Twenty of his victims were first and second graders. Six years later in Parkland, Florida, seventeen more students were killed, and the same number injured by gunfire at Stoneman Douglas High School. And all of these massacres had at least one common denominator, there was an angry young white male with his finger on the trigger.

The ban against civil lawsuits can be found within the language of the Protection of Lawful Commerce in Arms Act, first sponsored by Senator Larry Craig of Idaho. The law was enacted during the George W Bush administration. Where's the integrity in a federal law that prevents victims of gun crimes and their surviving family members, from bringing lawsuits in negligence against arms manufacturers and gun distributors in state and federal courts? Because the 12-gauge Savage-Stevens that killed Kyle Velasquez, the 9-mm semiautomatic that fatally wounded David Sanders, and the TEC-9 that killed Daniel Mauser—all these guns are weapons of war. The gun manufacturers and the sellers had to know what these products were capable of when they landed in the wrong hands.

In the USA, we have a long and established legal tradition of holding the cigarette, pharmaceutical, and automobile manufacturers legally responsible for the damage their products cause. It is practically un-American to let those who manufacture and distribute the weapons used in public massacres off the hook of civil liability for the damage done by the negligent use of their products. According to authors Canipe and Harrtman of Reuters News Service, through April of 2021 and including the Boulder grocery store massacre, more than two thousand living, breathing Americans have been killed or wounded in mass casualty events since the 1999 Columbine Massacre.

\*     \*     \*     \*     \*

Back in Washington and after three hours of trying to keep up with Frank, I am too tired and too hot to care much about what did or didn't happen out on the highway this morning. The sign outside says simply, Café. Frank smiles from the porch and holds up what looks like the remains of an ice cream sandwich as I ride into the parking lot. He's sitting on a shaded bench surrounded by the pine logs of a front porch built onto the cinder blocks of a one-story rectangular building. Through the window, there is a cluster of empty tables. The sign on the door boasts of air-conditioning, but all I can see is the ice cream freezer at the opposite end of the porch and the colorful, larger than life pictures on the front displaying the assortment of cold goodness.

I lean Daedalus against the shady side of the building and join Frank on the porch. On my way to the freezer, I get distracted by the glass-covered face of an antique analog thermometer, hung in a shady spot high on the wall. The red indicator hand is over one hundred degrees.

# CHAPTER 6
## A RACE TO KAMIAH

*July 13, 2017*
*Kamiah, Idaho*

"Get off the highway!" howls a mocking voice through the open passenger window of the pickup's extended cab. A dark, late model truck roars past as I straighten up against the handlebars and take my eyes off the road to see who—or what—is shouting at me. *Was that laughter I heard in the background?* Seconds later, a nearly identical truck zips by following close behind, but this time, the windows are shut.

The road is narrow here, cut between outcropping rock and a tight bend in the wild and majestic Clearwater River. Sunlight beams through tall cedars, flooding the sparkling water with low angled light. I can only spare an instant for looking around and holding the line of the front tire as it tracks the white line of the highway's edge. It feels important to see the person behind the harsh words or at least the back of their head. *A couple of rednecks probably, whiskey on their breath, out for a morning drive.*

But no. The redneck idea is my own built-in bias creeping out into broad daylight. What I can see through the back window of the passing pickup, is a perky blonde ponytail sticking out from behind a baseball cap in the middle of the back seat, the left arm wrapped around the shoulder of a much smaller person, but the right arm still raised in the direction of something offensive and just beyond the window, the finger still pointing.

This is no time for surprises. To stay on the road, I have to drill my eyes onto the white edge of the shoulderless highway. *Keep the tires on the asphalt, and keep pedaling through this turn.* And as I look down, there on the tarmac is the one true reptile I have been expecting to see ever since the day of high heat riding across the flood basalts in central Washington, a young rattlesnake, passing beneath my ankle and foot. But already flattened into oblivion by hundreds, possibly thousands of truck tires, like the ones that just passed me by.

Our group of five cyclists is intentionally strung out along the highway. The two-lane road has almost no shoulders. We are pedaling on a warm weekday morning through a pleasant river valley that is beginning to fill with traffic. The traffic consists mostly of recreational vehicles and pickup trucks, looking for a tempting spot to pull off the highway to cast a fishing line, or maybe just to pause for a longer look at the beams of sunlight reflecting off the river. Next are the intermittent short-haul truckers, loaded with long logs of fresh-cut cedar and bound for a distant sawmill. Least, in terms of numbers, are the cars and trucks with Idaho license plates, the locals, going about their daily routines, people who know the river in all its seasons, with favorite places deeply lodged into their long-term memories. I have already stopped several times this morning to appreciate the overwhelming beauty of this river, and perhaps understand why the locals would feel possessive about it. There is majesty in the sun-draped boulders and steep rock walls, and in the fast water that runs through them.

All morning, the cars and trucks have found a way to pass without incident. Like all the other cyclists in our group, I have a long flexible aluminum pole extending from the back frame of my bike. Mine has a miniature US flag attached, and right below it, a pennant of fluorescent orange. For the four-wheeled traffic on both sides of the highway, I want to be easy to spot from a long way off. The pennant and my green reflective jacket may have already saved me from serious injury today. To use them routinely feels like a confession, or at least a declaration, that I am vulnerable and exposed. Today, they remind me that the long game is to reach home at this journey's end, safe and sound.

Unless the bike and I are facing into the wind, I think that I can hear the difference between a car or a truck or a big RV, from the sound of the engine as it approaches. And if a horn is involved, I like to think that I can guess the mood of the driver as well. Oftentimes, it's a friendly little toot like Mr. Rodgers is behind me and wants to pass. But the long and blaring ones are out there too. Those drivers have no interest in sharing the road with a cyclist. For every one of those, there will be a car headed in the opposite direction that slows down enough to give me a thumbs up. Every day on the bike, another mixed bag of interactions, ranging from the friendly to the frantic, with people and circumstances over which I have no control. All of these fellow travelers with their ready supply of mixed messages can only be constant reminders that the source of my happiness comes from within, from the ability to crank on the pedals until I can reach the next lunch stop or rest break, until the sunset that comes at the end of the day.

Short-haul truckers are getting paid by the load to haul cedar logs. They whoosh by in a curious blend of freshly cut cedar and diesel. I'm not saying that all of them seem to be in a hurry, but the ones that are feeling the press of time let me know with a blast from the air horn and the sound of a big engine that is not gearing down. Others use their gears to hang back and wait for a better time to pass, then make their move with a quick blast of the horn. And some pass by on the other side, empty and returning for another load, waving from inside the cab.

This morning all the travelers on the road, especially the cyclists, are fortunate. We all find the grace to make it through that narrow stretch of sinuous and well-traveled and breathtaking-in-its-physical-beauty highway without incident. This morning is a self-propelled, experiential ride governed by the mysterious distractions of a fast and wild river in full summer, deep inviting pools of frigid water, sandbars and sunbathers basking in reflected light, all of them intriguing from the slow-motion perspective of a bicycle. But the most compelling visual of all, odd and unexpected, is yet to come—a young mother in a red bikini and baseball cap, her blonde hair pulled back in a ponytail, watching her children as they play by the river in the sunshine.

Two days ago, we stopped in Waitsburg, Washington, and spent the night at the county fairgrounds right outside of town after an eighty-two-mile day; not bad for five aging—don't even mention the word retired—cyclists, all of us in pursuit of good health and happiness. After showers and freeze-dried dinners, Frank, Gerry, and I went looking for the local pub to finish the day with a brew. Forrest watched us remove our panniers from our bikes to lighten the load and then stack the gear by the covered picnic tables where we would later roll out the sleeping bags. "Don't stay gone for too long," he cautions.

"Sure, Dad," teased Frank, unplugging his cell phone from the electrical outlet where it was recharging. "Look at that. Still plenty of signal way out here."

"For another couple of days," replied Don, rising from a comfortable position inside his sleeping bag to make his point. "Wait until we get *inside* Idaho. There's nothing at all. Not unless you want to pay the fee to hook up with a local provider."

"Take something to lock your bikes together," Forrest warned, revisiting the subject of getting to the bar. "Don't make it easy for someone to steal one of those bikes." But by the time we reached the town's only brewery, it was closed for the day. Gerry made a prediction: our luck would improve the next time that we three disappointed cowboys slipped away for a brew.

The next morning we slept in a bit, catching up from yesterday's long ride. We backtracked into town for breakfast at a nondescript-looking café on Main Street. Once inside, however, everything turned distinctive. The eggs and cinnamon rolls were a particular delight. The day was off to a pleasant start. Standing on the sidewalk after the meal, it felt like I might be standing on a corner in Waitsburg—as opposed to Winslow, Arizona—in my bicycle gear. (I'm such a fine sight to see.) *There's a girl, my lord, in a custom-made T-shirt, slowing down to take a look at me.* Her shirt was dark purple. Across the front, it read, "Resist Mediocrity!" The smile on her face made it easy to strike up a conversation. Once I mentioned being from Colorado and on a bicycle trip across the continent, the smile on her face grew even warmer. She, too, was an ardent cyclist and, a newcomer to Waitsburg. She also had a dream—to one day own and operate a bicycle hostel out of the new home she was searching for along the Lewis & Clark Bicycle Trail. Resisting mediocrity was both motto and creed, and her reason for leaving Colorado. She had moved out of Boulder after living there as an artist for many years. "But," she explained, "it just got too crowded and entitled." Waitsburg was a small town in the intermountain west that wasn't stuck on itself, a safe, affordable place to live, and a summer destination for cyclists. To complete our triad of circumstantial connection, she too, was originally from northern Ohio. I promised her a copy of my next book if I ever got around to writing it.

A day later, we crossed the Snake River and the border into Idaho. We had to stop at the state line for a Kodak moment, a group selfie of the five of us and the bikes sandwiched between the twin cities of Clarkston, Washington, and Lewiston, Idaho. As we posed for each other in front of the colorful welcoming sign with our bikes, a younger man sauntered up and offered to help out with the picture taking. He snapped a thorough series of photographs while taking the opportunity to promote his local independent business. "If any of you guys want some pot, you'd be smart to stock up in my shop. You won't find it this easy once you're over that state line. My store's right over there," he said, pointing to the other side of the bridge.

We all thanked him profusely for helping with the photography and for the advice on where and how to stock up on legal marijuana. But not for me, I am too dependent on and grateful for a healthy set of heart and lungs. The conversation did make me feel good though, about living in a country where borders are defined by differences in the law, rather than border guards, passport checks, and another language to navigate.

The five of us rode into Lewiston together and quickly found a local restaurant filled to overflowing with workday lunch customers. There was comfortable seating by the bar, where everyone but Forrest, the group vegetarian, tanked up on a large hamburger and fries. The cities and towns would get smaller and smaller from here, at least until Missoula. This was the perfect time and place to check for messages, and to send one that said: "Hello, Lee. Just crossed into Idaho. Will be out of internet range for a few days."

\*   \*   \*   \*   \*

"Hey, Dad!" It was Lee trying to get my attention as I hustled around the bedroom doing my last-minute packing for a long weekend with a couple of jogging friends in Steamboat Springs.

90

Lee's eager-to-get-going voice carried upstairs from the front part of the house. It was a Friday morning. School was out for the summer, and Lee, on her way out the door.

*Maybe she wants to wish me luck or something.* I walked over to the top of the stairs and looked over the rail. She was standing on the lower level of our split entry house, one hand looking at her watch, the other hand on the doorknob. Everything about her said sixteen-year-old in a hurry. I noticed for the first time that her beautiful auburn hair has been cut short for the summer. "How's Lee this morning?" I asked, feeling that natural parental interest in slowing down the conversation. "Like your hair," I said, remembering once again that the color was so much like her mother's.

"Doing all right, doing all right," she answered, looking up at me through sunglasses and a straight face. "Da, I'm trying to line up a new job. Got to get going here. But I wanted you to know... you're so into the Columbine thing...did you know that one of the gun sellers is going to be on *Good Morning America* this morning?"

"No way," I replied, truly surprised that anyone was coming forward so quickly, and once again displaying my ignorance of anything related to daytime television.

"For real. Thought you might want to know," she said with an approving nod. "You have fun this weekend."

"Thanks for letting me know." Then, I took a breath and added, "I really do like your hair that way."

Even behind the sunglasses, the words of approval seemed to make her face light up, not quite a smile, but close. "You have a good time with Peggy and your friends over there in Steamboat."

Coming from that father place, I answered, "You and your brother stay safe this weekend. Take care of things around here."

"The pets are in good hands," she said, "the house...maybe not so much."

"Pretty funny, Lee."

"I do my best."

"See you Sunday night."

"For sure," she replied. Car keys in one hand, she pulled open the heavy door with the other and walked into the attached garage. It closed behind her with a solid click.

*What an amazing kid!* I smiled from the stairwell. *What a lovely girl!*

It had already been a stand-out week. On Tuesday, all the Columbine students, those that were willing and able—for the first time since the massacre—reconnected with the building that was their school by returning to clean out their lockers. Students had two hours to go back inside to retrieve their backpacks and cell phones and everything else abandoned in order to flee for their lives. Their parents were allowed in as well (Cullen). It had to be emotional for all concerned. As a parent, I was behind the students and their rights to retrieve their personal property one hundred percent. But as a county attorney, I had to verbalize for maintaining the integrity of the crime scene until the investigation was ready to let it go. It was stressful, trying to live in both worlds, a kind of discontent that often woke me up in the middle of the night. It would take years to learn to see the good in both positions; and by good, I mean the kind that lasts, the kind that benefits everything it touches, like clean water.

The cleanup and the physical work of reconstructing the school building would go on throughout the summer, much of the labor done by community volunteers. These unpaid men and women were not only renovating the building, they were blessing the work with their sweat and tears, working together to rebuild a school for the students and teachers to return in August. The school district had open enrollment, a policy of allowing qualified students to enroll in the school of their choice from a range of available options. As the work of rebuilding began, one favorite talking point in the media was to speculate on the size of the pending drop in Columbine High School enrollment (Cullen). The media's distaste for ambiguity was ripe to bursting that summer. But within the community, we understood that it was still too soon to cast aspersions about whatever changes might be coming; way too soon for the returning students to be interviewed or harassed by intense strangers with microphones seeking answers to personal questions, reporters intent on finding the right student to explain why anyone would want to return to Columbine.

It was the summer for reconnecting with an old friend from high school to see if he might be interested in getting back together to do a twenty-six mile jog, or to celebrate the end of the millennium, or both. I had settled down in the intermountain west. Terry moved to the southwest. Maybe this was one of those rare friendships that wasn't meant to end after college all because Dallas, Texas, was holding its annual marathon on a Sunday morning in early December. I wanted to stay over for two nights and have time to talk, rest, and recover, before returning to the twin stresses of work and family. Surely the kids could get through another long weekend together. Each one was so independent. Caring family members lived close by in case of emergency. Sadly for me, there was one less mouth to feed at home. Cody was gone.

It was also the summer that the parents of Dylan Klebold took the remarkable step of sending letters to the families of the victims. What incredible courage it must have taken to write those letters, to acknowledge their role in the tragedy, and then to reach out to the other families. In contrast to the ruthless arrogance of the NRA's leadership, the Klebold's were willing to shed the mantle of silence and secrecy in favor of a deeper allegiance to their beliefs in character and virtues. Their efforts towards atonement were like a beacon of light shone toward the higher ground of hope; maybe a dim one, but at least it was out there for the Columbine community to read and consider, and for anyone else to notice.

*   *   *   *   *

Geographically, our cycling route would take us across the skinny part of Idaho. The first night inside the state, we camped together at a US Forest Service campground under a picnic shelter at a shady spot above a prominent bend in the river. It was about half full of car campers and RVs. The nearest convenience store was miles away in the wrong direction. But we were able to find a neighbor well-stocked with lite beer and willing to trade some for cash, as long as he could hang out with us later that evening around our campfire.

So, there were six of us that night, drinking around a fire, talking, and getting to know each other better. Long after dark and as things were getting loose, a band of coyotes came down to the river to drink. They were close, but I never saw a thing. Nor did I hear anything above the sounds of the river. It was their scents that gave them away, startling a few domesticated camp dogs into full alert. Those few stalwart four-leggeds rose to their feet on cue and let loose a fury of fearful barks and yips directed at their distant cousins. The coyotes responded in a chorus born of the wild places they still inhabited, deep resonant howls and barks practiced and perfected together over lifetimes of foraging for food and defending the pack, and for however long it took to satisfy their collective thirst, the forest rang with their declaration of war. But in the next heartbeat, the quiet returned. The pack had moved on without even a skirmish, without revealing fang or claw, and making no further claim of a superior right or ownership in the stream. The coyotes quenched their collective thirst by raising their voices at just the right moment, for as long as they needed, and nothing more. After which, the camp dogs settled back into uneasy silence close by the legs of their owners.

After the serenade, we just had to share exaggerated stories about open spaces and the wild things that inhabited them. But when the conversation started to lag, I took a chance and asked a general question that I hoped would circulate through the well-lubricated group, a topic that I had enjoyed around different campfires with other groups of men. I rerouted the conversation by asking the open-ended question, "What one thing made you the man you are?"

By some strange conjunction of planets, coyotes, and beer, everyone sitting at the campfire that night was willing to share a piece of personal history. Without any mention of Columbine— that would have muddied the water too much—I told a humorous story about being and becoming a single dad. Then, I concluded that the heart-opening experience of raising children into adults was for me the essential ingredient in becoming a man. In my experience, the circuitous route to manhood, or humanhood, had little to do with guns or sex. But we had three veterans in the group. I expected at least one of them to tell a tale about a hunting experience or their military service. But, neither of those subjects came up in our impromptu roundtable. Nor did anyone mention career or awards, or the car they drove, or the size of their home, or who they shared it with. Out of respect for those men who shared their stories that night, I will not go into individual details, except of course for my own. But I can reveal that a stunning plurality of four, identified the same heart-opening experience of raising children into adults as the essential ingredient or path to manhood. And a fifth man shared a story that I would categorize into the same heart-opener category, that getting remarried after a painful divorce was the turning point in his path.

Late at night we finally put out the fire and crawled into our sleeping bags, and for me, it was absolutely worth it. Tomorrow held the promise of another full day on the bike. I lay awake in my sleeping bag listening to the Clearwater River, looking forward to the ride and glad to be part of this group, wide awake and remembering with deep affection how each of my dependent children had devoted much of their childhood to creating his and her own unique and individual self. And once developed, they felt compelled to use that vital force of consciousness to declare themselves free. After tonight's campfire, I can feel it echoing through the generations, this process of emancipation, remembering my own, a scene in which I finally stood up to my father and said the equivalent of, "No. I am not you," after years of thriving under his care and nurturance. Like so many before me, I left home to create a family of my own.

Listening to the river, I also thought of Kyle—a youth destined to be dependent upon others all of his life due to the developmental delays—his murder in the library, and I thought of it for the first time as a failed emancipation; not for the victim, but for the boys who killed him. Their emancipations failed because Eric Harris and Dylan Klebold found it simpler and easier, even as juveniles, to access weaponry capable of destroying a significant piece of their community, instead of accepting the emotional and psychological challenges of emancipating from family.

\* \* \* \* \*

Lee was right about the *Good Morning America* interview. Usually, I took no time for daytime television. *Maybe today is the time to start. Because I've got the whole day off work. Steamboat is less than a four-hour drive. There's plenty of time for both.* I ended my travel preparations, poured another cup of coffee, and started channel surfing. It didn't take long to find the show. *Who was this gun dealer about to unveil himself to the world; a wanna-be terrorist with a middle eastern accent and a keffiyeh on his head? Or an outspoken redneck from last month's NRA convention?* In either case, I expected the interviewee to be older and male.

The show began with blonde and stately Diane Sawyer reminding the audience that the theme for today's show was, "The accessibility of kids to guns like what happened in Littleton, Colorado at Columbine..." But across from Diane Sawyer, appearing from some remote location through a closed-circuit television link, stood an unsmiling female teen. She looked numb, blonde, and dressed in a plain dark jumper with a beige-colored crew neck blouse. The camera showed little in terms of background and the young woman was only visible from the waist up. She looked straight at the camera and into my home television set, blinking often, but the eyes never looked away. Around her neck, a thin chain of gold gleamed. My TV set did not have the kind of resolution to see whether or not it held a crucifix, but I would have bet money that one was there.

Diane Sawyer opened the interview by describing her guest as, "The young woman who accompanied Dylan Klebold and Eric Harris to the gun show where three of the four guns were purchased." ("Robyn Anderson on *Good Morning America* (June 4, 1999)") Sawyer was laying a foundation, clarifying for anyone watching for the first time, that three out of four guns fired by the Columbine murderers were purchased from local merchants during business hours.

The girl's name was Robyn Anderson. She was from the A-list of Columbine students, the kind that doesn't believe that bullying exists in their school because they don't experience it. A-list typically students spend their daytime hours fully engaged in school activities, in the youth group at church, and in the case of Robyn Anderson, receiving the highest possible grade in every class. But school performance was not the point of the interview. Instead, *Good Morning America* had selected her because of her reckless affinity for two of the "bad boys" at school. She was "sweet little church girl, Robyn," a nickname taken from one of Eric Harris' private journals (Cullen).

The interview was brief, lasting little more than six minutes and the questions were limited to Robyn's role in buying the guns, her relationship with the murderers, and what it was like to go to senior prom with Dylan, only three days before the massacre.

Looking thoughtful and pensive, the famous television reporter looked directly into the image of the young woman on the closed-circuit TV screen and asked her first question, "What would have stopped you from accompanying them and helping them buy the guns?"

As a lawyer watching and listening, I recognized a soft-ball kind of question, slow-moving and right over the plate, one that sets up the premise—not to a judge or jury, but to the worldwide audience of reality TV—that Robyn Anderson was not the real purchaser of the guns. The question was leading. It set up a foundation, totally unproven, that Eric or Dylan must have been the purchaser, anyone but Robyn. But watching as a parent, the question made me cringe. Daytime television was allowing a coconspirator to proclaim her innocence, while acknowledging complicity. Diane Sawyer was handing to Robyn Anderson, one A-list person to another, the equivalent of a "Get Out of Jail Free" card. She was asking her audience to take it for granted that: *OK, so maybe Robyn was there in the room, but she wasn't the one buying the guns.* And then I got it; Diana Sawyer could do all of that and more any weekday morning, because this was reality TV, and she had star power. Justice would just have to take a back seat.

Robyn answered: "I guess that if it had been illegal. If I had known it was illegal, I wouldn't have gone." And here, I could feel myself beginning to fume. *Why don't you ask her, "Who put the shotgun that killed Kyle into the hands of your boyfriend?"*

Her face may have appeared stern and sober, but the questions by Diane Sawyer were generous gifts, wrapped up with shiny paper and bows. This was a setup. Her question had no wrong answer; any response by the recent Columbine graduate that came close to being related to the topic would reaffirm for the audience the specious foundation that Eric and Dylan were the purchasers, the only purchasers, and that Robyn was there only as a friend, a helper of sorts. "If I had known it was illegal." Her words sounded like those of a thief or a forger, someone caught in the act of taking something that wasn't theirs, and then admitting to the act but simultaneously asking to be let off the hook by suggesting, "I didn't know anyone would be hurt." Or the time-honored standby, "I was just following orders" (Young, 2017, p. 349).

"I was eighteen and they were both seventeen at the time." ("Robyn Anderson on *Good Morning America* (June 4, 1999)").

"So, it was legal to purchase the guns if someone eighteen years old was there?" Diane Sawyer asked.

"Yes," Robyn answered, at last explaining to the audience that three-fourths of the bloodshed, death, and destruction of Columbine was funneled through the gun show loophole. She was explaining to a nationwide audience how terribly simple it can be for a disenfranchised teen with money, to walk into a gun show and buy a gun, legally, with no need to wait around for a pesky background check.

Diane Sawyer never asked about the individual transactions or the specific weapons they purchased that day. There was no denying, however, that she and her friends bought three, from three different unregistered sellers, two shotguns, and a 9-mm semiautomatic rifle for Eric, an AR-15 manufactured by Hi-Point Firearms of Mansfield, Ohio. They paid cash. They didn't try to bargain. The guns cost between $250 and $300 apiece (Erickson, 23). But the audience never got to hear any of those facts or figures. The only question that even came close was when Diane Sawyer asked, "What did they tell you they wanted the guns for?"

"They really didn't say anything in particular. I just kind of assumed they were for hunting or collecting. It was just the sort of thing they would be into…the guns."

"But did you say, why?" asked Diane Sawyer.

"It was just in their personality trait I guess," replied the implacable young woman. "Something that they enjoyed, found interesting. It just didn't seem odd at the time, no." ("Robyn Anderson on *Good Morning America* (June 4, 1999)").

I wondered: if anyone had cleaned out Robyn Anderson's locker for her? If she had gone to the makeshift graduation ceremony with the remainder of her class? Because her senior class did graduate on schedule and several weeks before her appearance on *Good Morning America*. The ceremony was held on a beautiful blue-sky day, ripe with the abundance of spring. But even with all that good weather, the participants did not see the light or warmth of day. It took place indoors at nearby Chatfield High, a traditional rival, away from the prying eyes of the curious, and especially from the cameras and microphones of the vigilant press. Columbine still occupied a dominant position for both national and local media. Principal Frank DeAngelis could have sold expensive tickets. He didn't.

During her interview, Robyn was never asked any specifics about the different weapons she purchased or about the three different merchants who sold them. Robyn was never asked how Dylan reacted after she gave him the 12-gauge Savage/Springfield pump-action shotgun, the weapon that he would later use to shoot Kyle in the back as he sat at a computer table inside the school library (Erickson, 30). Or how Eric, also seventeen at the time, reacted when she gave him a similar make and model of shotgun, the one that he would later use to evacuate his own skull (Erickson, 55). Robyn never had to answer if either of her friends had talked to the gun dealers about how best to saw off the barrels and butts of the shotguns in order to increase the spray of buckshot and turn them into deadly weapons (Erickson, 23).

From the line of Diane Sawyer's questioning, the November 1998 shopping spree to the Denver gun show was turning into something like a trip to the convenience store to buy a six-pack of beer for some underage friends. The gun show loophole was never mentioned by name. If any good was to come from this interview, it would arise from the point that three of the four gun dealers were local businessmen, selling legal products…to juveniles.

Lastly, Robyn was asked about going to the senior prom with Dylan on Saturday night before the massacre. She explained that she was the one who wanted to go. She had asked him, as a friend, to go with her. With this shift into questions about the prom, the mood swung toward the predictable, until Diane Sawyer asked her about a comment made by one of Robyn's friends in a different interview with a different reporter, "The fact that you and she left the school just minutes before the attack began. Did you have some warning?"

"No, none." Robyn Anderson replied. "We were in a hurry to get out of the school only for the *pure* fact [emphasis added] that it was lunch, and we were only allotted forty minutes to leave, get lunch, and come back to class. So it wasn't unusual really, to be trying to hurry to get out ("Robyn Anderson on *Good Morning America* (June 4, 1999)"). The face of the girl answering the question looked so young and innocent. But buried within the fine print of her answers, I sensed a "tell", the kind of quirk that gamblers talk about to describe a glance or a motion unconsciously displayed, that reveals the strength or weakness of the teller's hand. Robyn gave away the weakness in her response when she emphasized this one fact above all her other statements, describing it as the "pure" one. The extra emphasis reveals the point of deception, the place in her story, where the coverup begins, and a deeper truth that she is just not ready or willing to face.

Which brings up the question, when did Dylan tell her? And how much did he explain? It was my belief that few seventeen-year-old boys could keep that kind of secret from their prom date only a few days from the planned and pending attack. Or perhaps Robyn knew on that Sunday afternoon in November, the day she bought the boys their first guns. Either way, there could have been time and opportunity to give out a warning. But how could she betray the boy who took her to the prom?

*　　*　　*　　*　　*

Eighteen years later by the Clearwater River in Idaho, the high-pitched voices of children at play penetrate the low roar of fast water. My stomach is growling. *There must be a good stopping place up ahead for a solitary cyclist to stop and cool his tired feet.* I want to kick back, have a snack, and watch the warm sunshine dance across the shallow stretch of river. But two dark pickup trucks are parked at the turnout, both with Idaho plates. In the distance a barefoot woman in a red bikini walks along the clean sand of an elongated brown sandbar, talking with her friend, a short-haired brunette in a one-piece suit that reveals little about the way she might have looked back in high school. Both of them wear sunglasses, but only the woman in the bikini wears a baseball cap, her blonde ponytail protruding from behind. Ahead of them, three children of disparate heights and ages laugh and splash their way through the thin line that separates warm sand from freezing water. Two middle-aged men are standing near the driver's side door of the closest truck, still in their street clothes, arguing, their voices raised and accusing. "The dealer said that it was impossible to lock yourself out of these newer models!" the younger one complains.

His friend provides a terse reply, the words unintelligible.

I pedal right past on Daedalus, aware of the irritation and anger over whose fault it is that one set of keys got locked inside the truck. *Welcome to Idaho, an open carry state.* I am willing to speculate that in addition to coolers, picnic baskets, and towels, each pickup has at least one weapon on board. It could easily be the popular 9-mm semi-automatic Glock. But neither man is talking about which gun to insert into the family outing. They are making plans instead, to return to town, riding together in the remaining pickup to retrieve an extra set of keys.

And how good it feels to pedal past them on my self-propelled machine. I give them a wide berth, but as I inch beyond the last truck, I realize that I am regaining the lead in an unscheduled, improbable endurance challenge, by competing with the simplest, most efficient machine in the contest, the one with the fewest components to break down. Because I am the visitor here, a guest passing through their state, and because they have the guns, I won't lord my surprise upset over them. Far better to let them figure it out for themselves.

Weight can be a major factor on a bicycle tour. It generally comes down to the question of personal risk and how much of it any rider is willing to accept. In planning for this one and talking with friends about decisions made in similar circumstances, I made a conscious choice to approach the ride with an open heart. In dealing with other humans, I decided to put my faith in my communication skills, my sense of humor, and a working cell phone. When and if it comes to being confronted by warm-blooded mammals with sharp teeth and claws, I am packin' a four-ounce aerosol can of pepper spray, right there in the front pannier pocket. Including the pocketknife, which is stashed with the cooking gear, that's all I want to carry. Redundancy is the key to deciding what to pack.

Further upriver and still within sound of the children, I pull off the road for my turn in the sand. I take off my shoes, get out some lunch, and trade my bike helmet for a baseball cap. My feet slide easily into painfully cold water. *No way am I going in any deeper.* The current is fierce. I pull my ankles out of the water and warm them in the sun, barefoot feet in no hurry to return to the captivity of bicycling shoes. When it's time for leaving, none of the other cyclists have caught up with me. *Surely, I would have noticed if someone had passed by.* We are traveling across the skinny panhandle section of the state. Cell phone service is nonexistent. On the bright side, there will be at least one more night of camping near the soothing sounds of one of Idaho's majestic rivers.

Frank is waiting for me on the manicured lawn of the US Forest Service building in Kamiah, Idaho. It is the greenest spot in town, a restful place with lots of warm, late-afternoon sun, but rather subdued in comparison to the sand bars and fishing holes of the Clearwater River a few short miles behind us. I catnap on the grassy lawn for a while, unconcerned about what might have happened to the other guys. But when my eyes open, the first thing I see is Frank sitting next to his bike, staring down the empty road and shaking his head. He comes over to ask, "They couldn't be ahead of us, could they?"

"No way, Frank," I assure him, but thinking to myself, *The retired engineer is showing.* "I have not seen anyone but you since we left camp this morning. Those three guys were all huddled up together when I took off. I was right behind you."

"Yeah," agrees Frank. "That's what I remember too." In years past, Frank has completed multiple triathlons. He is in fantastic shape for a man of any age. His resume includes pedaling across the country at least once before, following the original cross-country bicycle route called US 76. In this group, he is almost always the one out in front, waiting for the rest of us to catch up, just like the worrisome end to this beautiful day in the middle of Idaho.

"Frank, there's no way all three of those guys got ahead of us," I tell him, "me maybe, but not you, not without us seeing them or hearing about it."

"I'm going to wait here a while longer," he says.

"Come on," I say as the sun starts slipping behind tall cedars. "Let's go find a beer and something to eat."

Five minutes later, he's still pacing around the yard, looking down the only road through town and scratching his head. "So Frank," I call out. "What did you think of that mama bear in the red bikini?"

"What bear?" He asks. "What red bikini?"

"Come on," I say. "Let's go get some dinner and I'll tell you all about it."

"You saw a bear?"

"Not exactly," I tell him. "But I did win a race with two pickup trucks."

"No way!"

"Come on. I'll tell you about it over dinner."

"OK," Frank agrees. "Let's go find a campsite."

## CHAPTER 7
### AND THEN WE WERE FOUR

*July 15, 2017*
*Lolo Pass, the border between Montana and Idaho*

I am sympathetic, but not surprised the next morning to find Frank pacing back and forth across the campground, ready to ride, but uncertain how to explain that his bike has developed a safety issue during the night. The sky is still grey with predawn light. Our tents are next to each other in a private campground, less than a mile away from the lush green lawn of the forest service building where we spent much of the previous afternoon, waiting for three members of our group to appear. Frank is packed. He looks not just ready, but eager to go, all four panniers are balanced and full and resting on the frames that secure them to the front and rear wheels. My gear is spread out in disarray across a nearby picnic table, precisely where I left it before going to sleep. "How about some coffee before you take off?" I ask.

"Yeah, caffeine sounds good," he answers and lifts the closest pannier off the front of his bike, sets it on the ground, and points to what appears to be a side-of-the-road repair performed with plastic cable ties. He's pointing to the end piece of the frame where the metal arm attaches to the wheel hub. I take a few steps closer to get a better look. All I can see is a swarm of black plastic ties, wrapped tight, and securing two pieces of unrelated metal together. I admire the ingenuity. But, I don't ask for details.

Frank gets out his utility cup and explains that it's not safe for him to be riding with the rest of us anymore, not on a fast downhill, and not with this broken piece of metal near the hub of his front wheel. "That makeshift repair made with nothing but plastic ties won't hold for long. The baggage frame could work itself loose anytime. I don't want someone else to get taken out on a fast downhill because my bike's got a mechanical issue."

I listen and nod, agreeing that there is a problem, but not convinced that it is mechanical in nature. *This whole repair thing smells like a ruse to provide a clean way out for him. I'm pretty sure that Frank is fed up with waiting and having no way to communicate with anyone except me.*

As the water in the percolator starts to make that boiling sound, I reach for his empty cup and spin the conversation in another direction. "I don't feel like waiting around for those guys either. If something bad had happened to one of them yesterday, a traffic accident with some kind of physical injuries, there would have been lights and sirens going back and forth all afternoon long. I didn't see or hear one single emergency crew. Did you?"

"I don't even want to think about that," Frank replies, avoiding the question entirely. "I just want to get this bike over the pass and safely down into Missoula. I can get a plane back home from there."

"Meanwhile, those guys are probably waking up to a fantastic stealth campsite on a soft sandy beach with a great view of the river," I persist, handing Frank his hard plastic cup filled with aromatic, steaming-hot brew. "So, when are you taking off?"

"Soon as I drink this varnish remover and put the cup away. I can't make it all the way into Missoula in one day. I plan to stop tonight at the forest service campground. It's big, right on the river. You can't miss it. Meet me there tonight and we can ride into Lochsa together tomorrow morning." Frank is speaking about these locations with the familiarity of a cyclist who has "been there and done that," multiple times. "Lochsa Lodge, that's where you should stop and wait for the others. Lochsa has showers and washing machines and great food. Beautiful spot. That's where we're all headed. But I don't plan to stay there long enough for everyone to catch up. It wouldn't be safe. I've got to get this bike to Missoula and into a box for the trip home."

"So, Frank. Let me ask you something completely unrelated. Was I out of line two nights ago, when I asked about the manhood thing around the campfire? Did that piss you off at all?"

"I thought it was fantastic," he responds, "One of the better memories on this trip coyotes and a great campfire! And the reason we went on for so long…after running out of beer…was that question of yours."

"Yeah, that's how I remember it too. But this morning I'm wondering if all that talk isn't part of the reason we got dogged last night."

"Robert, it was just the right question for that campfire circle. You gotta believe in yourself that much," he says, standing up from the bench of the picnic table. "You put the idea out there. Everybody seemed willing to take their best shot, including me. Don't waste your time second-guessing yourself. There are no dress rehearsals out here."

"So, you're takin' off?"

"Yeah," he responds, leaning forward and giving me a fist bump. "Hey, thanks for the java."

"Don't worry about me," I tell him with a smile. "There are only a few paved roads around here. I can find my way to Lochsa. All I have to do is stay on this one, right?"

"That and pedal. It's all uphill from here until you get to the pass. But I gotta leave now and go make some miles. Can you explain to those guys what happened?"

"I'll take care of it. It's been really good riding with you, Frank."

"You too, Robert. Keep the rubber side down."

\*     \*     \*     \*     \*

All the talk about coming of age and watching my children emancipate into adults has churned up a lot of memories. The ones that keep me preoccupied have their roots in the summer of 1969—the beginning of my senior year in high school—the year of Woodstock and the landing on the moon by American astronauts. I was seventeen and like everyone else in my circle of friends, more interested in stimulation than politics. But it was impossible to ignore the shooting war that raged on the other side of the globe, growing in body counts and costs, and all of it undeclared. Up until that pivotal year, military service was a duty, readily avoided, by enrolling as a full-time student into college and staying there. But all those assumptions were about to change with the signing of an executive order in Washington DC.

Like every summer in northeast Ohio, the days were hot and muggy. Most of my evenings were filled with busing tables and washing dishes at a local restaurant. That left a lot of afternoons to make good memories at an abandoned limestone quarry with my best friend Terry. We dared each other to dive into the grey watery depths, first from one ledge and then another, until the day came when we both stood at the top, nothing but forty feet of humid air separating us from the unforgiving surface below. To lean forward and step into thin air was a lesson in balance; what it meant to give in to gravity. To dive head-first was a taste of the sublime, because a good dive included that moment of apogee, an instant of awareness that flight might one day be possible with the right set of wings. The thrill was part of my fascination with Greek mythology in its infancy, especially the story of Icarus. Even then, I knew there had to be more to the story.

A darker side to that summer was that Terry's parents were splitting up. Terry was grateful for every hour in which he could be gone from the house he called home, but that meant leaving behind his little sister and brother. Their family was broke. Somewhere in midlife, his father had climbed into a bottle and never came out. His Mom had more pressing problems than whether or not her oldest son was going to college.

In the face of declining popularity, the sitting president sent shock waves through my entire generation by giving the draft a facelift and turning its selective rules into a lottery system. The first history-making draft lottery was held on December 1st, 1969, and televised to a national audience ("Vietnam Lotteries"). I don't remember watching or even caring that much. At seventeen, all I knew was that it didn't affect me, yet. Besides, I had grades to keep up and authors like Ray Bradbury and Tolkien to read, a part-time job at a local restaurant, and girls to ponder and desire from afar. But the student deferment was history. Within the eligibility pool of that first lottery were impressionable young superstars like Bruce Springsteen, Bill Murray, and Sylvester Stallone, as well as future presidents Bill Clinton, George W. Bush, and Donald Trump; and best-selling authors in the making like Tim O'Brien, Philip Caputo, and Karl Marlantes. Two years later, another round of the same annual lottery would change the course of my life.

I can still see my father's eyes, feel his hand on my shoulder, and hear his words on the day I graduated from high school. Duty and honor were important to him. It was not in his DNA to disparage a sitting US President—at least not a Republican one—or the war in Vietnam. But the massacre at Kent State University, so close to our front door, gave even my dad pause to reconsider. The closest he ever came to being critical of that war was when he shook my hand four weeks after Kent and said, "I spent enough time in uniform for all of us. You shouldn't have to go." H. R. Haldeman, in his 1978 memoir about his years as chief of staff in the Nixon White House, *The Ends of Power*, identified Kent State as the turning point in the Nixon presidency, the "beginning of his downfall slide into Watergate." Decades would pass and I would have children of my own before I understood that when my father said those heartfelt words on graduation day, he was giving me his blessing.

*   *   *   *   *

Years later and alone on a bicycle in Idaho, my day fills with the stark serenity of tall cedars, sunlight, and the sounds of rushing water. There's no fear in it—not yet, anyway. I have plenty of water and freeze-dried food and the day is warm. Frank is up ahead, making plans to pull the plug of his participation in this journey soon, and three more cyclists are following in the distance. Whatever this feeling is, it's not fear of isolation. When they do catch up, we'll be a new group of four, a different kind of symmetry perhaps, but doable; something like stopping for beer on that first day and not being able to share it. This time, it's information I've got, but no one to hear.

*Maybe I'll follow Frank into Missoula, make a right-hand turn, and head south towards home. Maybe I'll follow his lead and call the whole group thing off. I could finish the summer with a long ride through beautiful country, solo, through Yellowstone and the Tetons, and be home before Labor Day with a raft full of good memories to keep me writing all winter. I might even bring out some of the sad ones, from Columbine, just to help with the balance.*

The twisting spine of the continental divide is not far ahead; on the other side, civilization beckons in the small university town named Missoula, Montana. But first, there's a bustling commercial outpost on the Lochsa River, a place to rest and re-group before doing the pass over the Bitterroot Mountains. *How long should I wait for the others to catch up? Do I retrace my steps, start giving up miles to go looking for them? Or keep going into Montana and hang out with Frank until his flight leaves? At least there'll be internet service in Missoula. And I could catch up with the latest text from Lee!*

Ever since Columbine, there's comfort in the stillness of remote places like rural Idaho, and not a single one of those choices has to be made right now. With every crank of the pedals my endurance is building. With each day's additional milage, the well of my confidence grows. Today is for riding next to this wild and scenic river, a self-propelled visitor moving through majestic forests shimmering with filtered sunlight. *Good thing I've got my shades on.* Most mornings, I wake up before the sun eager to get back on the bike. I'm feeling grateful to be alive for the first time in years. And no! I can't share the names of the drugs I'm taking. Because I'm not taking anything: no antidepressants, no antipsychotics, no tranquilizers like Xanax, Valium, or Klonopin, no opioids like oxycontin, and no psychotropics like marijuana, methamphetamine, or mushrooms. Nor do I take any statins or steroids.

If drugs are not behind it, then these feelings about the pleasures of vitality must be coming from the inside. Balanced on the bicycle seat, I see them as seeds of light telling me in no uncertain terms: *This body is really enjoying all this attention. The heart, lungs, and legs want to keep right on doing exactly what they're doing.* Medical science has described it, this renewed energy, in terms of recalibrated brain cells and nerves coming back online (van der Kolk). For all these reasons, I am eager to reach a lodge with restaurant-style food and take a rest. I haven't eaten indoors since Lewiston just after crossing the border into Idaho.

The same new research suggests that, in fact, there is no "recovery" from traumatic events like Columbine—no doorway to walk through into a better life. According to van der Volk's work with returning veterans, and also with ordinary people who have experienced and endured traumatic events within their own homes and communities, the reintegration of suppressed memories happens incrementally, through repeated entries into the labyrinth of time and memory, and that for many, the physicality of jogging, riding a bicycle, or hiking can be the catalyst for healing (van der Kolk). So, if I need to revisit the knowledge that a solitary youth on my caseload never got up from his seat at a computer terminal inside the Columbine library, then let the memories come on back and share this bicycle saddle. It's better here within the peace that nature can bring, to feel and touch and taste and remember the stressful stimulation of those years, a better place to start trusting again in the people around me.

Such is my frame of mind when another cyclist approaches—unexpectedly—coming from the opposite direction. I take my left hand off the handlebar and point toward the pavement. He reciprocates. We each want to talk, but Doug can't stop for long. Actually, he's competing in an endurance race, crossing the USA on a bicycle. He explains that the inaugural race was in 2014. Twenty-five people completed it, the fastest one taking less than eighteen days, which coincidentally is about the same length of time that I've been on the road. His descriptions compel me to glance at the trip odometer. My total mileage is somewhere between six and seven hundred.

"This year about one hundred and fifty people entered," Doug explains. "I like this one because of the synchronized start. The race begins on both sides of the continent at the same time."

"So, your paths cross in the middle somewhere?"

"Eventually," he nods with a smile. "We all follow the bike route called US 76, the same one AdventureCycling.org set up a long time ago." As he says the words, I get an intuitive hit that this Transamerica bike route is calling like the Sirens of Greek myth. "But doing it as an endurance race only started a few years ago," Doug continues. "Their staff monitors everyone's progress. Most start on the west coast."

"And you didn't mind being different," I say with a smile, "Good for you. This Transamerica thing sounds intriguing to me, just the route, not the race part." And as I say the words, the bright colors of butterfly wings sail past and then return, perhaps drawn to the colors of our shirts.

"Definitely. You should do it. Fabulous way to see the country, the small towns, and these two-lane highways. The entire route is marked with road signs you can follow. But they're not always easy to find. Best to use a cycling app. Google maps will take you there, too."

"And you're goin' east to west."

"I was living in Norfolk, Virginia, when it started. Just out of the Navy," he replied. "There were lots of good reasons to start at that end."

"My daughter was in the Navy too. I used to visit her in Norfolk," I say. "She was on an amphib called the Saipan. Did a lot of work with the onboard computer systems to keep them up and running."

"What was her rate?" asked Doug.

"I can't remember—something to do with computers. But I do remember how good it felt to drive to Norfolk from Denver and take part in a tiger cruise the first time Lee returned from the Persian Gulf." Revisiting the memory brought instant tears to my eyes, but they didn't stop me from blubbering on with the rest of the thought: "It was one of the best days of my life."

"That's cool, sir," Doug replies with newfound formality. I start assuming that he has spent enough time with talk and wants to get back on his bike to finish the race. But then he adds, "Say, before I take off. I've got a favor to ask."

"Sure. What is it?"

"If you're interested in US 76 or anything about the race, you should check it out on my blog."

"I'll do that, as soon as I can get a decent internet signal. What do you call your blog?"

"You're gonna laugh."

"Is that really the name?"

"No. It's just that most people laugh out loud when I tell them the real title," the young vet replied, pushing his punch line a few more seconds into the future. "My blog is called: Rideallnight@wordpress.com."

After confirming the words, Doug takes off on his gradual descent, heading for a distant beach, the edge of the continent, and the end of his race. And it does make me laugh. *Great title. Easy to remember until I get to a stopping place and feel like writing it down.*

*　*　*　*　*

One Sunday morning during the spring of my first year in college, my Dad showed up unannounced at the door of my dormitory room at Allegheny College, a small liberal arts school just across the Pennsylvania line from Akron. I was still asleep. A year had passed since four students were killed, nine more wounded, at Kent State University a few miles from our home. The bullets were fired by members of Troop G of the Ohio National Guard from M-1 rifles, the standard-issue service weapon for US armed forces during World War II. Both my parents were proud, justifiably so, of the roles they had played in winning that war. But the home they created, our home, often felt like living inside a broken mirror, the pieces only loosely held together by the wooden frame; because their intimacy with the war never ended, their values and beliefs never evolved into a legacy of peace worthy of the name. At least, nothing they were able to pass on to their children.

Yes, there was a treaty. Rationing and shortages came to an end, but the hostilities and the backroom wars kept coming. And no matter which president occupied the White House, my parents' collective DNA would not allow them to question the chain of command or to criticize the undeclared and ever-expanding war in Vietnam. Nor could they pass up the opportunity to heap scorn and ridicule upon anyone who spoke out against it. It was often easier during those high school years of the late 1960s to be small and silent or even invisible inside our home, so as not to offend.

His visit began with a knock on the door, one that lasted long enough to rouse me from bed, put on a pair of jeans, and open the door, expecting to find another student with something on his mind that couldn't wait. But there was Dad, alone and silent, standing in the hallway wearing his traveling hat, a short-brimmed woolen cap with a herringbone weave, the one he always wore on cool mornings for long drives.

"Hi, Dad," I said. "What brings you to Meadville?"

Instead of answering or even saying hello, he stood there looking me up and down for long, expressionless seconds. Then he said, "Get a haircut."

112

It took a while to answer him. Deep waters were churning in this unscheduled confrontation with my father's authority. I do remember that I was not about to widen the door or invite him in. When Dad was my age, he was already in the military, drafted into the army a few days after the bombing of Pearl Harbor. He spent the next four years within its chain of command, obeying orders and being a good soldier. When the Korean War started, the draft board called him up again and he served two more years in uniform, in a different war. But he rarely talked about any of it. In the rare moments when he did, it was clear that he had no love for the military, and yet, he was an ardent believer in the virtues of duty, honor, and country. Both my parents were patriots.

I also had to contend with the natural deference of a son toward his father. I had been dependent on him, and respectful of his ability to provide and protect throughout my childhood; that made it easy at first, just to stare at my bare feet with a dry mouth, wondering where the right response was going to come from. But, somewhere deep inside I must have realized that this dependency was nothing more than a habit, one that I might be ready to break. The answer came to me out of nowhere. I looked up and simply said "No."

That hit a nerve! Because his next words out of his mouth came with a snarl that ended with, "And I just paid my last fucking tuition bill!"

"Fine," I answered without hesitation or emotion. "I was thinking about dropping out anyway."

"And that would be really stupid!" he yelled, loud enough for any of my neighbors to wonder what was going on out in the hallway. "Just try it. You'll be wearing olive drab in a heartbeat."

"Don't you read the papers?" I asked, pushing back into a pregnant topic where I knew the facts cold. "The draft is a lottery now!"

"I knew that," Dad insisted but less forceful now, looking away and down the still empty dormitory hallway.

"But don't you get it? I'm 1A, just like the rest of the kids in this dorm. Student deferments are history."

"Oh," he said, clearly starting to figure it out for himself. "Well, what's your number then?"

"Don't have one! The lottery for my birth year will be held this summer."

"Oh," he repeated. We stood there in silence looking at one another, standing in the hallway of the freshman men's dormitory. I didn't have anything else to say. Dad reclaimed the lead by suggesting, "Let's go somewhere for breakfast." And we did. Early on a Sunday I could only think of one place that might be open, a diner out by the interstate that served breakfast all day long. He asked me if I was coming home for the summer.

When the national draft lottery was held in August, my birthdate was number 300 out of 365, a number so high that all the pundits agreed, there was no chance of being drafted into the army during my nineteenth year! It felt like I had won the lottery, except that no money would change hands, and, the high number would combine with the cultural aftershocks from Kent State to inspire me to look outside the family home for guidance on how best to emancipate. Years later, my daughter Lee, bless her heart, would remind me at a soul level of the significance of this family history, when she found the need to assert her own free will and independence. Dad never spoke of my hairstyle again. How could I not respect Lee's need to test her metaphorical wings by enlisting, even if it broke my heart?

*    *    *    *    *

Back in Idaho, signs are beginning to appear announcing that my destination is close at hand. The highway expands to include a wide shoulder covered with crushed gravel. Traffic lanes glisten with a recent coat of paint, as simple asphalt takes on a bright and welcoming look. There's an electric lightness filling my body, an awareness that I will soon be stopping to rest. I see road signs for RV camping, for groups on motorcycles, and arrows pointing toward the campgrounds for organized groups of cyclists and their support vehicles. It feels like Idaho's version of Disney's Magic Kingdom, a commercial island in the middle of tall cedars and pines, carved out of the Clearwater National Forest, and a complex staging area for the ironmongery of recreational camping in all of its 21<sup>st</sup> Century variations. Daedalus and I pass a neat diagonal row of enormous metal boxes on wheels that partially fill one parking lot. The RVs bear names like Fleetwood, Coachman, and Airstream. Dream, Eagle, and Revolution are also in the mix; but by any other name, each one portends a sedentary lifestyle that I intend to forestall for as long as my body permits. Another sign directs me toward the main administration building, promising a dining room as well. It's been too long since I ordered food from a menu. I'm excited.

There's a grassy spot for bicycles in front of an immense cabin built entirely of cedar logs and surrounded by a well-tended garden with colorful blooms. I don't linger for any longer than it takes to observe that Frank's bike is not here. Inside are large opposing dining areas, serving both firefighters and a large group of young international cyclists in the midst of their cross-country tour. Frank was right about stopping here to rest. But he chose not to linger any longer than it took to eat something, catch his breath, and then take off for the pass and Montana. Off the back lies a spacious deck, more flowers, and the occasional butterfly. I will soon be following the same road. The only question is when.

The hostess has sectioned off the different dining areas between those who would arrive with sweat stains and those without. I find myself sitting at a small table, close by another late-in-life cyclist. He introduces himself as Jack, another west to east cyclist. "The food is good," he says, "the portions plentiful, and the showers hot." His words and a glimpse of the whole grain pancakes are all I need to know before deciding to stay and wait for my friends to arrive; that and an omelet with joe feels like the ideal meal for a body craving protein, carbohydrates, and fluids.

The meal is superb, as promised, and I linger on the patio watching darkening clouds gather into a thunderstorm. I leave the table with just enough time to pay the camping fee and set up my tent before cold hard drops start to fall. I pull the last pannier under the rainfly and close the zipper. Safe inside, I listen to the raindrops hitting the ground, the occasional and overpowering crack of distant lightning, and readily succumb to the sheer pleasure of an afternoon nap.

The next thing I remember is the familiar sound of the three overdue cyclists, picking out spots for their tents, but they waste no time in setting anything up. Instead, they head straight for the dining room, probably feeling just as depleted as I when I finally reached this place. I give them a generous head start and then join them in the dining room.

Gerry, Don, and Forrest are sitting together in the section dedicated to tourists who sweat. Lively conversation fills the expansive room. Lightning strikes have started several wildfires on the Montana side of the border. We will likely pass close by in the coming days. A new crew of firefighters has arrived, consuming more food with the same relentless intensity. Don sees me come in and motions for me to join them. He's asking the waitress for a second plate and offers me a generous slice of well-proportioned, whole wheat pancake. I order another hot brew.

We make plans to do Lolo Pass in the morning. The pedal to the top is at least ten miles, all of it uphill. It will be a long slow pull. These procedural parts in the conversation come easy, as if I've been transported into the lodge and to this table through some kind of time portal, as if the group had never split apart. I ask if anyone noticed the dead rattlesnake flattened into oblivion on that first stretch of highway. I offer a quick summary of my unofficial race to Kamiah with two pickups and their drivers. But neither topic gains any traction. The conversation rolls on into other directions, with no one volunteering any information about where they've been or what they've been up to for the past two days; as if reality is some kind of moving train and only the present matters. But I feel it like an elephant has entered the room, and no one is willing to talk about it. *No one has even mentioned Frank's name, as if his absence is explanation enough.*

The lawyer in me is not about to give away that kind of information, not yet anyway, not until things loosen up. Otherwise, how could there ever be any interest in travelogues like the one I intend to write. Life is better—reality itself is better—when it's part of a shared experience. And it is clear to me that this new collection of four cyclists is something entirely different from the group that came together around the last campfire.

116

Later at the campground, Gerry breaks out his guitar and rediscovers that he and I know a lot of Jim Croce and Paul Simon tunes in common. After a couple of songs, I break the ice and say, "Too bad Frank's voice is missing."

"Yeah," Gerry agrees. "It is too bad. Where'd he end up?"

Neither one of the bicycle patriarchs is much into sing-alongs. But they do like to sit back and watch. Both their heads turn toward Gerry and me as the question hangs in the air.

"He's on his way to Missoula," I say, loud enough for everyone in the campground to hear, but nothing more in terms of explanation. I'd rather be singing at this point in the evening.

"I figured as much," says Forrest, christening the group of four.

Thirteen miles of highway separate Lochsa Lodge from Lolo Pass on the continental divide, a geographical and cultural border between Idaho and Montana, in addition to 1,800 feet of elevation gain. It takes us all morning to do it on our heavily laden touring bikes, but once at the ridgeline, Montana welcomes us as only a place known for its Big Sky can. The top of the pass is the place for Daedalus to extend his wings. There is nothing quite like the empowered awareness that comes with a long downhill run on this bike; not the untrammeled excess implicit in *free will*, but in the artistry and craftsmanship found within the flow of *free choice*. On Daedalus, there is a balance between gravity pulling us downward with relentless precision and the uplift created by the wind moving across the curvature of the wings. My eyes want to look away from the road's surface and get lost in the scenery of a blue-sky day. But *free choice* kept them glued to the highway looking for rough spots in the pavement...something like the original wing builder's advice to his youthful son several millennia ago…that once you're off the ground stay in the middle zone; because arriving safe and sound at the final destination is the highest good.

From Lolo Pass into Missoula is another forty miles. They go by quickly, because of the gravity described above and because of my encounter with a Montana soccer mom driving two pre-teen boys to practice. All of us are bound for Missoula. Their

SUV slows down to pass with a friendly kind of honk. The driver pulls over onto the shoulder and stops. A woman with short dark hair hidden beneath a baseball cap leans out the window, offers a friendly wave, and motions for me to come closer. She didn't have to ask twice. I am already locking the brake levers with the short bungee cords wrapped around the handlebar, already slipping my cellphone into the back pocket of my shirt, and taking the Click-Stand from its plastic mount, the one that secures it to the bottom of the crossbar. Two young boys in the back seat watch as I set the rubberized tip on the roadside and then lean the bicycle's entire weight against it. I walk toward the forest green Subaru, smiling at the soccer players in the backseat splitting a large pizza. The young driver asks, "Are you part of the group with three other cyclists?"

"I sure am," I say, still wearing my helmet and sunglasses.

"They're stuck on a hill several miles back," she says, tilting her head like she has a secret to share. Then she confides, "One of their bikes has a flat. I'm worried that you're going to get way out ahead of them."

"It's still early," I reply, taking out my cellphone as if check-ing the time, but more interested in how strong the internet signal might be, this close to a city with an interstate running through it. "There's plenty of time for them to catch up."

"The boys and I don't like seeing you all alone out here on the highway. I can take you back up there if that would help," she suggests. It must have been clear to her that mine was a situation in need of some management, her logic not unlike the instincts of a wise Montana sheepdog protecting its flock. "You could leave your bike right there in the tall grass…no one will mess with it out here…and then when you're ready, I'll bring you back."

But on my side of the ledger, I am eager to reach the next city and hopeful for another text message might. Frank should be there too, hanging out in Missoula while making plans to fly back home. I graciously decline her offer. "If it's only a flat, they'll be coming soon enough."

She gives me an approving nod, looks back at the boys in the backseat, and opts for plan B. "Then, at least let us share some of this pizza with you."

"You are too kind!" I declare. "I'd have to be crazy to say no to drive-up pizza delivery!"

"Share a piece with this man," says the driver and in a flash, the back door pops open. Two boys appear, one with a pizza box in hand. Savory aromas fill my nostrils.

"Yummm," I say, lifting a drooping slice into both hands and taking a sizeable bite of still-warm crust, the layers of cheese, garlic, and sausage. The taste is a greasy delight. "That is delicious," I say, smiling first at one boy and then the other and meaning every word. Their generosity is so spontaneous. Taking the second bite, it occurs to me that I might have passed through some kind of time warp, because Idaho was never like this. She interrupts my daydream by upping the ante, again. She hands me a napkin and asks, "What do you think, boys? Should we give him another piece?"

This Montana family has no fear of being kind to a passing stranger on a bicycle. In their eyes, I am more a curiosity than a threat—something to slow down for, and perhaps even a chance to offer assistance. After the sirens of Idaho in their full-sized pickups, a pizza-bearing concerned mother in a Subaru feels like a breath of fresh air, her willingness to trust quite remarkable. *Maybe this is just the way it is in Montana.* Indeed, I would soon discover how safe it could be on this side of the divide to strike up conversations with people of different generations, to ask strangers for help, and even offer assistance to a solitary woman, alone in a stalled car on an empty stretch of highway.

Pizza returns to the menu that night as we all meet up for a farewell dinner with Frank. We fill the evening with as much laughter and good cheer as five guys who have spent seventeen days together, riding seven hundred and fifty miles through parts of four different states, can muster. I do my best to keep the sadness at bay, but one of us is leaving and taking his liberal political bias with him; leaving me with two conservative ideologues and a third man who would cast his next ballot in Ireland. In his serious moments, Gerry is worried about the future of the Irish economy, if and when Britain dumps the euro and returns to the pound sterling. It is a pressing political problem back home.

Soon after the food arrives, Forrest announces that he has some work to do back at the motel and gives Frank a heartfelt goodbye. But once he's gone the good fellowship of the evening seems to evaporate. Don will be the first to open his mouth and affirm it. With the last of our beer draining away, the conversation works its way toward the inevitable farewell. Until Don, another retired engineer, looks around the table and declares, "You know, all this great technology we have, all of it came from inventions created by white people."

*Where did that come from?* No one else is speaking. I am tired, but my beer-impaired brain knows a challenge when it hears one. While I search for the right response, Don starts reaching for the bill and his wallet.

"Einstein," I reply, staring back across the table at him. "Relativity. Einstein was Jewish."

Don glares back but says nothing in response.

But I do. "Einstein barely made it out of Berlin before the Nazis took over," I say, pleased with what feels like a strong response.

Gerry tries to slow things down by asking if anyone would like to see a picture of his daughter, the little girl he and his wife adopted from Romania. Out comes his cellphone and he starts flipping through photos. When he's ready to pass it around, there's a closeup on the screen of Gerry and a smiling young woman with a sparkle in her eyes, brown skin and gorgeous dark hair.

Frank puts a cap on the controversy by demanding to pay his share of the bill. Then he adds, "It's time for this liberal Californian to get some sleep."

# CHAPTER 8
## HOW TO PACK

*July 17, 2017*
*Missoula, Montana*

"Hmmm," says the formerly enthusiastic tour guide. "The experienced cyclists like to get their loaded bike-weight down to around seventy-five or eighty pounds."

Bright early morning sunlight beams down on us as we stand on the loading dock of the Adventure Cycling building next to a mechanical scale set up for the sole purpose of weighing touring bikes and their loads. This is the last stop on my membership tour. Daedalus hangs from the padded hook of the block and tackle, immobilized but balanced on the crossbar. The young woman stares at the pointer on the graduated scale, shaking her head like a disappointed teacher forced to deal with another late assignment. I'm steadying the bike with both hands to keep it from slipping. I can't see the numbers. "What does it say?" I ask.

"You are right at one hundred pounds," she says with unequivocal gravitas, her brown eyes locked on the circular dial.

"Ooops," I answer back in my outdoor voice, ready to accept full responsibility for yet another rookie mistake. *No wonder my tires are showing wear. What was I thinking when I packed a collapsible camp chair?*

Frank was still here in Missoula when the four of us arrived, waiting for a plane to take him back home to California. So was a message from my daughter Lee, waiting in the ether of the internet, and, a package from my wife, Marceil, waiting for me at the local FedEx store. She works for the state in health care management-fulltime and has an office close to the capitol. I believe her when she says that she still enjoys her work and the heightened energy of being downtown in the daytime. As for recreation, she dances. I am excited to open the package; hoping to find a note inside with words of affectionate encouragement, along with the used but original bicycles tires that Daedalus came equipped with. Like a lot a busy people, Marceil owns a competent bicycle, but rarely rides. She would rather dance in a hotel ballroom to the sultry beat of West Coast Swing music. I partner with her, not on the dance floor, but in traveling together to vacation destinations of her choice. My wife is supportive of me in these riding adventures. And with this package from home, I will soon be swapping out Daedalus' tired tires in the comfortable workspace provided by Adventure Cycling for its members, as soon as the tour guide and I conclude our business.

Missoula is a jumping-off point for an array of bicycle tours and trails. Thousands of touring cyclists pass through this city of about 75,000 residents every season. Some are riding coast to coast across America like the four of us, others are on shorter jaunts to destinations like Glacier National Park or the mountains of British Columbia. During the summer season, dedicated Adventure Cycling staffers are on hand to meet and greet member cyclists with a hearty welcome, cold beverages, and ice cream treats. Inside, there's a comfortable seating area for hanging out with other cyclists, and, internet access with workstations for anyone with business in need of attention. The décor is all things bicycle with lots of memorabilia from the Bikecentennial ride of 1976. There is even an annual wall of fame and a Polaroid camera for anyone wishing to commemorate their tour with a photograph.

The tour guide pushes the brass hook out of the way and says, "For anybody carrying this much weight, this is the part of the tour where I strongly recommend a visit to the buffalo soldier exhibit over at Fort Missoula." The tour guide pauses to let the words sink in and then adds, "One hundred years ago there was an army unit stationed here. Part of their training was with bicycles."

"I didn't know that," I reply, suddenly curious and wondering where the tangent is going. "More stuff I never learned about in school."

"Oh yeah," she replies, smiling once again. "It was one of those segregated all-black units. Those guys, with heavy gauge steel bicycles, fully loaded with all their gear: each one weighed in at fifty-nine pounds." She says, looking right at me to make sure that I'm getting the numbers right.

"Wait a minute," I protest, getting into the conversation. "Fifty-nine pounds for a steel bicycle, gear, and a rifle, and bullets?"

"You know what?" she says, undeterred. "I've been doing this for a while, and you are the first person to ask about the weight of the rifle…and I'm just not sure."

"It's a subject I care a lot about, ever since Columbine."

"OK. Tell you what. If you are really into history, and bicycles, go over to that museum and check it out. They've got black and white photos of those men, their bikes. And someone over there will know the answer."

"I really don't think there'll be time for the museum tour," I try to explain. "The guys I'm traveling with may not want to stay in town another night."

She nods affirmatively, shifts back into energetic tour guide mode and says, "Then start throwing away, or giving away all your extra stuff."

"That, I can do," I assure her, "And thanks for the tour, and the advice."

"Just sayin'," the experienced young staffer continues, adding the final tweak to her recommendation. "Your tour will get easier—and a lot more enjoyable—by taking twenty pounds off that bike." She wishes me luck and returns to her station behind the counter. The tour guide is a cog in the wheels of a significant nonprofit organization: one whose mission is to make the world a better and healthier place by inspiring and empowering people to travel by bicycle. Its offering to the nation and a world-wide riding community is a system of vetted bicycle routes crisscrossing North America. Today, this work encompasses over 44,000 miles in the US and Canada ("About"). Its monthly magazine provides entertainment and content to more than fifty thousand members worldwide. And in years past, Forrest has been a regular contributor. He's hoping to make a comeback with a story about this trip— Old Men Bicycling Across America—with the theme that it is never too late for rediscovering the bicycle. He also plans to pitch the story to the magazine's editor later this morning.

Back in the mid-1970s, the vision of the founders was little more than a glimmer in the eyes of four young enthusiasts, with a big idea for celebrating the USA's two hundredth birthday: to lead an organized group of cycling enthusiasts on a vetted route across the continent, one that took advantage of prevailing winds and back roads instead of interstates. They managed to enlist about two-thousand like-minded cyclists in the tour, and on May 14th, 1976, the staggered start of their coast-to-coast ride commemorating the USA's bicentennial began. It was the birth of the Transamerica Bicycle Trail and with it, recognition of bicycle touring as another way, perhaps even a better way, to take a long vacation, and rediscover the USA.

*    *    *    *    *

The Colorado legislature convened on January 5th, 2000, filled with good intentions and to *do something* about the gun violence in Colorado. Among my friends and colleagues, the wave of popular support for limiting the access of impressionable teenagers to assault rifles was palpable and growing. But once inside the legislature, this favorable majority would find itself in direct opposition to the NRA's more nuanced demand: unregulated gun markets.

America is awash with guns. According to the ATF, the USA imported a total of 4,305,851 handguns, rifles, and shotguns in 2018 (*US Bureau of Alcohol, Tobacco, Firearms, and Explosives,* "Firearms Commerce in the United States: Annual Statistical Update 2020"). This latest statistical report lists five leading suppliers, by order of magnitude: Brazil, Austria, Turkey, Italy, and Germany. It is no coincidence that foreign corporations, headquartered in these same countries, are generous supporters and contributors to the NRA. Brazil's Forjas Taurus bestows a free NRA membership on buyers. Italian gunmaker Beretta has donated at least $1 million into NRA coffers. Austrian gunmaker Glock, the maker of the most popular handgun in America, between $250,000 and $500,000 (Lichtman 159). Through their donations, foreign gun makers can purchase the NRA's proven ability to influence US lawmakers; because of it, neither Kyle Velasquez nor Daniel Mauser will ever see the inside of a voting booth.

No one in my circle was surprised when the Colorado Senate and House of Representatives came up with competing bills on the gun violence issue. The opposing legislation wound its way into different committees, hearings were held, and a who's who of Columbine survivors and family members testified, including Robyn Anderson. Ms. Anderson returned to Denver to testify before the house judiciary committee, to lend her support for universal background checks and to close the gun show loophole, at least in Colorado. She testified on January 27th, 2000, in a public hearing at the Colorado statehouse, offering the same salient facts first explained to the *Good Morning America* audience. This time under oath, she explained the important distinction between *private sellers* and licensed gun sellers. "While we were walking around, Eric and Dylan kept asking sellers if they were private or licensed. They wanted to buy their guns from someone who was private—and not licensed—because there would be no paperwork or background check." She testified to her role in the transactions. "I didn't want to put my name on something that I wasn't going to have control of. They bought guns from three sellers. They were all private. They paid cash. There was no receipt. I was not asked any questions at all. There was no background check. All I had to do was show my driver's license to prove that I was eighteen. Dylan got a shotgun. Eric got a shotgun and a black rifle that he bought clips for. He was able to buy clips and ammunition without me having to show any ID." And she concluded with the words, "I wouldn't have helped them buy the guns if I had faced a background check" ("Congressional Record, Volume 146 Issue 11 (Wednesday, February 9, 2000)").

But the Colorado legislature adjourned that spring with neither bill coming to a vote, including the one Ms. Anderson supported with her testimony. I was not surprised—disappointed, but not surprised—when both bills died in committee, even though political polls were showing that at least 70% of the Colorado electorate wanted something done to prevent juveniles from getting their hands on guns through the gun show loophole. A similar measure was bogged down inside the US Congress.

Undeterred, local heroes like Democrat Denver Mayor Wellington Webb, Republican Mary Estill Buchanan, former Colorado Secretary of State, Republican John Head, a well-known Republican trial-attorney, and grieving father, Tom Mauser, made plans to create and circulate a petition to make background checks a prerequisite for any gun purchase in Colorado, and with the goal of placing the issue on the November election ballot (Soraghen).

To aid in these efforts former President Clinton came to Denver to attend an MSNBC townhall and show his support for the initiative. Tom Brokaw hosted. On May 2nd, 2000, the Colorado governor and state attorney general—one Republican and one Democrat—signed their names originating the petition, the one that became ballot Initiative 22. It was the first of its kind in the nation. Organizers needed 62,438 signatures in order to get the initiative on the ballot. They had twice that number when the deadline for submission arrived (Cullen 301).

*    *    *    *    *

Undaunted by our divisions, the five of us plan to reconvene this morning outside the Adventure Cycling building. After the tour, Daedalus and I find a shady spot of grass, an outdoor workspace dedicated to bike repair and maintenance. Marceil has come through, again; the replacement tires are in good shape. I turn the bike upside down and remove the front wheel. My conversation with the earnest young staffer has been a game-changer, leaving me with more on my plate than a solitary morning in Missoula can hold. I want to bike over to the park and check out the museum. *Why did I never learn about a black buffalo-soldier bicycle corps until the reggae song by Bob Marley became popular? Why weren't those history lessons taught in the public schools I attended? What happened to those men and their bikes?*

Thinking about education reminds me of Ben and Lee. I take out my cellphone to scan through the photos and reread the latest text from Lee, sent while I was pedaling my way through the wilds of Idaho. She wrote: "Sounds like you got yourself in with a good group of guys." I shook my head rereading it. *If you only knew about the farewell dinner for Frank last night.*

Outside on the lawn, the old tire comes off the front wheel. I take out the inner tube and lay it inside the nearly new tire, check the rotation marks, and coax both of them back onto the rim. All

126

around me people are working on their bicycles, lubricating chains and gears, adjusting brakes, and a few, like Frank, disassembling them to pack into shipping boxes. Constant activity and intensity fills the air. Above the din, I can hear Gerry's voice coming from a retail counter where he searches for a souvenir cycling shirt. I can hear Forrest too, his voice friendly and boisterous. He must be acquainted with a lot of employees, or else he's putting on a good show.

I lift the second tire free of the chain and repeat the process. Rear wheels always take longer, at least for me. In the background, Forrest's voice drifts away. *Maybe his meeting is in another part of the building.* Ten minutes later, I'm leveraging the rear tire back over the rim and hear Forrest's voice again. It's intense this time and angry. Then, the sound of the outer door opening with a sharp bang. *I need more time.*

Speaking of a commodity loosely defined as time, the next time I find myself in the planning stages of a bicycle tour, everything gets laid out on a big table or chair; then half of that gets left behind. Absolute essentials like food and water, items with redundant uses or applications, those get to come along on the trip. But, for the rest of the items left on the table…it would have to be something close to the heart like a cellphone or a journal, select items with an inherent ability to add value to the journey far beyond their weight. *But why wait for the next trip? This heavy glass jar full of peanut butter is not getting out of Missoula alive.* I will leave it on the shelf inside the kitchen.

I'm reaching for the tire pump when Frank comes over to help. "The boys are waiting for you out front," he remarks in his cool Californian cadence. "Can I give ya a hand with that?" he asks.

I set the bike back up on two wheels and squeeze each tire between a thumb and forefinger. "Almost there," I say to him. "It's going to be a lot different without you around. Gonna miss having you out in front of me all the time."

"Yeah," he says. "It's been a good ride. Groups can get tricky though. Things change, right in front of your eyes. It's not always easy to adapt, all the different temperaments, shifting alliances and loyalties. It's a lot like high school," he concludes, "with money."

We laugh together at his joke and exchange man hugs. "Look me up the next time you're in Denver," I say to him, meaning every word, and making a mental note to describe this situation in my next text to Lee.

"You bet I will," Frank says, walking away and into the building.

*I better get going here.* While I'm putting away bike tools, inspiration strikes. I get out the cellphone and type: "Funny you should mention the group thing. We are now down to four. It wasn't pretty. Stay tuned for updates."

\*     \*     \*     \*     \*

Dylan Klebold was a lefty. Once investigators were able to safely enter the building on that first day, the murder weapons were found with the discovery of the killers' bodies in a separate section of the library. The 12-gauge Savage Springfield pump was there, the one used to murder Kyle (Erickson 55), but Dylan took his own life by shooting himself in the temple with a TEC-9, a weapon frequently associated with 9-mm toting malefactors, made popular by the *Miami Vice* television program during the 1980s. A Swedish manufacturer named Interdynamic AB designed the unwieldy pistol, but this foreign corporation had no legal market for it at home. Taking aim at the USA, the Swedish company created an American subsidiary, Interdynamic USA, where the semiautomatic pistol, with its cumbersome twenty- or thirty-round magazines that hang down in front of the trigger guard like the limp penis of a Texas bull in midsummer found a niche retail market. The remains of the two murderers were close together. Eric Harris had evacuated his cranium with one squeeze of the trigger on his own 12-gauge shotgun, sawed-off to about twenty-six inches in length. Nearby was his Hi-Point 995 carbine, a "Made in America" assault rifle manufactured in Mansfield, Ohio (Erickson 55).

During that long ago shopping spree with Robyn Anderson, the retail merchants of the Tanner Gun Show were not selling the TEC-9. It was illegal to manufacture, own, or sell one at the time. Dylan was only seventeen when he bought his from the friend of a friend. He paid $500 cash (Erickson 23). The buyer and

128

seller met through their mutual friend, Philip Duran, another Columbine graduate who had once worked at the same pizza shop. But because there was a law on the books prohibiting the sale, Philip Duran would face criminal charges for his role as an accessory to the Columbine murders, for connecting Dylan with Mark Manes, the gun's owner, and yet another former Columbine student.

After the bloodshed and destruction, both Duran and Manes came forward and admitted their complicity to law enforcement. Each one faced criminal firearms charges because there was a law on the books named the Public Safety and Recreational Firearms Use Protection Act; a law that classified the TEC-9 as a dangerous assault weapon and prohibited its sale ("103rd United States Congress"). The same law banned the possession and transfer of "large-capacity ammunition magazines," like the ones carried by both Dylan Klebold and Eric Harris as part of their private arsenals into a public school inside my community. This extension of the Brady Bill provided the legal teeth used to convict and sentence two Columbine co-conspirators. This ban on certain specific assault weapons was adopted by the 103rd Congress under then-President Clinton. It passed by a narrow margin and only after a ten-year life span, a sunset provision, was imposed on the laws that made the TEC-9 illegal. To be enforceable after 2004, the law would have to be renewed by act of Congress.

The original Brady Bill had its origins in the wave of popular support for reasonable limits on buying and selling handguns in the wake of the 1981 assassination attempt on Ronald Reagan, like the one used to wound the popular sitting president. Its background check requirement was later expanded to include any firearm from a federally licensed dealer, manufacturer, or importer. Banned purchasers included felons, fugitives, domestic abusers, and the dangerously mentally ill. Former presidents Jimmy Carter, Gerald Ford, and Ronald Reagan, all supported it (Lichtman 129).

The common sense, the gunsense, behind the federal ban on certain assault weapons proved its worth to the nation in the aftermath of Columbine by streamlining the prosecutions of Mark Manes and Philip Duran. These defendants would have separate sentencing hearings, months apart, providing at least two opportunities for our devasted community, still simmering with anger and loathing, to witness the scales of criminal justice in operation. How fortunate for community safety that the assault weapons ban was still good and enforceable law at the time of the shopping spree with Robyn Anderson. It meant that Dylan had to look elsewhere for his poorly designed and difficult to shoot straight TEC-9. And it explains why Manes and Duran both went to prison, while the gunsellers of the Tanner Gun Show and Robyn Anderson all walked away without so much as a slap on the wrist. Nonetheless, under the Bush/Cheney administration, that same law would be allowed to sunset in 2004 and because of it, the TEC-9 became available for purchase in retail gun show stalls.

Four years later, the NRA would lose their spokesperson. Heston died of natural causes in 2008, leaving his guns behind. But instead of getting lost in a circular debate over whether a state or the nation had the right to take poor Charlton's hunting rifle away, governments that care about public safety should instead start taxing and regulating gun ownership and sales, and on the individuals who want them; the same legal mechanisms used to manage our cars and trucks. So many households seem to have at least one, or two, or ten; which makes the NRA's fear-based invective about taking guns away nonsensical. Hercules of ancient myth could not accomplish it.

*     *     *     *     *


I had made a commitment to the young staffer, a promise to lighten the load. But there is only time that day for making a few easy choices before rejoining the group and riding out of town. I'm still carrying a quart bottle of water given to me by the pizza delivering trail angels, hidden but not forgotten, deep inside one of the panniers. Sure, it's extra weight, but I will soon put it to good use, camped that night on the bank of the free-flowing Clearwater River, and grateful for their kindness and generosity with every swig.

The next day we intersected the weaving path of the Blackfoot, another scenic river still resonating with the natural beauty described both by Norman Maclean in his 1976 memoir *A River Runs Through It* and the well-known movie that followed. His book is one part coming of age story set in the early 1900s, about a father in Missoula who gave his two children essential lessons about independence and self-sufficiency by teaching them how to become fly fishermen. But his book is also a eulogy, written by the family historian to preserve the memory of his younger brother, who was murdered on a Saturday night in Montana by an unknown assailant with a gun. *It's way too late for me to learn fly fishing. At least I was able to teach Lee and Ben how to ski and instill in them a love for the mountains in winter. Maybe there's something in this tourist-on-a bicycle-business, that I can use to help preserve the memory of Kyle. Maybe even do something about closing the gun show loophole, nationwide. Maybe.*

When election day arrived in the year 2000, 70% of Colorado voters approved Initiative 22. Universal background checks on all gun purchases became state law. It was a result accomplished at the ballot box, by petition and the initiative process, and the only way the legitimate voice of the registered voters would be heard in the aftermath of Columbine. Colorado was the first state to close the gun show loophole within its borders. Oregon was not far behind. But in the vast majority of states, the loophole is still wide open and fully capable of funneling weapons of war into the hands of juveniles without any weapons training ("Https://Ballotpedia.org/Colorado_Gun_Shows_Background_Checks,_Initiative_22_(2000)").

All morning long we have been cruising across a sun-drenched plain with rolling green mountains in the distance. I'm feeling drained and hungry. Far ahead I can see a tiny blaze of white, looking out of place amidst all the earth tones. Pedaling closer I see Don standing next to a white marker, straddling his bicycle at a distant road intersection and staring at the map spread out across his handlebars. There is no traffic in sight or sound, but in between Gerry is not slowing down…the vertical tricolor of his homeland proudly waving…on a beeline towards the wooden pole of a stop sign. Like a jouster in a medieval competition, Gerry rides straight at Don before sliding into an abrupt stop. He throws his head back and lets out a good cleansing laugh. *It looks like we're about to take a break.*

I am closing the distance on both of them, near enough to see that the white spot is actually a homemade advertisement created from a single piece of copier paper and stapled into the wooden pole. A series of nines have appeared on the mileage counter and will soon flip into the one-thousand-mile range. Such a small event, but out here, anything related to milage seemed to burn with a bright significance. I pull up next to my friends, catching my breath and reaching for the water bottle.

"This is lunch," says Don, folding up the map and slipping it back inside his handlebar bag.

I look around for a building or even a few houses. But there is nothing in sight except the three of us, a whole lot of nature, and a gravel road following the contours of a hill until it disappears from view. But I have faith, faith in Don's announcement, and the faith engendered by a single piece of signage bearing the cartoon profile of a happy bicyclist pedaling hard. Below the picture are two printed words, "Cyclist Friendly." That's all it said. But this piece of local artwork has just demonstrated its ability to glean the passing two-wheeled tourists out of all the other vehicles that pass by on this two-lane piece of blacktop, the one that shortcuts the distance between Missoula and Great Falls. State Route 200 was a "blue highway" in the truest sense of the words.

Blue was the color of the ink used on the foldable state highway maps of my childhood to identify the secondary roads, the ones made obsolete by the construction of the interstate highway system. Every state had its own map, its own colors and design. But blue was the color for the roads that connected the small cities and towns. Another favorite book of a similar vintage was *Blue Highways*, first published in 1982. Its author took a nostalgic look at the remarkable restaurants, people, and places that defined those neglected destinations, with their all too often declining economies and populations. The book even included an infallible system for finding the best of the best in delectable home cooking at affordable prices. To do his research, William Least Heat-Moon circumnavigated the entire USA, but he was not self-propelled. He wrote his travelogue from behind the wheel of a conversion van.

Our leader from the back of the pack pedals into the gathering and says, "Gentlemen. There is an amazing restaurant on the other side of that hill."

"What are we waiting for?" asks Gerry.

"Couple of pictures," answers Forrest, leaning his Surley against the wooden post while the rest of us gather in for another group selfie from multiple cameras. I take a couple of my own. I want to memorialize the sign with some life-sized cyclists for scale, expecting the stop to make a good memory.

Around the next bend stands a large wooden sign welcoming us to Ovando, Montana. The buildings are a curious blend of hundred-year-old, wind-blown structures, most of them storefronts dedicated to selling impulse items to passing cyclists, trout fishermen, and the random tourist drawn in from the highway. But the mainstay, the anchor of the town, is its celebrated restaurant, the Stray Bullet Café. Ovando includes a bicycle hostel found within a large teepee for anyone who has reached their limit for the day and wants to stay over. Even with all the local color, there aren't quite enough locals to add up to a town, not according to Google. The search engine describes Ovando with its fifty full-time residents as a census-designated place (CDP).

With Daedalus leaning against a long porch rail in front of the building, I follow my friends into a high-ceilinged room filled with sturdy wooden tables and chairs, and customers. Their cars and pickups dominate the parking spaces in front. On my way to the table crowded with bicycle helmets, I check out the quintessential western bar and mirror lining the back wall. At one end sits an old-fashioned cash register, the kind with mechanical keys and a glass window. At the other, a large calendar fills the lower corner of the mirrored surface. *That's one.* I sit down and order a second breakfast with coffee, and then scan the potpourri and paraphernalia adorning the walls. Right away I spot a second calendar hanging on one of them. *There's got to be more than just two calendars in here. This restaurant is made for lingering.*

The four of us talk and laugh for a while but only till the food arrives. At this point in the journey, we have all become dedicated consumers of calories. One by one my friends finish their second breakfasts and leave to wander around this eclectic CDP, check the air pressure in their tires, or just rest in the shade. I find myself appreciating the downtime, a few minutes away from everybody else, alone in a busy restaurant with time to look around and find a third calendar, this one displaying the brightest and shiniest in farm implements, hanging next to an ancient newspaper framed and mounted on the wall. I take my coffee and wander over to scan the frontpage news from another age. I was curious to learn which story caught the eye of the café's decorator-in-chief, someone who cared enough about that specific story to frame it behind a pane of glass and mount it on the wall.

The article inside of the Stray Bullet is a story featuring the 25th Infantry and Bicycle Corps as they leave Missoula on the first of July 1897. They passed through Ovando on their way to St. Louis, Missouri, to make a statement in a world enamored with bicycles. It was years before Montana became a state. *I wonder if they made it.* The story explained that after the end of the Civil War, the US Army assembled four African American units, the Buffalo Soldiers, and posted each one west of the Mississippi ("U.S. Army's 25th Infantry Bicycle Corps: Wheels of War"). But the unit stationed at Fort Missoula was the only one riding or pushing bicycles. There is a black and white photograph of six lean and stoic soldiers fording a shallow river holding bicycles over their heads—with rifles slung over their shoulders. Each bike has a large canvas bag draped across the handlebar and another storage bag strapped to the inside diamond of the frame. The men are all African American; the army they served in, segregated.

A second photo shows their commanding officer, a young 2nd Lieutenant, West Point graduate, and bicycle enthusiast named James A. Moss. His mission: to prove the value of the bicycle for military purposes. Under his leadership, the 25th Infantry and Bicycle Corps intended to demonstrate to the chain of command that bicycles were faster and more reliable than cavalry for transporting armed soldiers over long distances. Hence, the nineteen-hundred-mile trek to St. Louis. Rifles and bullets were integral to the success of this mission. To help with the public relations efforts, an embedded journalist from *The Daily Missoulian* was invited to accompany them. And of all this interesting history, the fact that drops my jaw and leaves it hanging wide open is the date of their departure from Fort Missoula. The Buffalo Soldiers began their quest on July 1st, 1897. My individual bicycle quest began in Astoria, Oregon exactly 120 years later.

How stunning the synchronicity that I was following in their footsteps, and their bike tracks. What a relief that Daedalus' frame, also made from welded steel, was so lightweight and durable. My chainring and cassette offered a wide range of bicycle gears. For the men of the 25th Infantry, there was only one. Nor was I burdened with a bolt-action Krag-Jorgensen rifle, each one adding ten additional pounds to the daily load, and that did not even include the weight of the individual bullets ("U.S. Army's 25th Infantry Bicycle Corps: Wheels of War"). What a blessing, that all I needed—or wanted—to protect myself with, was a four ounce can of bear spray.

Sitting down at a nearby table, I imagine that most of those men in the 25th Infantry put on their uniforms for the same reasons that my father put his on when he was drafted into WWII at eighteen in 1941; and for all the same reasons described by John Adams in a letter to his wife Abigail Adams dating from 1780s: so that *their* children would not have to be soldiers and risk their lives in war. Instead, the future president wrote that for his children, they would have the liberty to be farmers or shopkeepers, artists or mathematicians, and philosophers or poets ("Letter from John Adams to Abigail Adams, Post 12 May 1780").

I can look back across all these generational divides, and believe that each individual went to war, or at least into the military, in the hopes that their children and grandchildren would not have to do the same. If so, none of them realized it. *Maybe I can do something to help break this endless cycle. Maybe I should start by advocating that all of us fathers provide our children with bicycles—instead of selling them guns—and safe places to ride them.*

I am still absorbing the article when Gerry walks back into the restaurant in his fluorescent riding vest and helmet. "Robert, the boys are about ready to leave."

"You know what Gerry?" I reply, without even stopping to think about the many ways this decision could unravel. "I'm going to stay here awhile longer. History is dripping off the walls in this place. And I still haven't sampled the pie. It must be fantastic. There are at least three different calendars in here. Why don't you stay a while? I'll buy. What kind of pie are you liking today?"

"You'll have to explain a little more about the calendar thing," Gerry answers, looking toward the window and shaking his head, torn with indecision. "Another day for the pie, OK? I'm going to keep up with the bicycle patriarchs. Catch you down the road, Robert."

25th Infantry and Bicycle Corps as they leave
Missoula, Montana, July 1897

We Begin
From left to right: Robert, Forrest, Frank, Don & Gerry
Fort Stevens, Oregon, July 2017

Frank fixes a flat on the side of the road, July 2017

Robert on Daedalus near Portland, Oregon, July 2017

Medusa's Head' Hayfield Art near Belt, Montana, July 2017

Bicycle Bunk House in Dalbo, Minnesota, 2017

Daedalus near Itaska Park, Minnesota, August 2017

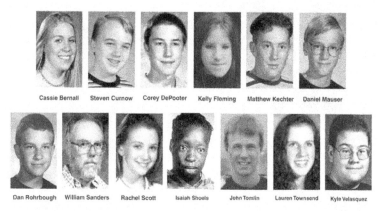

Cassie Bernall   Steven Curnow   Corey DePooter   Kelly Fleming   Matthew Kechter   Daniel Mauser

Dan Rohrbough   William Sanders   Rachel Scott   Isaiah Shoels   John Tomlin   Lauren Townsend   Kyle Velasquez

Victims of Columbine School Massacre, April 20, 1999

Memorial for Victims of Columbine School Massacre,
Littleton, Colorado, April 20, 1999

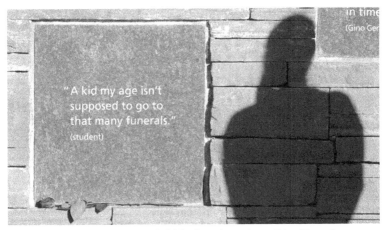

Columbine Memorial Marker (courtesy Sky News)

Columbine High School Main Entrance
Littleton, Colorado, December 2021

Thanksgiving
Lee Case holding Earl the Grey, Robert, & Ben Case,
Littleton, Colorado, November 2017

Thanksgiving
Robert with father and mother, Roy and Marjorie Case,
Littleton, Colorado, November 1999

Celebrating Another Graduation: Recruit Training
Robert with Lee & Ben Case,
Chicago, Illinois, December 2001

Lee Case aboard USS Saipan, February 2003

Bike trail between Carbondale and Hotchkiss, Colorado, June, 2019

Robert on the road to Independence Pass, Colorado, June 2019

CHAPTER 9
BIKES, BUFFALO SOLDIERS & THE STRAY BULLET

*July 18, 2017*
*Ovando, Montana*

Bicycles in the 1890s were a commercial phenomenon, a craze sweeping both sides of the Atlantic, in tandem. On this side of the ocean two brothers, Wilbur and Orville, opened their own small business, the Wright Cycle Company, in a storefront and within walking distance of their home in Dayton, Ohio. Their new, state of the art "Safeties" were easier to ride and more affordable than the high-wheelers that preceded them in the commercial marketplace. The bicycle was undergoing a technological transformation: both wheels on the Safety were the same size and this next generation in two-wheeler design included a chain for transferring power from the pedals to the rear wheel. On the other side of the Atlantic, impoverished but up-and-coming young author, H. G. Wells, was getting out of London on the weekends, going further and farther across the English countryside than ever before, because he was riding a bicycle. One of his earliest novels, *Wheels of Chance*, captures Wells' respect for this new mode of travel with the bicycle as catalyst for emancipating his lower-class main character from the quota-driven demands of city life, into a life of travel, mobility, and adventure, at least on the weekends.

The same winds of change were blowing into Missoula, Montana, where Lt. Moss caught the fever and made a formal request for authorization to convert the 25th Infantry into a bicycle riding unit. Moss had already lined up the A. G. Spalding Bros. of Chicopee Falls, Massachusetts, to supply at no cost to taxpayers brand new heavy-duty bicycles for the entire unit, in return for field test results and branding rights. The outcome was that the entire unit received top-of-the-line Safety bicycles, starting with thirty-five pounds of welded steel in the frame. The wheels had to be durable. The soldiers got six more pounds of steel in each one, covered over with an inflatable tire. The US Army supplied everyone with a ten-pound blanket-roll of Civil War-era gear, tents and poles, blankets, underwear, socks, and a toothbrush; all of it engineered to fit inside a handlebar bag that tethered over the front wheel ("U.S. Army's 25th Infantry Bicycle Corps: Wheels of War"). Forty young and fit enlisted black men volunteered to pedal, push, and pull those heavy-duty rollers overland and across wide prairies, broken only by railroad tracks or rutted trails. There were no highways, blue or otherwise.

I pick up my bike helmet, walk over to the counter where the cash register sits, and ask for my check. That's when I look down and notice the fourth calendar, a foldable, desktop model sitting right out in the open next to the stack of receipts being counted by a muscular waitress. I blurt out the words, "The cherry pie is unbelievable!"

She looks up with a smile and tells me, "You're good. Some other table paid it forward for you."

"Did he have an Irish accent?" I ask, remembering Gerry's departure and the seed he planted as he turned toward the main doors. From now on I will be visualizing Don and Forrest as the team of bicycle patriarchs, inseparable, and so alike in their histories and values. Real nicknames come from the heart. In time, theirs might even grow into something more accessible like "the Pats." Long ago, my prodigal daughter reminded me of the incredible power of nicknames in a series of letters she sent home from boot camp.

"Oh no. It wasn't him. It was a young family. They were making a game out of watching you pouring over that old newspaper. I guess they just wanted to help you out in return."

"Are they still here?" I ask.

"Long gone," she replies, shaking her head and continuing the receipt count, "you enjoy the rest of your ride."

I leave the Stray Bullet grateful to that unknown young family, and intent upon passing along this generational wisdom of my own; the more calendars on the insides of the cafes and restaurants of blue highways America, the better the food. For the engineers, there is also a scale running from zero to five. A zero equates to an interstate pit stop. Don't bother. If the place has only one, then get ready for prepared food, assembled in New Jersey. If there are two, then it's safe to order, but only if fish trophies are present. A three-calendar place comes with an inherent recommendation: *can't miss with the farm-boy breakfast*. Four calendars send a powerful signal: *try the homemade pie, too*. And five, the loftiest rank of all: *keep it under your hat. They might franchise*.

Walking through the other businesses in Ovando, the man behind the counter in the fly-fishing store claims that at least one thousand bicyclists pass through here every summer. I do the math. If each one drops ten, or twenty, or even one hundred dollars into the local economy, then the bicycling community represented a major infusion of income for these out-of-the-way but historic places. There have to be other regions in the vast and diversified country that have yet to awaken to the potential of bicycle tourism. For that to happen, we cyclists need safe places to ride.

The distance from here to Great Falls, Montana, is less than one hundred and twenty miles. I can cover it on Daedalus in two long days of smooth asphalt and good weather. According to Lt. Moss' reports, he and his bicycle-mounted infantry also averaged fifty miles per day, but moving across open ground. Leaving Ovando in 1897, I have no doubt that the 25th Infantry reached Great Falls in the same number of days. But the comparison ends there. Theirs were long, grueling days, with a lot of time devoted to pushing and pulling heavily loaded bicycles across a roadless landscape. Today, we are blessed with blue highways.

So, as afternoon evolves into evening twilight, it can be mystifying when the land returns to the sky its more vibrant colors, and the highway reveals its natural cast of blue. The pull of the journey is strong at this hour, when the sirens of the open road raise their irrepressible voices in song. This is the time of day for coming around a bend and finding a band of cyclists up ahead, all of them in dark uniforms and riding old school bicycles, for pushing the pedals harder in an effort to catch up, but finding that no matter how hard

I try, the distance never closes. Until I see Gerry stopped up ahead and waving his arms, his bicycle turned around and waiting for me on a wide spot on the shoulder. He calls out in a welcoming Irish lilt, "We've found a lovely spot in these pines for a stealth camp." I pull over and stop in time to give his front tire a gentle nudge. We exchange high fives, and he points the way towards a place in the junipers where the Pats are busy setting up camp.

*   *   *   *   *

After my long weekend getaway in Dallas, Texas, I drove straight to Littleton from the airport and found Ben at home, alone, and happy to see me. We ate takeout pizza for dinner, just the two of us. Seated at our sturdy kitchen table, we shared a laugh after he teased me about the mystery man in Texas who never came to visit or even call, at least until a few months ago. "So how was it?" he asked. "Did you and Terry hit it off?"

"It was great to see him again," I replied. "He wants to meet you guys someday. I hope he gets the chance. We were such good friends back in high school. It was great to talk with someone who's known me for as long as he has. We've both changed, a lot."

"So, what about that marathon?"

"I was hoping you'd ask. Check this out." I said, showing him the bib I had worn during the race. Small, reinforced holes were punched in each of the four corners where safety pins could attach. Across the top in royal blue letters on a white background, it read, "The Dallas White Rock Marathon December 5, 1999." At first glance, it was nothing more than a plasticized piece of paper about the same dimensions as a paperback book.

"Yeah, what about it, Dad?"

"Look. I was number 1111," I replied, pointing to the numbers that filled the center of the bid in a large serif font.

"Somebody had to have it."

"And that somebody was me," I said, wiping my hands on a napkin before picking up the bib and moving it away from the greasier aspects of the meal. "I can't explain it, but having that number on my chest made me feel like being in Texas and reconnecting with Terry was exactly what I was supposed to be doing last weekend. I haven't felt that kind of confidence in a long time. Drawing that number was like an affirmation that maybe the tough times we've been going through were for a reason, that there's some kind of higher purpose out there, one that eventually we get to figure out."

"Sounds like you're on a roll, Dad," Ben replied. "Here. Have another piece of pizza."

"Thanks," I said, smiling at Ben as he handed me the box. It was good to be home. I felt like staying up for a while, maybe even going out somewhere for dessert after Lee arrived. But then I noticed the FAFSA forms, untouched and sitting in that same spot on the Formica countertop of the kitchen desk. On the plus side, Lee did complete the form on the grant application offered by the Knights of Columbus, the one that required a personal essay. Picking up the page, I could see that she had thought about her answer before spending the time and effort to get to a final draft. It was polished, articulate, and well-organized, and a scathing indictment of Christopher Columbus and his misdeeds in the Caribbean, explaining in meticulous detail why she would never take a single dollar from an organization bearing his name.

As I read the words, my ego felt like a colorful balloon being stuck with a pin. Once I was finished, I felt exhausted. All I had left in the tank was enough energy to drag my body upstairs and unpack, leaving Ben downstairs with his homework and the TV. All three bedrooms were on the second floor, the doors accessible from a common landing. There was a small office with a bookshelf, an office chair, and a pine top table holding the keyboard and printer to a Mac computer; I'm guessing the same place where Lee created her essay. I set my suitcase down on the floor outside my bedroom door to turn around and take one more look at the empty table where she had poured out so much buried hostility, only to notice that one of the lower panels in Ben's bedroom door was broken through.

I called out to him from the top of the stairs, "Hey, Ben. You never told me about your weekend. How was it?"

"Fine," he yelled back.

"How'd your door get broken, then?" But Ben doesn't answer this time. "Come on up here, would ya?" I call out to him.

That was all it took to get him started. Lee still wasn't home. The physical evidence was irrefutable. He spoke with detachment about the argument they got into, right before he went into his bedroom and locked the door. She was upset and yelling. She didn't like being locked out.

"After the panel broke, she calmed right down," he added.

"Did you let her in?"

He shook his head no.

"This wasn't the first time was it?"

Again, he shook his head.

"You didn't do anything wrong, Ben," trying to sound as sympathetic as I could make it. "And I'm sorry about your door."

"Yea. Lee said she was sorry, too," Ben added, both of us looking at the damage from the outside. Then he opened it and we both walked inside. He showed me the hole in the sheetrock of the wall, about knee high, a matching memento to Lee's temper.

"Anything else you want to tell me?" I asked.

"That's it. There aren't any more holes."

\* \* \* \* \*

In Montana the sun is high overhead. My three companions are trailing far behind. The shadowy mountains are behind us now, mostly, replaced by wide-open vistas that seem to erupt from every high point in the landscape. I'm sweaty, ready for a break, but unwilling to stop and wait on the remaining three cyclists in our group, not when there's a city up ahead with a population of almost sixty thousand. My last shower was two days ago back in Missoula. I let it go, the inclination to stop and wait, and ride on with my thoughts, alone.

By midday, I am pedaling down the main street of Great Falls, Montana, happy just to be here. It feels like a parade of one, passing by an assortment of restaurants and motels, even a storefront with bicycles to rent. There are signs for fast food, beer, and happy hours. The occasional pedestrian points or smiles. Sometimes, I wave back. It feels so familiar, like the joy of coming home again after a long separation, even though it is for certain that I've never been to this city before. Riding into the shadows of one

150

commercial office building after another, I feel comfort in their cool shade. Once through the downtown, sunlight beams in from all sides. I pass a series of traffic lights. There's the smell of moisture in the air as a stately river comes into view. It seems out of place, far too broad for this arid land.

Daedalus and I pedal straight for the bridge with its expansive lane for both bicycle and pedestrian traffic. Balanced on the saddle, it feels like the bike knows the way, and won't consider stopping until we find an ideal place on the other side to rest. Today, we have the bike path to ourselves. We can cross at our leisure. Humming a tune of my own design, I look around, keeping the balance with the momentum from the pedals, and appreciating the unadorned beauty on both sides of the Missouri River. The word oasis comes to mind.

For the rest of the world, this is a Thursday afternoon. Lots of people are still at work, like Lee and Marceil. I will stop in the shade of the park on the other side of the river and send each one a text, letting them know I made it to Great Falls, that all is well, and that I'm thinking and caring about them. There's enough juice in my cellphone to check for text messages, but only because I've been carrying a little something that no one else in my party is burdened or bothered with. And no, it's not whiskey. That's not my style. I'm talking about a solar array that straps onto the front frame in the mornings and gets transferred onto the back in the afternoon. In planning for this trip, I wanted as much connectivity with the outside world as I could handle. That meant having the capacity to recharge the battery in my cellphone, even if we were camped in a place without electrical outlets. The single panel of this array can trickle up to 3.5 watts into the detachable storage battery for as long as the sun shines. Then at night, I can recharge the cellphone by direct connection to the storage battery using its charging cord. The system is made by voltaicsystems.com. I'm grateful to have it along for the ride. Then, I'll send a text to Don, the only other cyclist in the group connected to the internet, to let him know that I'm in Great Falls and looking for a campground, instead of a motel room.

It is a fine thing that once learned in childhood, we humans can remember how to ride a bicycle after setting one aside. The same is true for the chimpanzees and orangutans that get the opportunity to learn. (Penn) The bicycle itself contributes to the balance. A well-aligned, riderless bicycle, with its handlebar free to turn, will roll down an incline upright and straight and without falling over. The speed varies depending on the design. Different teams of engineers and scientists have made the studies and agree. Physicists have given it a name—intrinsic stability. But the bicycles tested in their laboratories were brand new machines, tuned and balanced, their chains and gears spotless and well-lubed. Daedalus needs some of that TLC. There are several bike shops in this city to choose from. It's a good thing the group plans to stay over in Great Falls for two nights.

Tall, leafy cottonwoods line the riverbanks. Birdsong is everywhere and I see a few black-necked Canada geese floating on the water. The only other birds I can identify with confidence are the large white Rocky Mountain pelicans. Three of these massive and graceful birds adorn the river as I cross the bridge. This is the location where the Lewis & Clark & Sacagawea expedition ended the river-borne part of their exploration into what was for the white men, uncharted land. Two hundred years ago, the expedition traveled up the Missouri River by boat, encountered impassable waterfalls—the ones the city is named after—and headed overland by caravan and on foot, hoping to find a way to the Pacific Ocean.

On the other side of the bridge a city park is filled with the irrepressible sounds of children at play in a public swimming pool. Instantly, a hot shower and a dip in that pool leap onto the day's agenda, just as soon as I get some authentic independent diner food inside my belly. But even before that, I stop and find a picnic table near the riverbank. It's close enough to watch a steady flow of car and truck traffic moving across the bridge, but the sounds of the cars, trucks, and RVs are drowned out by the cacophony of young voices issuing from the pool. I'm in a location close to the center of the city, but there's no one else in sight. It sure feels like solitude. I find a spot close to the water's edge, remove the bicycle shoes and socks and soak my feet in the cold water of the Missouri River, until the chill starts to creep inside.

\*   \*   \*   \*   \*

The search for a campground in Great Falls leads me to Rick's RV & Camping, with its easy access to Interstate 15, and a meeting with two Honda Goldwing riding buddies on their way home to Florida from a motorcycle trek to Alaska. They stopped in Great Falls to meet up with friends and to watch an air show this weekend. Like me, Bill and Ed are dedicated tent campers. The three of us, so far, are the only ones staking a claim to the compact grassy area set aside for tents, and surrounded by a sea of behemoths on wheels that are the bread and butter at Rick's RV and Camping. The motorcycles Bill and Ed ride are equipped with trailer hitches and both of them bring along a vast array of camping gear, coolers, and clothing. Our styles are quite a contrast, but we are the only ones in sight riding on two wheels, a fact that Bill wastes no time in pointing out, after rising from his collapsible camp chair and strolling over to my pannier laden bicycle to say hello.

"Nice rig you got there," he says with a perfectly straight face, his hand extended in greeting. "What kind of mileage you get with that thing?"

"I like it," I replied, returning the smile and gripping his hand in the middle of a warm Montana afternoon. "It runs on all the food and drink I can put into the tank. My name's Robert."

"Not Rob or Bob?" he asks with the interest of a gregarious man. Bill looks like he could double for Santa Claus during the holiday season. "I'm pleased to meet you."

"It says Robert on my birth certificate. It took a long time for me to accept it. But now that I have, I'm sticking with it."

"Sounds like you got aa story here, Robert. Maybe you can tell it to us when there's more time." Bill was the kind of person who did everything about meeting someone for the first time well: the eye contact, the interested look on his face, and the offer, "Would you like a cold beer?"

"Not right this second. Can you give me a few minutes to get set up and cleaned up?"

"You got it," he promises. "So, what sort of business did you leave behind in order to be out here on this sunny Thursday afternoon?"

"I like to carry my business around with me wherever I go."

"You some kind of investor?"

153

"More of a bicycling poet," I say with a grin, pointing toward a hardback book still in the grip of Bill's left hand, the forefinger marking his place. "I'm a writer now, out to capture all this in story, the people and the places. I want to get it all down on paper. Maybe some day I can explain to anyone who cares to listen how fulfilling it is to ride across the USA on a bicycle."

Bill admits to being an avid reader, one who prefers to spend his summers in cooler climes with a good supply of unread books inside his motorcycle trailer, leaving his wife to the sunshine, the grandkids, and the Florida beaches. He loves to read, almost as much as his friend Ed. But Bill is the mouthpiece. He's the one who takes the lead in talking about books, authors he enjoys, and the places they've been together on their motorcycles. Ed must have overheard, because he stands up from his camp chair to wave. He's tall and lean. I'm already guessing that he won't have much to say until there's more time to get acquainted. *If I were to travel with these two for any length of time, I would nickname them Thick and Thin.* "When you write that book," Thick continues. "I promise you that I will be among its readers. Might even buy a box of them to pass around to my friends if this memorable encounter can find its way into the pages," he suggests with an easy laugh.

After a hot shower, I return to the campground just in time to get a call from Marceil. It is good to hear her voice and assure her that all is well. "Yes, I'm safe and sound," and I try to explain how it is that Great Falls, Montana, might qualify as an oasis, at least during the summer. So many things to get done in the short span of two days, including taking Bill up on his offer for a cold one. I walk over to their campsite and renew the conversation. As he hands me a beer from his cooler, the phone starts buzzing with another text. "Aren't you the popular one," he observes without breaking a smile.

It's from Gerry on Don's phone, telling me that they are sitting down for an early dinner at one of the chain restaurants by the fairgrounds. He asks if I'd like to join them. *Maybe it's time to mend some fences.* I text him right back, "Sure would. I'm on the way."

\* \* \* \* \*

Even after the physical challenges of the marathon week-end, I was too upset to sleep. Ben and I stayed up and started a movie. We didn't have to wait for long. Lee walked through the door and came downstairs to see what we were up to, gave me a big hello, and asked about the weekend in Texas.

I told her the weekend was great, and, that I knew about Ben's door. She wasted no time disputing it, admitting to the deed and then concluding, "I've already apologized to him."

"That's what he said, too," I replied, working to keep it conversational and adding, "You're going to pay for a new door."

"Just tell me how much," Lee answered, shifting into her implacable voice. She'd been balancing part-time jobs and school-work for the last year and had a talent for saving her money to spend lavishly on things that interested her.

"Yes, I will. You can count on it. And this is your chance to explain about the hole in his bedroom wall. When did that happen?"

"I'm not sure," she said.

"But it's been there a while?"

"Oh yeah," said Ben, jumping into the conversation for the first time.

Lee glared at him for a second, then dropped her gaze.

I let the silence hang in the air. Nobody spoke until I said, "Ben, I want to fix your wall right away. I can buy some sheetrock mud and start patching it tomorrow. We'll repaint it next weekend. It won't cost me anything except for my time. I'll give that away to you both. But in return, Lee, I want you to list the names of some colleges on those FAFSA forms."

By this time, we were all standing around on the landing at the top of the stairs. The doors into their bedrooms are a few feet away. Earl the cat has joined us, purring audibly from around Lee's ankles. Lee looked down approvingly and squatted down to pick her up, almost low enough to be face to face with the broken panel.

"I've already apologized to Ben," she said, more to the cracked door than to me. "And I'll pay for a new one." But then, she stood up to her full height and gave me with a look of stoic seventeen-year-old defiance and said, "But the FAFSA forms and Christopher Columbus, not gonna happen."

155

"How do you expect to go to college then?" I asked.

Lee rolled her eyes and turned on her heel. With Earl in one arm, she reached for the doorknob to her bedroom with the other. "Goodnight," she said, closing the bedroom door with the predictable, "click."

*     *     *     *     *

Alone in Great Falls and even though Bill has offered to keep an eye on my stuff, I tuck the panniers and all the gear away inside the tent and close the zipper. What a relief it is to get back on the bike without all that weight. Daedalus feels incredibly light and responsive. *Or is that the beer talking?* Bill and Ed look up and wave from the other campground. I ride off towards the other end of town as Thursday afternoon turns into evening, Google maps showing me the way. I'm hungry. I'm tired. And this route promises to be the most direct path into the center of town. It takes me to a traffic light where I stop, confronted by an intersection with the same four-lane road that I ventured down earlier in the day. But now, it is filled with cars and trucks, and all of them experiencing a renewed sense of urgency.

These vehicles move like they're on a mission, to distant suburbs and daycare centers on both sides of the river, or maybe to meet friends somewhere for a drink after work. But my destination, by Google's calculation, is only a few blocks away. Here on the ground and in real-time, they promise to be blocks filled with confusion, honking horns, and the press of traffic. The safer option, of course, is to cross the highway when the traffic clears and take a longer route, toward a dinner that has already begun without me.

*Should I infuse myself and the bike into the flow of traffic?* This is an Icarus moment: the youth from Greek mythology who flew too close to the sun. *He keeps showing up no matter the age.* I have to choose between good judgment and moderation, or cutting off a few minutes of travel time by risking a shortcut onto a busy four-lane road during rush hour.

I wait on the side street, considering the options. Directly ahead the traffic light turns to green. *But wait, there's more.* An arrow indicates that it's OK to turn left now. And there's no traffic! It's all stopped behind the red light. It feels like the universe is giving me a sign, showing me that it will indeed be OK if I make that turn, hit the pedals, and follow the shortest route into a right-hand lane that will soon be filling with much larger four-wheeled gas guzzlers.

Daedalus and I make the turn. We glide into the right-hand lane, as far over as we can go. There is a gutter, but no shoulder. The curbs are high. Traffic swiftly catches up from behind and then sweeps ahead, somehow finding room—except for the car directly behind me, the one with the horn blaring its disapproval. There's no need to turn and look. No need even to glance into the rearview mirror on my handlebars. I can tell from the revving sounds of the engine that the car is right on my tail. The horn blares again. Up ahead, a storm sewer appears, just a few seconds away, its metal grates lining up in just the right width and orientation, to grab a bike tire in its iron maw and bring this bicycle to a screeching halt, but leaving the rider in midair and moving forward at a speed not that much less than the traffic intent on moving past. The horn blares again, expressing its outrage. But I am stuck in the gutter with no way out, nothing to do but keep moving, my hands deep into the D's of the handlebars, pedaling on until I come out of this tunnel, or there's some kind of impact. That's when I see the storm grate pass underneath the wheels. I can start to breathe a sigh of relief. Because my turn is right there, half a block ahead. But this is also the moment when the car behind me decides to make its move. The vehicle accelerates to pass, the beater remnant of a once dignified and sedate Honda sedan, precisely the kind of car I have watched other parents drive for years and then pass on to their children. The driver has decided that this race with the bicycle isn't over yet. The edge of the door squeezes closer, pressing me into the curb. Anger surges out of my mouth as I scream at the driver to move over, never taking my eyes off the concrete curb on my right. Until my front tire slides into it, the Honda shoots ahead, and I fly over the handlebars, shoes and feet still firmly attached to the pedals.

# Chapter 10
## A Great Fall in Great Falls

*July 21, 2017*
*Belt, Montana*

"You motherfucker!" I scream. All of the rage directed towards the grey Honda, decrepit and departing from the scene of my accident. My hands are shaking. I can't remember flying over the handlebars, or my feet releasing from the pedal grips, or even the impact of my face, chest, and forearms trying to merge with the sidewalk. What I do remember is leaping to my feet onto this smooth expanse of concrete, balanced and upright. My left hand clenched in a fist, all except for the middle finger, and those two words streaming from my mouth with rage and anger. Disappointed, I watch the car move away at a constant speed. The distance between us keeps increasing and I repeat the invective, but more subdued this time. The rage and anger are ebbing away, like run-off after a storm on its way to a sewer. The Honda's turn signal flashes on. The driver inside takes the next right and moves on out of sight. But many others are slowing down. I can feel the eyes of these strangers behind the glass windows of their four-wheeled vehicles, staring and pointing. They will all keep moving though, except for the one who decides to stop and offer assistance to the man in bicycle gear bleeding from the hands and forearms.

But the next voice I hear doesn't come from the direction of the street. It's in the background, calm and mellifluous. *It wasn't your fault. I saw the whole thing. How come cars and trucks get four lanes, and bikes get none?*

"No, it wasn't," I say, staring spellbound at the sanguine stains seeping into the palms of my gloves and long-sleeved shirt and in total agreement with this assessment of fault. "But I'm the one getting up from a face plant." *And how long has it been since I used the MF word in public? How many decades?* Inside my head, memories of confrontations between older teenage boys come flooding back and listening spellbound as one after another sprinkled the F-bomb into the discourse. It felt like the words were on parade, and I got to watch. *Funny, how the same words came tumbling out today like a preprogrammed response, and so parallel to the bicycle analogy: once learned, never forgotten.* "Maybe never with that kind of intensity," I say as if someone is listening.

There is no use denying it: the rage was blind, like an explosive volcano venting from some deep, untapped reservoir within my spleen, or maybe another random organ with a long memory. And the raw anger flowed until the pressure was released. *Good thing there was no weapon around to fire in the direction of a fleeing car...*

I turn around and see a young man in tennis shoes and a baseball cap, bent over and looking down at the bicycle lying on its side. "Poor Daedalus," he says, the voice sympathetic as he reaches for the handlebars and lifts the bike up and onto two wheels. He walks the bike in my direction and then leans it toward me. "Nice work getting back on your feet so fast," he says, sounding like a coach or a therapist rather than a random pedestrian. Then, he looks at my face and says, "For what it's worth, both of your tires still have air in them. That's a plus, right?"

But instead of trying to meet his eyes, I look down to steady my hands and reach for the bike. "Oh yeah!" I say, responding in two simple words but meaning, *Oh yeah! I am so happy to be walking away from this one.* "And thanks for coming over to help. Hey, wait a second. How do you know…"

"You ought to have somebody take a look at those hands," says an insistent voice from the direction of the street. Startled, I turn away from a clean-shaven young man in wire-rimmed glasses and see another man, slightly older and bearded, striding towards us in business-casual shoes. Behind him a shiny SUV sits with its emergency flashers on, completely blocking an entire lane of traffic. "That was quite a spill!" He says. "You and the bike went flying."

"Your hands are going to be tender and sore for a while, but you're going to come out of this OK," says the first one to speak.

"Where did you come from anyway?" I ask, turning back toward the voice of the younger man, still curious and more interested in that thread of the conversation.

"From that parked car right over there," says the bearded Samaritan. "And how's that head of yours doing?"

Looking in the direction of the street, I say, "I don't think my head hit a thing." But just to be sure, I lift my right hand and tap the helmet with a knuckle. The palm, I can see, is oozing blood through the fabric of its glove. There's also blood on my forearms seeping into the long sleeve of the nylon bicycle shirt. I twist the wrist and lower the arm. Then, shake my fingers with a sigh of relief, "Good thing I had that helmet on. The gloves, too."

"Yeah," the more recent Samaritan agrees. "But let's have the EMTs check you out and be sure. I'm going to call an ambulance, OK?"

"No," I tell him. "Don't do that. I'm supposed to be meeting some friends for dinner." I look up and down the sidewalk, confused by the sudden disappearance of the other trail angel. *That's weird. There wasn't even time to say thank you.* I focus on the businessman in the flannel shirt instead, while taking mental inventory of the first aid kit back at the campsite and definitely not wanting to incur the expense of an ambulance ride.

"I think your friends will understand if you're late," says the bearded man, standing close enough for me to notice how few white hairs it contains. His head is nodding as if confiding in me. "You don't want to go to dinner like that. Get yourself cleaned up first. Relax for a while."

"You're right about that," I tell him, scanning the sidewalk now for spare bicycle parts and wondering if I can pick out the spot where my chest and forearms hit.

"If there's nothing broken on you, you are one lucky guy," he continues, returning to the original topic of discussion. "You know, we've good a couple of good emergency clinics here."

"How far?" I ask, looking past him into the dark windows of the cars voluntarily slowing down in order to watch for blood or broken bones. No horns are blaring now. I can feel their eyes on me, fixed on the unidentified cyclist involved in the crash—the bike is upright and in his hands—good thing someone has stopped. He's talking with someone from the community. "I want to take a look at the bike," and walk Daedalus through a small circle.

"Couple of miles on the other side of the river."

"That's the wrong direction. I've got a campsite about the same distance away, but it's due south of here." And while saying the words, I'm spinning the wheels and watching the rotation. Neither one appears to be bent. I can see broken spokes though, on each one. I check the brakes. *They're working fine. This conversation is talking me into getting back onto the bicycle and pedaling back to the campsite.* I look into his face, read the compassion in his eyes, and say, "I really appreciate that you stopped to help."

"But I stopped to call for an ambulance."

"And I'm feeling good enough to ride."

"OK, then. I'm gonna take off. Be careful on that bike," he cautions and returns to his car and his plans for Friday evening.

"Thanks again," I call out as he opens the door and slides behind the wheel. The emergency flashers go out as traffic resumes the flow, its inherent sense of order restored. But watching the line of cars start moving, I can feel my shoulders starting to slump, the legs feel tired and weak. *If I'm going to ride back to Dick's, I've got to go now.* I lift a leg to straddle the bicycle seat to slowly push the pedals down an empty sidewalk toward the next crosswalk and traffic light. More than anything, I want to go home. But the closest I can get is my tent and the tender mercies of Dick's RV & Camping.

\*   \*   \*   \*   \*


Back in Littleton and while the Colorado legislature tied itself into a knot over how to stop juveniles from buying assault weapons, Lee provided her answer to the "What are you going to do about college?" question. It was only her junior year when she announced during dinner, "I'm staying home tonight. Got an important meeting tomorrow, early."

"Tomorrow's Saturday," I replied, finding myself once again in the role of parent-with-no-clue-what's-going-on. It was a part I never felt comfortable with, but it seemed to be happening with greater frequency with each passing birthday. "What's happening tomorrow?" I asked. "Why so early?"

"The Navy recruiter I've been talking with has a Saturday morning meeting for all the potential recruits," Lee replied, scanning my face for disapproval, surprise, or anger, any one of which could have reflected my feelings in that moment. But, the main thing I felt was overwhelmed.

"I had no idea you were talking with a recruiter," I said, trying to sound more curious than judgmental. I knew the value in not letting my face get in the way of the emotions underneath. But implacability was for courtrooms and negotiation. We were at home, at the sacred family space of the dinner table, eating tacos and black beans with a tossed salad on the side, one of the half-a-dozen meals that I could throw together in thirty minutes or less after getting home from work. If Lee went through with this enlistment idea, then our days for sharing meals like this were numbered. I didn't want to forestall any of those family feasts with an angry outburst at this one, or, by giving in to that instinctive parental need of mine for control. Besides, Lee was six months away from her eighteenth birthday. She wasn't asking for approval, just support.

"When did all of this happen?" I asked, leaning into the dinner conversation just a bit, to know more, a lot more, and with nothing to gain by getting upset. Ben was creating another taco from the assortment of food bowls in the center of the table. None of this information was taking him by surprise, but I could see that he was taking careful mental notes.

"Right after your trip to Dallas," she answered without skipping a beat.

"Oh," I said, but feeling like a long line of dominoes was falling one at a time onto a hardwood floor, and I was getting to watch. "Have you signed anything yet?"

"Some pre-commitment forms."

"You're still seventeen…"

"Dad! I'm not enlisting tomorrow," she insists, cutting off my sentence with the alacrity of a sprinter coming out of the starting blocks. "I'm going to graduate first. I want to spend one last summer in Littleton hanging out with my homies. Then I'll enlist, in September."

"Oh wow," I replied, realizing that lots of planning had preceded this conversation. She would be a senior in high school in just a few months. In fact, it reminded me of the conversation I'd had with my Dad on the subject of college. "That's really soon," I said, feeling the catch in my throat but trying to sound encouraging.

I've heard more than a few middle-aged comedians make jokes about the uncanny ability of their teenage sons or daughters to deliver with precision the exact words or comment that can cut to the quick at the most inopportune time. I've had those moments too. But this wasn't one of them. My daughter respected me enough to share her dreams with me, and to bring up the topic over a meal. Her proposal was a plan that echoed, with a kind of reverse twist, the story of my coming of age, the college dormitory scene where I had a confrontation with my father over the length of my hair, face-to-face, instead of going behind his back. I was proud of her too—she was showing me and anyone who cared to listen that she had the confidence to make her own way, on wings of her own design.

The next morning while Lee was gone for her meeting, Earl the Grey, her feline companion came round to check on the status of her dinner bowl. It pleased me to scratch her ears for a moment and remind her, "Don't worry, girl. You can stay here just as long as you want."

\*     \*     \*     \*     \*

But at the scene of my great fall in Great Falls, I am reminded of what can happen at the intersection between the human desire for order and predictability, and our fascination with danger, violence, and crime. Journalists and writers have been taking advantage of these quirks of character for a long time; the one that supports the old newspaper editor's adage, "If it bleeds, it leads." It's one of the reasons so many of them stayed focused on the Columbine story for so long. Within the impacted communities surrounding the high school, we lived and worked and went to school burdened with the competing desires for everything to return to normal but keeping our eyes and ears on alert for the next breaking news story. I have revisited that stress every time another angry man with a semiautomatic weapon—and the reveal almost always shows a young white male—acts out his anger and rage on another vulnerable population inside a public place. The list has become so long, no one can possibly remember Columbine as an isolated incident. Angry, disenfranchised men with assault rifles continue to maim and take lives inside our schools and churches, concerts and theaters, places I once assumed to be safe and secure, and with increasing regularity. Yes, the human heart can be a dark forest. But, so too, is denying the fact that juveniles having access to that level of weaponry isn't a clear and present danger and getting away with the denial because it is someone else's kid that's doing the bleeding.

At least, these are the important memories that I have selected for this bicycle journey, blending them now with the pain of landing face-first on one of the finer sidewalks in the City of Great Falls, Montana. I was in a hurry today. I took an unnecessary risk. I guessed wrong and paid a price in terms of injury to myself and damage to Daedalus. The crash was another lesson in humility, which is fast on its way to becoming a theme for this third and final trimester of life.

*     *     *     *     *

As winter turned into spring during that first year of the new millennium, the same one in which Philip Duran was sentenced to emancipate inside a Colorado prison, grief revisited our Littleton home. Lee's favorite pet died on a cold and dreary weekend, killed by a reckless driver, and grief returned to our family. This time tragedy's epicenter wasn't five miles away. It was inside our home, seeping into the walls from the street outside where Earl the Grey was struck, trying to make it back into her own front yard. Lee was devastated. And I could feel the security of my psychological perch on suburban life starting to slip.

Late at night when the house was quiet, I worried that with her precious cat gone to her final reward, Lee too, would leave and find her bearings in the military and like so many before her, become fixated on those new connections with comrades at arms, all of them members of the same team that civilians like me cannot join. Deep inside, I wanted both Lee and Ben to emancipate well, and eventually, to tell their coming-of-age stories to my grandchildren, or even write them down for a larger audience. I still intended to keep my job, to maintain the income stream that paid the mortgage on a house that neither one wanted to live in for much longer. My plan and my hope were to provide a stable enough platform for each of them to have a clean launch. But now with Earl gone, my deepest fear was that once Lee enlisted, Littleton would become nothing more than a place she came from.

Ben escaped from our grieving household by going to Spain for spring break with a group of foreign language students in his class at school. I loved it when he returned and told me how glad he was to be home. In his teenage exuberance, he remarked that he didn't care if he ever traveled overseas again. But then, he surprised me by taking a job that summer with a landscaping company where most of the crew spoke a Latino variation of Spanish, the one spoken in Denver's neighborhoods and streets. Ben wanted to spend the summer outside in the open air. He spent it immersed in Spanglish.

*    *    *    *    *

Two nights after the great fall, I awaken feeling good about returning to the quest, even if it includes saying goodbye to two new friends, Bill and Ed. The swelling in my hands is receding and I'm feeling some vitality returning. The plan is to regroup as four and get an early start. But before leaving the campground that morning, I challenge myself with the less than arduous task of finding an object of beauty to commemorate the day; unaware that one of the funniest moments of the entire trip is coming. The Little Belt Mountains are close. We want to get through them before we camp.

Once back in the saddle, I find that it may be difficult to limit myself to just one thing that captures the imagination. First, is the picturesque place named Belt, Montana, sitting in the moist and protected bowl created by sheltering mountains; second, are

165

the wide-open expanses of wheat fields, cattle, and hay on the gentle flanks of the mountain range; and third, an immense human head carved from a cylindrical bale of hay by a local artisan. But before I gain the perspective to recognize it as a piece of art or even a larger-than-life roadside attraction, I see only a dark looming object far ahead making me scratch my head and wonder, *What the heck is that?* The mind keeps on repeating the question, unable to focus on anything else until the answer is revealed in bicycle time. The sculpture stares fixedly toward the highway behind a barbed wire fence, a weathered hay wagon for a pedestal. I have to bring Daedalus to a stop and then, get up close and personal, before recognizing the face of a woman with snakes for hair. She is Medusa, the guardian goddess of Greek mythology. None of us can ride past without stopping to admire the ingenuity, the stark beauty. All of us return to our bikes without being turned to stone.

Late that afternoon the four of us stop again, another mechanical breakdown. I'm at the back of the pack, pushing my pedals up the wide shoulder of a four-lane highway, one of those three percent graded hillsides that cars and trucks regularly ascend without anyone inside even noticing that the elevation is changing. Gerry stops to get off his bike about halfway to the top. He shouts something, but he's too far ahead for me to understand. I watch as he lays down his bike against the hill, walks back to the roadway, and bends over to pick something up. Higher on the hill, the two bicycle patriarchs are riding together toward the distant summit. They won't realize that something is wrong until at least one of them turns around.

When I catch up with Gerry, he's busy wiping away the grease and dirt from the threads of a bicycle pedal that has detached itself from the crank. "The threads look OK," he declares, holding it in my direction.

"Can I help with something?" I ask, appreciating Gerry's decision to lean the wheels against the hill and keep it upright, instead of removing the panniers and then flipping the bike over so that all its weight rests on the saddle. Maybe he just wants to align today's repair with the adage about keeping the rubber side of the tires on the ground. But there is not a scratch on that saddle of his.

When Gerry bought everything brand new back in Oregon, he splurged on two items. One, of course, was his miniature guitar. The second was his all-leather saddle, the point of daily contact between his Hibernian backside and the frame of his bicycle for almost two months. When the sun is high and the view unobstructed, the surface of that saddle shimmers like dark honey.

"I'll fix it right here," he says with an understandable blend of confidence and impatience threading into his voice, Then, he lays down on one shoulder beside the stricken two-wheeled machine. "Let me have a moment here with this."

From the 1970s onward, bicycle seats have gone through extensive changes. Today's market is saturated with brands and models, and the seats constructed from an assortment of materials like vinyl, molded plastic, titanium, Kevlar, spray adhesives, and something called gel. Manufacturers compete every year for bragging rights over who has the latest in design or technology. Through the decades, brands have been guided in varying degrees towards either lighter-in-weight or cheaper to make. Except for a solitary British company that continues to produce a variation on its original design, the one that came into production during the heady days of the booming 1890s and while the US Army's 25th Infantry was still a bicycle riding unit. A descendant of that company is still making and marketing the same saddle design, using techniques passed down from artisans of one generation to the next (Penn). Gerry, apparently, appreciates this tradition. For his second pedal across America, he has equipped his bike with the all-leather Brooke's bicycle saddle. For today's roadside repair, he does not intend to put a scratch on it.

I hang back, fixing the small bungee cords around the brake levers to hold Daedalus in place on the hillside and remain standing still straddling the crossbar. Gingerly, I take off the gloves to give my bandaged and lacerated palms some air and remind myself of the several ways in which the challenge of finding a source of beauty in today's ride has been fulfilled. Near the top of the hill, Forrest and Don have turned their bikes around and are returning, giving up ground to discover what the holdup might be. I'm grateful to be back on the road with these guys; grateful too, that it's not me holding a damn bike pedal in one hand while scooting around on the ground in a constant search for just the right position. Cranks are designed with opposing threads, one clockwise and the other counterclockwise. The design is supposed to keep the pedals in place while riding and most of the time, it works. In the comfort of a well-lit and warm garage, out of the wind, it might not be much of a chore to determine which one is which. But thousands of miles from home on a desolate highway, with threads that a rider does not want to strip, the job could grow into a challenge that consumes the fading hours of any day.

So, the three of us wait. No one notices a short convoy of large brown trucks that pass us by on the highway. No one notices the sand-colored one, its emergency flashers on and leaving the highway. We don't even notice the two, camouflage fatigue-wearing figures who leap to the tarmac from its air-conditioned comfort.

But fast-stepping down the wide shoulder, they are coming towards us. A youthful voice rings out, "We've got water!" breaking through the reverie of a late afternoon break. There's an urgency in the words that cuts through my daydream, a sense of pride and determination in the tone.

"So, do we," says Forrest, scratching his head and turning to watch the young national guardsmen stride right past him as if he weren't there.

"Probably heat stroke," says the identically clad partner, carrying what might be a first aid kit.

The last guardsman to speak approaches Gerry's prone figure, still flat on his back on a large rectangular sleeping pad. The first responder kneels on the ground near his patient. Without a word, he pushes the tip of an open water bottle against the patient's face.

"It's nothing of the sort," growls the irritated Irishman, pushing the water bottle away with one hand and sitting up with an uncooperative pedal in the other. "The *damn* pedal fell off! And, I want to get this thing back on while there's still daylight! Can I get some peace and quiet here?"

# CHAPTER 11
## A SPECTACULAR FAILURE

*July 23, 2017*
*Mosby, Montana*

It is early morning. Out of nowhere, a sudden breeze rips across the highway and pushes my bicycle off the kickstand, over the hard-packed shoulder of a remote Montana highway, and down the sloping bank on the other side. Raucous laughter erupts on my right. Spittle flies into the air, as each one of the Pats throws back his head and laughs. Shame and embarrassment flood my face, anger too, as I watch the bicycle and all the gear somersault over the steep embankment. Next, I groan, audibly—it feels like high school all over again—shake my head and turn away from the laughing duo leaning against the nearby guardrail, their bikes safe and sound and propped up against the rusty curves of metal. They seem to be inseparable.

Far away an emergent sun breaks through the implacable horizon, highlighting a line of low clouds in shades in orange and pink. The colors are warm and inviting, but the air around me sends a chill up my spine, a chill that's got nothing to do with the bicycle patriarchs and their mischief. The younger, more vocal of the two, punches his old friend on the shoulder and explains, "That flyin' bicycle...Got to be the funniest thing so far this summer." Three weeks into the ride, across three states and one continental divide, I am still the newbie, making a rookie mistake. They lean against the guardrail as if it were a throne, exuding a shared understanding that knowledge filters down from the top of the pyramid, into a broad base where newbies survive as best they can. Theirs is a top-down style of communication that I remember all too well. It is the same one I grew up with during the 1960s, the one practiced inside my home and throughout the industrial city in Ohio where we lived.

I walk to the edge of the shoulder, hearing nothing but the sound of the Pats slapping each other on the thigh, like teenage boys in colorful cycling clothes, and recalling in generous detail the way my technologically impaired kickstand let go and slipped to the ground. The look on my face as I spun around empty-handed, grabbing for the seat, the rear frame, anything to prevent my reliable two-wheeled machine from tipping over and rolling down the hill.

I look down the hillside, expecting to see water bottles strewn across the slope with a bent bicycle lying somewhere near the bottom, one-wheel spinning helplessly with nowhere to go; expecting to see open saddlebags and freeze-dried food, hot chocolate mix, and cooking supplies littering the hillside. But the bicycle is standing on both wheels, as if something unseen holds it in place.

"What the hell?" The words form under my breath as I jog down the hillside towards Daedalus, seeing for the first time another man standing next to him. A V-neck sweater appears over a button-down shirt; then a baseball hat, and tennis shoes.

Looking like someone waiting for a school bus, the youthful vision inside my head voices, *Hey, boss. Look what I found!*

And I start to visualize a large Latino youth with wire-rimmed glasses. He looks right at me and smiles, holding the bike by the seat, balanced and steady in one large hand. He leans the crossbar in my direction, but before I can get there, the large youth starts unzipping the handlebar bag with the other. *He's opening it, the one with my wallet and cell phone inside.* "Hey, stop that!" I shout, while accelerating my steps. "That's my stuff in there!" And, is he big! A full head taller than I am. But it's not the threatening kind of bulk. He's smiling and a little on the flabby side.

*There's something in here I want to show you*, the young man says, still planting words inside my head, *And I don't have much time.* He reaches inside the bag for the brown, faux leather diary, the one with a north arrow stamped onto its cover.

"Hey! Give that back," I say, grabbing the opposite handlebar in one hand and reaching for the book with the other. "I brought that all the way from Denver!" And I've been keeping up with the entries ever since we left Astoria, Oregon, on the 1st of July. It was all blank pages then. And we were five cyclists.

The brown-skinned youth lets go of the bicycle seat, but he extends his arm, keeping the journal far out of reach like an older brother taunting a younger sibling. We're standing face to face, the bicycle still in between. He doesn't step back or even let go of the book. Instead, he thumbs it open, scans a page, and says, *Looks good…What are you writing?*

"Why is that any of your business?" I say, letting the irritation show. "Who are you? What the heck are you doing out here?"

*I'm here to help with some of the scenes in your book.*

"What book?"

*The one you're going to write after all this is over. A decent author would include a scene with that strong gust of wind. If that was me…Yah know?*

I look up at the silver letters on his baseball cap and read the word, "Rebels." "So, who did you say you are?"

*I didn't. But the name is Kyle.*

"Pleased to meet you, Mr. Kyle. Now give me back my journal. And, explain to me, why I should be listening to any of this."

*Sur-viv-ors guilt*, he replies, emphasizing each syllable and infusing each one for clarity. *We've met once before. Maybe you don't remember yet, but you will. It was in court, a long time ago. There was the hearing to decide whether or not I should go back home or stay in foster care.*

"And you wanted to go home, didn't you?" I say, feeling sympathetic all of a sudden, but still not remembering. "Even if it meant changing schools."

Kyle just nods.

"I worked lots of dependency or neglect cases, more than I can remember."

*I remember…one of them was mine*, Kyle replies. *I was really shy and timid once. Didn't talk much to strangers. You and the caseworker did most of the talking back in court that day, what little there was.*

"And you still look sixteen," I told him.

I resigned from the County Attorney's Office for good in 2014, feeling fortunate to be able to leave on my own terms—life was short, misery sure, and college was paid for mostly—fortunate to be able to coattail onto my partner's medical insurance and become a trophy husband.

Kyle doesn't answer. He just hands me the journal, steps backward away from the bike before reaching up to remove his hat with both hands. About two cups worth of blood and brains rain down on the ground behind him.

*Sorry about the mess. But I have to do something to jog those memories into place. I want you to understand how I fit into this story.* He shakes off his shoulders, places the baseball hat back on his head, and gives me the half-smile. *I'm at least one of the reasons you're on this trip, Dude…or this quest as you like to call it.*

"Everything OK down there?" It's Gerry, the fourth cyclist of our group calling out from the highway.

"It's all good," I shout back.

*Robert,* Kyle says, re-engaging with me and our conversation. *I need your help. Every spring and summer there are more massacres in more public places. There are too many copycats out there. Columbine is turning into just another statistic. If you don't write the book, no one will remember, not even you.*

"I can do this," I say, trying to sound confident, but feeling more like a solitary cyclist losing his bearings on the edge of the Montana prairie.

*Good, because once you're into the writing, you are going to hear that the ship of the Columbine story has sailed. But how many of those early books even mention my story? I was never a shining star in the high school world. Today, if some drugged-out, depressive teenager searches for Columbine on the internet, they'll probably find Dave Cullen's book. Read his book, Robert. Yeah! My name's in the dedication. But, you won't find me in the index!*

"You're really upset about this, aren't you Kyle?"

*How would you feel if you were nothing but collateral damage? There are way too many blogs and tweets out there, repeating the same misinformation. My murder had nothing to do with payback!*

"I've heard those stories too," I admit.

*I never bullied anybody in my life!* Kyle insists, the words reverberating inside my head. *There was nothing noble about getting shot in the back by Dylan Klebold. He didn't even know my name. Neither did Eric.*

"Eh, Robert, you all right?" The stoic Irishman shouts from the top of the hill.

*And Robert*, Kyle continues, rushing to finish. *Don't forget to close the gun sh…*

"What? Close the gun shit?" I ask, looking around, journal in one hand the bike in the other. "Kyle! What was that about guns?"

"Never carry one meself," replies Gerry walking right up to us and into the midst of the conversation. "Can't understand the fascination you Yanks have with them. They do a lot of damage, you know." Then Gerry drops to one knee, making a show out of sighting down the front wheel and frame. He brushes his hand along the spokes of the wheel. "Do you carry one in that handbag of yours, Robert?"

"A gun? No. I have nothing like that. Don't want the extra weight or need its threat. All I have is this can of bear spray," I reply, reaching inside the bag to show him a slender black aerosol can. "Got a pocketknife in there too." I don't show him the book of poetry, the reading glasses, or the pens and mechanical pencil. Inside, everything looks like it did when I left the campsite that morning, all the daily essentials within reach.

"I keep myself safe with the quick wit and charm," Gerry jokes without breaking a smile. "The bike looks OK?"

"So far, so good," as we each grab one side of the handlebar and push it back up the slope.

"I saw the whole thing," Gerry continues, never missing a beat and launching into his take on the course of the morning. "A big gust of wind comes up out of nowhere and pushes your bike down, like a playground bully might. You have no chance to stop it. But instead of falling down like gravity has a say in it, your bike flips over like it wants to fly or something. This bicycle's got talent!"

"Thanks, Gerry, for helping me out. I'm going to ride on ahead this morning. See you down the road."

"Not at tall," he answers, giving me a high five and heading back towards his Salsa Journeyman. It leans against the guardrail for support and right in line with the others, the tricolor of Ireland still hanging from the long flexible aluminum pole extending from the rear frame, and held there with a couple of hose clamps. He's been a breath of fresh air on this journey.

Before taking off, I twist around for another look at the hillside. No sign of Kyle, nothing but a trail of bent tallgrass. But there's not a doubt in my mind that only a few moments ago, we were talking together, and now, I'm feeling overwhelmed by an enormity of possibilities. Seeing Kyle again after almost twenty years has lit a fire of hope underneath all this potential. I make a promise to him and to anyone within earshot that tonight, wherever I am, I will update my journal with everything that happened today. *Perhaps the future book will be more than a bicycle travelogue.*

*     *     *     *     *

To help me deal with the stress at work and the grief inside our home, I enrolled in a not-for-credit creative writing class, in a not-for-profit educational program known as Colorado Free University. Of course, I wondered if I would feel safe enough to get personal in its group writing exercises. Driving over to the classroom early one Saturday morning, I felt a longing for anonymity. I did not want to be recognized. *Please god, just let me be another face in the crowd in a classroom full of grownups struggling with how to age better.* I also felt guilty about spending time in a motivational workshop taught by an instructor who promoted herself as a former attorney, author, and teacher. Her bio bragged that she had left behind a successful law practice, and a Harvard law degree, to teach others about how to feed and care for their creative selves. Her workshop was titled: "Unleashing the Fire of Your Inner Writer."

The classroom was set up with folding tables and chairs, arranged in the shape of a large U. There was plenty of room for the instructor to occupy the open end, deliver her motivational and personal stories and writing prompts while engaging everyone in the room with an abundance of eye contact, vocal variety and enthusiasm. Tama was standing at the front when I walked in, a gentle smile on her face, waiting for the dozen or so students on the attendance list that would soon fill her lair. A table sat near the door with white name tags. I wrote out "BOB" in magic marker ink, taking comfort in the camouflage of its palindromic, monosyllabic nature. Blank paper and Bic pens were laid out at strategic intervals on the tabletops. Per my usual, I found a seat with my back to the wall and watched the others arrive, fellow troopers in the army of disappointed professionals. My goals were simple, to find out if I could rekindle an interest in creative writing, but do so without calling too much attention to myself.

Lawyer-turned-writer, Tama Kieves, warmed up her audience with a few entertaining stories about who she was and how she had arrived at this latest incarnation in her life. She assured us that if we wanted to write, then we were in the right place: this was a hands-on workshop with fifteen-minute intervals to work on the writing prompts, including her recommendation that once the words began to flow, not to lift pen from paper until the end of the page. I could feel a hint of excitement in waiting for her first prompt to appear and already making plans to linger after class and buy a copy of her book, when in walked another attorney from the First Judicial District. I knew him, instantly, even in jeans and a Bronco sweatshirt. And this was not just another lawyer that conducted business at the courthouse from time to time, it was Jack DaVita, one of the juvenile court magistrates. I had appeared in his courtroom hundreds of times covering my "dependency & neglect" docket. *Please don't sit next to me, Jack!* I thought, not wanting him or his eyes anywhere near what I might be about to reveal on paper. *We can talk during the breaks.*

Jack and I were close in age, and I was pushing fifty. We probably had lots of background and experience in common. We worked in the same juvenile court system, the one that authorized Kyle to go home just in time to be killed. But anyone familiar with the fine print of the still unfolding Columbine story might remember his name and the metaphorical albatross that hung from around his neck. *Far heavier than the one I acquired in the Velasquez case,* I thought; because three years before our coincidental journey into this creative writing seminar, Magistrate DaVita had both Klebold and Harris as juvenile offenders in his delinquency docket and for over a year preceding the massacre. They both had priors, and like Kyle, had once been under the jurisdiction of the Colorado courts. But Klebold and Harris were in the system because of felony arrests (Erickson, 20-21).

The criminal acts that landed them in jail took place in mid-winter 1998, about the same time frame that Denver's professional football team was winning the Superbowl. It had to be bitter cold that January night, when Eric Harris and Dylan Klebold broke into an electrician's van on a lonely stretch of highway not far from their suburban homes, stole some property from inside, and got caught with the stolen goods a few hours later. Harris and Klebold were busted! Busted by the Sheriff's Office a full year before Columbine. Taken into custody, fingerprinted, and photographed, both were booked on felony arrests. Had either one been eighteen, it would have meant a long weekend in jail and a Monday morning arraignment. But because they were teens, the parents were telephoned and informed that their seventeen-year-old sons were in the county jail, having been arrested in possession of stolen property (Erickson).

It had to be a shock for the parents, that late-night telephone call, but only a warm-up for what was coming in another fifteen months. Any righteous parent, I believe, would have been full to overflowing with anger and worry after that kind of wake-up call. All of them drove to the jail that night to pick up their child. But wouldn't those same concerned parents, in the light of a new day, be considering what could be done to help their youngest son around this latest obstacle to college, family, and a career? And for the lawyers they would consult with, was there any way to keep this nasty felony arrest off their freshly minted criminal records? (Cullen).

The direction of the parents' hopes lay in the juvenile diversion program, one year of court supervision with terms and conditions. After successful completion, the underlying charges could be dismissed. Unlike Kyle, who once lived in the supervised care of a foster home, Eric Harris and Dylan Klebold could even continue to live in their family homes, assuming Magistrate DaVita allowed it, and continue to attend the same school, together. First, they had to get accepted into the program. And with the assistance of expensive legal representation, it happened.

Eric Harris and Dylan Klebold would spend their last year of high school jumping through the hoops of the diversion program, the watchful supervision of a diversion officer, and the oversight of the juvenile court. Under Magistrate DaVita, both Klebold

176

and Harris performed community service, went to school, maintained part-time employment, and participated in mental health counseling—which for Eric included psychiatric treatment (Erickson, 18). The two young Icaruses—or should it be Icarods?—lived at home, stayed in the same school, and kept in close contact as best friends. Klebold and Harris continued to stoke their respective rages on internet blogs. They continued to build a cache of homemade bombs in Eric's basement. And with a little help from their friend Robyn, acquired two shotguns and a 9-mm semiautomatic rifle at a local retail business through a conduit known as the gun show loophole.

When Eric and Dylan and Robyn went to the Tanner Gun Show in November of 1998 to purchase their weapons of war, the two boys had felony charges and criminal records. Had there been a background check requirement and a registered gun merchant willing to apply it, neither Klebold nor Harris could have passed. They needed Robyn Anderson and not just because of their ages. She was the only one with a clean record, but somehow that glaring detail never came up during the *Good Morning America* interview. Possessing any one of those three guns was a flagrant violation of the diversion requirements. The would-be murderers could have landed in jail months before the massacre had only Robyn Anderson, or one of the gun show merchants, had the temerity to report them to the authorities.

And what teenage boy could pass up an opportunity to brag to his girlfriend about the night he spent in jail? Of course, Robyn Anderson knew about her boyfriend's arrest. And if she knew about one, she then knew about the other. The only question worth asking, is when did she find out? Because if Robyn knew on the day of the shopping spree, then she was conceivably guilty of aiding and abetting, not just the violations of their diversion requirements, but the murders themselves. Criminal charges were never filed. Instead, Robyn Anderson was rushed in front of a television camera and vindicated on reality TV, declared "innocent" by "Good Morning America" and its viewing audience.

Why does any of this matter more than twenty years after the fact? Because it shows how Columbine and too many others could have been prevented, but only with universal criminal background checks and gun merchants willing to enforce them.

On the way home from the creative writing class, I drove straight to the bookstore, the same one that once employed Lee, and bought a journal. It wasn't my first, but I had forgotten the satisfaction of keeping one. Tama Kieves rekindled that flame. My first journal was filled with writings and drawings from an adventurous year abroad after winning the lottery—not the one with a jackpot assembled out of dollars—the one that allowed me to drop out of college with impunity and travel around Europe by thumb and by backpack. A young Icarus, I spent the first summer working on a construction site in Hamburg, Germany, as an unskilled laborer. It was a total immersion into their language and culture, except for those few on the construction site who had learned some English as prisoners of war inside the USA. Each one seemed to have a story to tell about how long and hard their struggles to return home after the war. There was time that summer for soaking up beer, watching American movies translated into German, and reading. I bought my first journal in Hamburg. It was thin with a blue cloth cover and beige binding, small enough to fit inside the top pocket of my backpack as a young traveler, and memorable enough to occupy a special place in my individual library, today.

\*      \*      \*      \*      \*

Today's route begins as a long gradual descent down a two-lane blue highway to a real breakfast at a truck stop/convenience store about an hour away. The highway, State Route 200—the vetted route for bicycle travelers by adventurecycling.org—straightens out now that we are leaving the mountains behind. The stops are fewer and farther between. For my purposes, it is the direct route across two hundred and fifty miles of high prairie separating Lewistown, Montana, the last town we passed through of any size, and the North Dakota state line. In between, there will be a few highway junctions with names, gas stations, and towns with declining populations.

I climb back into the saddle and ride. It feels good to be ahead of the others this morning, something like the release that can accompany that first cold beer. *Thank you, Kyle, wherever you are, for this renewed sense of purpose and vitality. I'm feeling alone and in charge of a bicycle, and drinking in the freedom of it.* On any other morning gravity would have taken control. Daedalus, the bicycle, would have fallen over and stayed down. But not this morning. Today, my spirit feels like I'm lifting away from something fixed and immutable, pushing away from a steady branch like a fledgling learning to fly, and hoping for the breeze to catch my wings. I will have plenty of opportunities today to sort through the flood of memories of Ben and Lee graduating from high school, so blended with Kyle and Columbine.

When I started working for Jefferson County, my children were still in grade school, and freedom—or at least my working definition of it—amounted to having choices. With a steady paycheck, freedom included being able to choose from the cornucopia of goods and services available within our community, far more than I could use or even afford during any given month. Month to month was how we lived, paycheck to paycheck. We had the freedom to rent different movies during the week. I could choose between community events or outdoor gatherings to enjoy as a family, which book to read next, or which restaurant to patronize—maybe the one with the big-screen TVs. We might watch half of a Monday night football game, and maybe even get loud. There was a steady income and some of it disposable. I was free to spend, free to choose from whatever was available within our price range. And there, my understanding of freedom got stuck for the longest time, right up until Columbine.

After visiting Kyle this morning and talking with him, the day is taking on a purity that could never be collected, quantified, or sold. Our meeting is stirring up a stream of vivid memories. *I've changed a lot since my unrequested participation in the Columbine clean-up crew—change is the operative word.* Twenty years down the road, it makes sense to up my game on the subject of freedom, to insist on a higher meaning, one that won't be mistaken for the numerous brands of beer that anyone can track, stacked like Lego building blocks against the walls of a neighborhood discount liquor store. If freedom can be reduced to selecting shiny objects for placement into a shopping cart, then liberty is nothing more than a stock or commodity listed on one of the stock exchanges, and possessed, by only a few with the deepest pockets. *Individual freedom has to mean more than that.*

So the freedom I am choosing—from the balanced perspective of this moving bicycle seat—comes with its own inherent energy. Freedom is a force to be wielded in rebuilding our communities and the roads and bridges that connect them to accommodate safe bicycle travel. Metals can be alloyed with other substances and become even more useful. I want the same for freedom, blending it with higher values. Alloyed with fear, freedom has produced the devastation of Columbine, and all the subsequent massacres in America's public places that have followed. I want to live long enough to see what can result when freedom is finally alloyed with compassion, kindness, and respect.

Here in this saddle, freedom means nothing more or less than being self-sufficient, self-propelled, and in charge of a bicycle. Every day of my journey is a test administered by the natural world. Each day, the test changes. It migrates into the physical, emotional, and psychological realms, and the scorecard, if there is one, won't get tallied until the end, when sunset signals that it's time for nourishment and rest, because another day's ride is coming.

I chose to stock up on freeze-dried dinners in Great Falls, knowing they would be necessary on this leg of the trip. Glendive is the next city of any significant population. Until I can reach it, my phone will not detect an internet signal. Last night before falling asleep, I reached for the map of folded, plasticized paper, to fix into memory the likely spot for this next day to end. I choose a place so remote that even though it had a name, no population was listed, at least according to whoever counted heads during the last census. Eastern Montana is like that when it comes to inhabitants. If a location has an unimproved campsite and drinkable water, it's good enough for the mapmakers. Today's stopping point is from the map. Today's destination has that much going for it and more. It is the location where the Musselshell River crosses underneath blue Highway 200 on its way into the Missouri River. Long before maps, nature made this countryside remarkable. Mosby should be difficult to miss on a bicycle.

The land is wide open here, full of unobstructed views that belie the inherent beauty of the landscapes; lots of space here, for filling with memories and affection for the people I care about and miss. I sent Lee another text with an update back in Lewistown, letting her know that I would be out of range for a while, possibly four or five days until Glendive. *Maybe that will tweak some interest.* The water bottles are full. I topped them off back at the last truck stop without waiting for the rest of the group. They will find me soon enough. Today, I want to feel the rotating pedals pulling and pushing the tires into a smooth rhythm induced by the land, over and through the undulating brown hills. Daedalus and I do the up-hill work. We enjoy a breeze on the other side. I stop along the way in towns named Winnett and Teigen for food, water, and a brief rest. Then, I can start all over again for Mosby.

At last, the sun is behind me, casting intermittent shadows ahead of a bicycle. We are moving down the highway, wings fully extended to catch the uplifts. There's no stopping us now. In front of us and extending away to the south, a long sinuous rim of rock dominates the landscape and defines a ridgeline beyond which I cannot yet see. It is the kind of landform a river makes in collusion with gravity over millions of years, just by running through it. This ridge has to be the high bank of the Musselshell River, which means that I am closing in on tonight's campsite with plenty of daylight left. I'm tired, elated, and grateful to be pedaling into what must surely be one of the last inclines, still eager for the next panoramic view that awaits at the top. I feel strong and competent. My body sings with the freedom of being fully alive. This trans-formational freedom is so much more than an ability to buy, or to choose, or to own, even a weapon as lethal as an assault rifle. This is the freedom to be.

And on the next downward stroke of the pedal, one of the links in the bike chain, the one that transfers the energy from my heart, legs, and lungs into the rear wheel, breaks.

## CHAPTER 12
## A TEXT FROM LEE IS WAITING

*July 24, 2017*
*Glendive, Montana*

*Something's wrong here!* The message flows from the nerves in my feet to the brain stem in an instant. *I get no resistance from the pedals!* I look down, just in time to watch the bicycle chain noiselessly play itself out into a row of continuous links stretched across the asphalt. Daedalus drifts to a stop on the slight uphill grade. I lean the bike against the collapsible kickstand and look around for signs of life. Nothing moves in any direction. *This is bad.* Nothing seems out of place, except for the length of chain laid out as straight as an arrow, neatly parallel to the painted white line separating highway from shoulder. A gentle wind blows from the south.

I take a swallow of water and remember my first flat tire, how it felt like all the life had gone out of the day. It took a while before things started to improve again. First, I had to remove the wheel, scatter tire levers, valve caps, and nuts all around, replace the inner tube, reinflate the tire, and return the wheel to the frame. It took time and effort. But, once the rubber side of the tires returned to the pavement, the tire pressure held. Life was good again. I was back on the road.

Here, in the middle of Montana, breaking a chain is the bicycle equivalent of losing your brakes in a car on that infamous hill in your hometown, the one with a railroad crossing and a stop sign at the bottom, known far and wide as Dead Man's Hill. A broken chain requires a spare link and a special tool for removing said bad link. I have neither. Nothing but a spare plastic grocery bag for slipping the collapsible metal pieces into as I pick it up off the highway. I tuck the bag inside the front pocket of the pannier with all the bike tools, the few that I did carry. I seal it away behind the Velcro closure, along with the illusion that I am some kind of free agent, capable of surviving on my own with a bicycle for some indeterminate length of time.

So, I wait. I look out from my perch near the top of the rise, look down the highway, and watch a dark moving speck grow into a vehicle and then a Subaru. The car with Montana license plates slows down. I am thinking about all the different ways there surely must be for cramming a bicycle and all this gear into a hatchback. The car pulls up alongside and stops. The window on the passenger side slides down so that the young driver can ask, "Are you OK?"

"Yeah, all except for this busted chain."

"Can't help you with that. Need anything?"

"I'm good for now with water and food."

"You need a pickup truck."

"Don't I know it."

"One will be along," the driver replies, rolling up his window. The car pulls away. The young man looks back through the rearview mirror and waves.

*I wonder if he has a friend with a truck.*

There's no need to look at my cell phone to understand that there's no internet here. I don't even need one to check the time of day. I can tell by the position of the sun how much light and warmth is left in it. And Daedalus and I have been standing out here by the side of the road for a long time—long enough to watch Gerry and the Pats approaching on their bicycles from a long way off. They are strung out along the highway, slow-moving dots coming steadily closer. Each one catches up in slow motion. Each one stops and asks, "What's wrong?" Each one offers the same assessment and mentions the campsite up ahead in Mosby. There's water there. Each one says, "Don't worry. Someone will stop."

This is how the late afternoon and evening proceeds: solitary cars and trucks pass by, all of them slow down, a few even stop and offer water or an energy bar, but all of them decide to pass a stranded cyclist by and keep going towards their individual destinations. I am waiting for the last one, the exceptional one in today's series of solitary cars and trucks with a driver willing to stand out; the one able to demonstrate that everyone who predicted, "Someone will stop," was right. I need a pickup truck driving trail angel with a heart as big as the one that got Columbine teacher Dave Sanders into so much trouble. He devoted an entire professional life to teaching high school and coaching basketball teams, but on the day of an unexpected massacre, he went down like the captain of his ship, insisting that others be saved first.

With the magnificence of that heroism in my head, I imagine that a great beast of a pickup truck is out there on the highway somewhere. I can't see it yet, but my heart it telling me that it is there...and it's big, a three-quarter ton. And it's coming closer.

I squint into the western horizon, but nothing has changed. Until a small dark dot appears. Something is coming down the highway, moving too fast to be a cyclist, and too big for a car. The dot grows into a truck! The driver sees me and starts slowing down. I can see duallies on the rear end and a solitary man behind the wheel. He's wearing a white, summer-weight cowboy hat. *The only thing missing is the Marlboro cigarettes—and for good reason.* The mighty truck pulls up alongside, its sides so high that from my angle on the shoulder of the road, I cannot see into the bed. It could be empty or full of stuff. But I can tell that it's an older model GMC, without the usual assortment of dings and dents. This is a well-maintained machine, someone's pride and joy and the proud owner sits behind the wheel, upright and imperious in his Sunday best. The passenger window slides down and the driver calls out, "Soon as I pull off the highway, you go ahead and throw your gear into the back. I'd help you with some of that if I could. But my balance isn't so good anymore...since the accident."

Excitement flows into my arms and hands. I feel strong enough to lift the whole bicycle and toss everything into the back in one heave. But then sanity takes over. I blurt out, "Just stay right there. I got this." One by one, I remove the bags from the frames and toss them over the high fender.

"I can take you all the way to Mosby," says the rancher. "It's got a bicycle hostel, or at least the start of one. I ought to know. I'm building it. The name's Don."

"Good to meet you, Don!" I reply. "I can't wait to see this hostel of yours," and right away remember the trail angel back in Waitsburg, Washington, the woman in the "Resist Mediocrity" T-shirt.

I notice that Don is trying to turn his shoulders and watch through the rear window. But he can't twist his back around. He speaks out of the side of his mouth for the words to flow in my direction and says, "I'm also the mayor, head of construction, and the garbage man."

I stop what I'm doing to laugh at his joke, before returning my attention to a silent Daedalus upright and just ahead of the rear wheel, looking for the right purchase to lift the bicycle up and over the shiny metallic barrier. I grip the crossbar's tubular steel with both hands. Then, come the tears as I look back on three weeks of travel and team building and realize that once these bicycle tires leave the road, I will lose something of immeasurable value, that sense of belonging to this band of eclectic cyclists meandering across the country. Membership has its privileges, a sense of camaraderie, and security. The loss of our friendship on wheels hurts. We were a resilient group of guys with a shared goal, able to adapt to changing weather, elevation, and even take a chance at recreating ourselves after dropping in number from five to four. The others will surely morph again in my absence. Ever since Kyle's reappearance this morning, life has become a lot more complicated.

"I used to live over in Lewistown," says Don, breaking through the memories and reminding me how fortunate I am to be sharing the road with this Montana man and his bad-ass truck, one who by all appearances is friendly and wants to help. "I used to ride my motorcycle all over these roads. That was before the accident." Here, he pauses in a story that he clearly enjoys telling. The man behind the wheel is not about to give it all away at the beginning. That was just a teaser.

Without another word, I bend my knees, pick up the bike, and lift. But on this first try, I can't extend my arms high enough for either wheel to clear the edge of the grey painted metal. Disappointed, I set Daedalus back down on the ground for a different grip.

*Let me help you with that,* says the mellifluous voice of a six foot three Kyle inside my head. The words resonate from my feet into my backbone where they merge into a flood of emotions. Tears gush. They flow down my cheeks and onto the red polyester shirt. And this time, the tires come off the ground with gusto. Daedalus slips easily into the bed of the truck. *Robert, just keep going,* declares the soothing voice. *Your bicycle's gonna have a new chain on it before another night falls.* At least, I think that's what he's saying; because it feels like I'm standing at a fulcrum in time and meeting my own destiny, getting an enjoyable glimpse into powers far beyond my comprehension, my mortality or humanity.

Wanting to make sure that I am understanding it right. "Did you just say tomorrow night?" I inquire, reaching for the passenger door.

"What was that?" says Don from behind the wheel.

I look at him and notice that we are close in age. "Don, I'm Robert," I say, lifting myself into the spacious cab. "Thanks for stopping."

"No problem," he replies, making eye contact and holding out his hand to shake. Then, he adds, "Hope you don't mind about the 9-mm," slipping the truck into gear and returning to the highway. At least he's not trying to show it to me and drive at the same time—which is a good thing—he's just letting me know that it's there. "Always carry one when I go out. Ever since the accident, I get anxious. Not to worry though. I trust you...so far."

It doesn't surprise me a bit that Don carries, not out here in sparsely populated Montana. In his simple introduction, he has shared both the fact of his head injury and the feelings of vulnerability that go along with it. I can respond with respect and sympathy for this pickup driving trail angel, without even thinking about the semiautomatic pistol he wants to carry inside this great beast of a truck. Uneasiness about the gun is nothing compared to how appreciative it feels to be in the passenger seat. "You can trust me, Don," I say, wondering if my three friends will find their way to his makeshift hostel tonight. There's an unimproved campground a little further down the road.

"Stayed too late at the bar one time too many," Don continues, circling back to his story and taking full advantage of his captive audience. "It was me and the Harley. I can remember deciding to leave the bar to ride home but after that nothing." Then he starts shaking his head and says, "Don't remember falling asleep at the wheel. Don't remember driving straight off the road. Don't remember the crash. But there was a silver lining," he declares, pausing long enough for me to ponder the extent of his injuries before moving on with his story. "There was a witness, somebody I didn't even know, following behind on the highway. Called for help with a CB radio. That's what saved me," he concludes. "That and a bunch of doctors and nurses putting my skull back together and fusing some vertebrae in my back. Without them, we would not be having this conversation and I wouldn't be driving this truck and picking stranded cyclists up off the highway."

\*  \*  \*  \*  \*

Lee's commencement from high school was on May 23$^{rd}$, 2001. By then, our family had grown to include an in-your-face, four-legged attention seeker. The dog was a Boston Terrier, a new puppy and a surprise that I brought home a few months after Earl the Grey's untimely death. Lee decided to schedule her enlistment for the first Monday after Labor Day in September and was expecting another graduation ceremony from the Navy equivalent of boot camp before the end of the year. First, she had to get out of Denver.

Older sister Christen, another daughter by their mother's first marriage, orchestrated and held an end-of-summer barbeque a few weeks before the scheduled departure. But all the good vibrations engendered by the party, the good food, plentiful beer, and gifts, dissipated into a national vacuum created by the inescapable current of history. The first Monday after Labor Day that year was September 11$^{th}$, the day of the collapse of the Twin Towers in New York City. There would be no leaving home that day. Airports all over the country progressively shut down and closed their doors, and all of Lee's precise logic and carefully arranged plans were swept aside as the world insisted on imposing its own agenda for the days, weeks, months, and even decades to come.

Lee and I soon quarreled about what it all meant. After she drove away from the house that day, I went into an emotional

187

limbo. She had been planning not just a goodbye, but an emancipation flight from home, and for at least a solid year. Everyone in our family circle was frustrated, disappointed, and angry; but no one more than Lee. She was eighteen, a high-school graduate, and headed into the military. This was not the ideal time for me to step into the shoes of controlling dad, and for a solid week I did my best to let that parental need for control go. In the few days that remained, Lee could spend her time partying, hanging out with friends or family, or being at home when it suited her. When she found her way home, she would be greeted at the door by an energic young dog, thrilled to have another human to play ball with. He was so full of attitude that the kids named him Buster. The name fit his personality to a tee. Even after his tongue began hanging down from one side of his mouth because of a jaw that would not close properly. He still blustered his way around the house, demanding attention, insisting that someone play with him. Earl could never be replaced, but Buster had no qualms about creating a niche in the family. I was there to get up in the morning, go to work, and answer the phone if anyone called. All I wanted was one more family dinner together before the airport reopened and Lee could get out of Denver. We always found a lot to talk about.

*　　*　　*　　*　　*

Riding across the Great Plains at sixty miles per hour and from the vinyl seat of an aging GMC pickup, the world looks different. The natural sounds are gone. There's no wind to distract, no downhills to look forward to, not even a destination on the horizon. Inside the cab of Don's truck, ten miles is ten minutes away. On a bicycle, it could be thirty minutes, or an hour or more depending on the winds, the weather, or the slope of the pavement.

Don explains that since his accident, he enjoys helping people, especially cyclists. When he picked me up, he was on his way home from church in Lewistown. It's his habit, his routine to go into town on Sundays. He likes Lewistown well enough but says that he couldn't live there—too many people wanting to know his business. There's a week's worth of groceries in the back of the cab. Don's going home, back to his mobile home in Mosby. At

188

least he was, until he saw me and Daedalus, standing by the side of the road, thumb out.

Don explains that he doesn't sleep that much and likes to keep busy. So, he bought this windswept piece of land out along the highway, hooked up his old mobile home to the truck, and established his residence in Mosby. "What's left of the Musselshell River runs right next to my place." And Don has a dream, a goal. He wants to spend what's left of his time on earth running a hostel on the Lewis & Clark Trail for cyclists like me that ride through every summer. He knows how far it is down that long highway from Great Falls to Glendive, and understands that he won't make any money doing it. He wants to cover his costs. That's all. His plans are a work in progress. He has already converted an old garage/machine shop into something like a small apartment. The bathroom and shower are plumbed in. There is even a washing machine. Don likes to stay busy, but he does get tired. When that happens, he takes a nap. That's how he's building his hostel, one small step at a time, and I have listened to more than one motivational speaker expound on this principle, the daily aggregation of marginal gains. I can relate to its wisdom. The same one carries cyclists across continents and motivates writers to turn their manuscripts into books.

Once we arrive, Don gives me a tour of the hostel. The interior walls of the bathroom are rough drywall, but the lights are on and the hot water works too. Anyone with eyes can see that Don's dream is taking shape. He says that he would rather be spending his time fixing up the hostel than watching daytime TV. He gets frustrated trying to watch those shows. He asks to see the broken bicycle chain, just in case he has a tool that he might be able to fix it with.

I retrieve it for him and try to explain, "Don, even if you could fix it, I don't have the replacement link to keep the chain at the right length." But I hand him the broken mechanical device anyway.

He takes the oily chain in one hand and rotates his wrist back and forth as if examining its value, "It doesn't take that much, does it?"

"What's that?"

"To stop you right in your tracks."

"No, it sure doesn't," I answer, nodding my head in agreement, reminded again of all of the careful planning that went into the decision for Kyle Velasquez to return to his life inside the family home, with just enough time to settle into the student body at Columbine High School before meeting with Dylan Klebold in the library.

"I can take you into Circle tomorrow, for sure," says Don. Circle is the next small town down the highway.

I mention Glendive. That's where, according to the map, the next bike shop can be found.

"Glendive is too far for me to think about right now," he explains. "I get anxious the further I get away from this place."

"We leave tomorrow morning?"

"Yeah. First thing."

"OK," I reply. "Well, wherever we stop though, make sure there's a gas station. I'm going to buy you a tank full of gas. Help cover your costs."

"We'll find one," he says, handing me back the broken length of chain.

\*    \*    \*    \*    \*

The most significant of the Boot Camp letters was dated November 11th, 2001, one of those eerie days when the numbers representing the date—at least most of them—all lined up like soldiers during an inspection, 111101. But those symbols were not soldiers. They had to be sailors, because the source of this particular letter was naval in origin. The letter was from Lee, and I missed my girl. She would send them—not an email—but multipage letters on paper and ink almost every week until boot camp graduation, or as the Navy preferred to describe it, recruit training.

Lee's letters made an impact, highlighting the days in which each one appeared in the mailbox, stopping time for a while, at least until I could quickly read through every page, let loose a thoughtful sigh, and then read each sentence and word all over again. In the wake of her boot camp letters nothing else mattered, and responding to one, in-kind, took priority over everything else at home or at work. The November 11$^{th}$ letter would be the sixth one to bestow its profound magic over the otherwise dulling cycles of daylight and sleep. I mention this one first though because within its pages lay the gift of a unique and powerful nickname. And like sentimental parents everywhere, I have kept every one.

The first letter was postmarked September 27$^{th}$, 2001, a seven-page typewritten form from the US Navy explaining item after item of pertinent details about the recruit training process. However, it opened in Lee's handwriting with a line that read, "Dear Dad." That was enough to keep me engaged all the way to page five, where the rigidity of the form gave way to a full page for Lee to add three handwritten paragraphs. She opened by explaining that:

> I finally got an opportunity to write you. Since I got here, I have been on hold w/about 30 other girls b/c no one can get a plane out here. That in itself hasn't been too bad, it's just that they don't start counting actual boot camp days until you get an entire division of about 94 people. My division just arrived today…so it looks like I'll be graduating in the first 2 weeks of December.

Her second letter described a typical day within that first week assuring me that,

> Boot camp itself is not so bad, as long as you listen…things are so simple here, but there is so much instruction that making your bed becomes a fifteen-minute job—no joking.

She described her days as eighteen hours long with nothing but marching. "Chow sucks, we cannot talk and only get 10 minutes to eat bad food." But eventually, the weekend provided some respite from the harsh routine.

> Saturdays we all go to church—it's the only place where you can talk and relax w/o getting

beat. (Beat is just what RTC's call extreme physical workouts meant to punish.)

Lee closes her final paragraph with,

> Since I've been here I've been sick, completely lost my voice and am just getting it back, so I am not thinking too clearly at the moment. Let everyone know that I'll write when I get the chance. I miss you guys—take care—write me so I have something to do. Love, Lee.

Ben and I had to wait a whole week for the next one.

\*     \*     \*     \*     \*

In the morning, I'm up before the sun, drinking fresh coffee and rereading the journal entry from last night. Mayor Don of Mosby, Montana, is awake too, ambling around the yard checking through the list of things he needs to do before he can leave. One of them is moving the truck from inside the garage onto the parking area where it sits outside, facing the highway. Daedalus got to spend the night indoors, laying flat in the bed of the truck. I still have some packing to do.

I stayed up late last night, sitting under the incandescent beams of a porch light, adding a lengthy entry to the daily journal about my rescue by pickup truck and back-to-back encounters with a ghost from Columbine. At first, the words flowed like dreams from the end of my pen, but when I reached the scene in which a new bicycle chain was promised—before another night falls—that was where fatigue overcame my need to finish the writing. In the light of this new day, it looks like the ink just stopped flowing. I close the book and watch trail angel Don continue through his morning checklist. Other than walking, he and his truck are the only game in town.

Don wants me to drive. He wants to rest up and save his energy for the trip back. I'm grateful for the opportunity. Circle is about seventy miles away on the map. It's the first place of any size with about five hundred people on the roster. The town is hard to miss because the highway cuts right through it. Don knows well the location of the hardware store. He provides directions. We walk inside and ask if they can help with a broken bicycle chain. They have no bicycle chains in stock. We get back in the truck and decide to go all the way to Lindsey, the next spot on the map. I never mention Glendive, my preferred destination; don't want to do or say anything to make Don more anxious than he already is.

Back on the road, I tell a story about a hot and challenging day on the bike that ended well with freshly grilled hamburgers, succulent french fries, and cold beer back in Roosevelt, Washington. Don responds with a story of his own about living in that part of the west because he helped to move a lot of dirt around back when the Roosevelt Regional Landfill was built, and he was an earthmover operator. From his days in eastern Washington, he starts on a list of all the different cities and states where he's worked as a crane operator. Of all the construction-related jobs he's done, that's the one he enjoyed the most. It kept him occupied all day, sitting in an insulated cab high above the major cities of both coasts, reading Zane Grey books, and watching the flow of people and traffic below. It was a lifestyle that he supported with the purchase of a mobile home and the same three-quarter-ton pickup that we're riding in this morning. Don lived the life of a nomad for a long time. But in terms of finding the right place to retire, he decided to return to his homeland on the high plains around Mosby. This is about as settled as he's ever been.

Don is still talking about it when we reach Lindsey, but there isn't much there, just a school, post office, and a few houses. We stop at the gas station anyway and ask if they know where we can get a bicycle chain fixed. From Lindsey, it's only twenty-five miles to Glendive, a city of about 5,000 that straddles the Yellowstone River. We can be there before lunch. Don says that he's willing to go that much further, but only to the first entrance onto the interstate. He doesn't want to take the time to drive into town. It's not that he doesn't like people. He's been gone a long time and wants to get back home.

He directs me to the parking lot of a large convenience store with multiple rows of gas pumps near an offramp to the interstate. Don says that he knows it well, and, he needs to pee. While I fill up the truck with gasoline, he lowers himself to the ground, shakes himself off, and finds his footing. Don reaches under the seat. He pulls out a thick looseleaf daytimer and a holstered pistol. Holding them in one hand and against his hip like a schoolboy carrying a couple of books, he shuffles gingerly toward the entrance and the double glass doors. All around me are reasons to smile; the profile of my well-armed benefactor with balance issues making his way to the head, the knowledge and gratitude that this man has brought me and all my gear all the way to the next city of any size, and, because my cell phone is pinging like the Rip van Winkle character waking up from a long sleep.

When Don returns, the tank is full, paid for, and Daedalus' wheels are back on the ground. I'm busying myself loading panniers onto the front and rear frames. Still smiling, I hand him the truck keys, tell him again how much I appreciate his hospitality and generosity. A mischievous part of me wants to ask him about needing his pistol to take a pee inside a public restroom. But he might not see the humor in it, especially since he's in a hurry now. I do not believe for one second, though, that Glendive is in danger of a potential terrorist attack. In my opinion, the only logical explanation for Don wanting to have his pistol close was to obviate his worrying about me stealing it, or anybody else for that matter. Either way, Don is now ready to roll. He shoves his gun and calendar back under the driver's seat where they belong and climbs into the cab of his truck. There's nothing left for me to do but stay out of the way. The big engine roars to life. Within seconds, Don and the big GMC three-quarter-ton are gone without a backward glance. John Wayne, the heroic movie star of the forties and fifties, could not have done it better.

I need a break too, to relax from the road, find something edible for an early lunch, and to check the phone for emails and texts. Inside the convenience store are premade sandwiches, ice-cold soda, and a wide array of salty and sweet snack food. But before sitting down to eat at one of the colorful tables, I ask the slender convenience store woman, "How far is it to the next bicycle repair shop?"

With the natural confidence of a local who knows everything worth knowing about the area, she leans forward in her polyester button-down shirt and explains, "You won't find one on this side of the border, not until you get into North Dakota. That's for sure." Even though it is not easy for me to hear these words without obviously registering some disappointment, the woman with streaked blonde hair adds still more evidence to support my growing belief that people in this part of the country take pride in their willingness to offer assistance to passing strangers, especially the ones on bicycles. "Maybe Dickenson," she says, adding specificity to her account, "That's about a hundred and fifty miles."

The good news is, there is a text from Lee. She's asking: "Made Glendive yet?" I resist the temptation to blurt out an enthusiastic monosyllable in response, remembering that Lee is not expecting me to be here, or even to read these words for another three days. There is time for something bigger and better than a monosyllable. I want a response that will keep the conversation going for a while. I need something better.

I scan through and respond to other emails and messages, say goodbye to the friendly woman behind the counter, and walk outside into the noonday sun. Daedalus and I park ourselves on the shoulder of another blue highway. There's a narrow bridge up ahead, and I can see the buildings of downtown on the other side. *Better to stay on over here where there's room for a car to pull off. But there's not a lot of traffic. Sure, there's an exit ramp off the interstate. But the cars getting off are only stopping for gas. Most get right back on the highway without driving into town.* All I can do is strike up a distracted hitchhiking pose.

Right on cue a middle-aged man driving a dark Chevy Blazer, bike rack on the back, drives by and stops. He is a man with hobbies. The back end of his SUV is full, loaded with cardboard boxes, camping gear, and black powder shooting supplies. "We can find room for your cycling stuff," he assures me and starts piling boxes on top of one another. "What happened to that bike of yours?"

"The chain broke yesterday afternoon out on Highway 200, just before the turnoff to Fort Peck," I say, handing him a pannier.

"You were out in the boondocks."

"Oh, yeah. Just hitchhiked into town this morning. You wouldn't happen to know where the closest bicycle shop is?" I ask, hopeful that a man with a bike rack would have one in mind.

And he does. He can't say enough good things about the one in Medora, near the entrance to Theodore Roosevelt National Park.

*And that's a whole lot closer than Dickenson.*

But he also goes on to explain, "If I had more time today, I'd take you over there myself." He even drops his voice to show some disappointment at not being able to make the trip, but then quickly adds, "But, I don't. So, I can't. Much as I'd like to."


If you limit yourself to domestic airline destinations and places that can be reached by travel along interstate highways, you are likely to have the mistaken impression that Medora, North Dakota, lies in a remote part of the country. But if you consult instead a trails map for self-propelled travel, you'll find it located at a prominent crossroads. This Lewis & Clark bicycle route that does a good job of following blue highways along a northern tier of states is taking me there.

Another piece of the crossroads that elevates Medora is its location along an ancient east-west trail that stretched between what are now cities named Seattle and New York City. In a time before written words, this earlier highway was named the Red Trail and intended for foot and horse traffic. After the same route became a blue highway, the name morphed into Old Red 10 or Old Highway 10. Maps of more recent vintage insist on calling it Interstate 94. But back in the day when Medora was high on Teddy Roosevelt's to-do list, the best way to get there was by train. Today, this small town is adjacent to the two cattle ranches he once owned and operated before becoming president in 1901.

Born in New York City, Roosevelt left the metropolis behind long enough to acquire a lasting devotion to the Badlands of North Dakota. To borrow from TR's description, it is a place of grim natural beauty. It is because of this historical connection that the Maah Daah Hey bicycle trail also passes through Medora, winding through the Badlands of the Little Missouri National Grassland and connecting his two former cattle ranches with over one hundred miles of singletrack. Singletrack is one of those intuitive words that expresses its own definition. It means a trail wide enough to fit a single bicycle and rigorous enough to demonstrate the need on the bicycle for wide tires and suspended front forks. Riders can select from the nine campgrounds scattered along its length to support each day's ride. Amenities include potable water, hitching rails, and fire rings (Haney).

And it doesn't end there. The Maah Daah Hey is a small section of a proposed Great Plains National Trail which, though still in the planning stages, crosses the USA from north to south, from the Charles M Russell National Wildlife Refuge near the town of Fort Peck in central Montana to Guadalupe National Park near the western edge of Texas ("Great Plains Trail Alliance").

With Daedalus securely fastened to the back of the grey Blazer, the driver weaves his way through Glendive. He takes us as far as the next entrance ramp onto I-94. It's early afternoon. The day is cloudless. There's no wind. It's a perfect day for balancing on a bicycle seat. But, that can't happen, not yet. I watch the Blazer drive away, as my heart sinks into my chest. *Now what?* He has deposited us into a commercial area on the east side of Glendive with at least two motels within walking distance, but few cars. There are quite a few of them though, trucks too, down on the interstate. *But we're out of sight. Stuck up here on the entrance ramp, right in front of the no hitchhiking sign.* Feeling uncomfortable, I take the bike by the handlebars to walk down the ramp to get closer to the highway and create some separation between us, me and the bike, and the sign.

*This is where I make my stand, the stand against encroaching boredom.* It takes a while before the sun moves into midafternoon. These are minutes that turn into hours without much traffic, except for a deputy sheriff that drives slowly by. Finally, another car comes down the road leading to the interstate highway ramp. *It looks like a grey Chevy Blazer. Could this be the same black powder guy, again?* My mind leaps to the completely unsupported conclusion: *The kind man might have changed his plans, whatever they were, and decided to take me the rest of the way into Medora after all.*

But, the car does not turn into the freeway ramp. It makes a U-turn instead. It stops. Now, the driver's getting out. He's waving. It is clearly the same bearded man and car. *He must have gone home, thought some more about the stranded cyclist, and come up with another idea.* Beaming with pride, he opens the tailgate, again, and pulls out a large piece of white poster board. He waves for me to come on over and see what he's created. The sign reads "Broken Chain" in bulging letters.

I thank him profusely for the second time today, but then feel the despair creeping over me as the dark grey tailgate recedes into the distance. *For a minute there, I thought that I might have a ride to Medora.* I try to remember his name.

CHAPTER **13**

A CHANGING OF THE CHAIN

*July 24, 2017*
*Beach, North Dakota*

The black powder enthusiast behind the wheel of the Blazer dropped Daedalus, me, and all the gear at a remote freeway entrance ramp, said goodbye, and then, drove away. But this trail angel was not the kind to stay away for long. He must have driven home, realized that there was one more thing he could do, one more act of kindness to perform, and I am now the proud possessor of a large homemade sign—bigger and better than a bumper sticker—that captures my predicament in bloated, hand-crafted letters. *I can advertise with this baby.* The man wishes me luck again, and we shake hands, again. I thank him for his willingness to help and watch the dark tailgate recede into the distance for the second time, a demonstration of just how personal the act of giving can be when it has room to grow. Again, the pang of regret as he drives away. *I'll take one order of acceptance, please, with a side of gratitude.* Now, all I need is some traffic.

Instead, I get sun. A ball of white heat lords over the little patch of windblown tall grass and asphalt, plodding across the sky toward a distant line of trees. Someone planted them like that, nice and straight to shield a house or a barn from wind and the elements; cared for the trees too, with a steady supply of water; because the climate here is dry. I distract myself with the memory of Lee's latest text and assign my bored intelligence to the task of imagining a clever response. Instead, I grow tired of holding up a sign with no one to see. My legs feel like they are ready to move. *Sunset is at least another four or five hours away.* I take a walk across the open expanse of brown vegetation and cast away plastic, but not before wedging the sign between the rear wheel and the crevice created by a couple of panniers, lying flat on the ground. *There's still plenty of time.*

My eyes are downcast, scanning the ground for anything crawling or even remotely interesting to break the tedium when I look up and see that Daedalus and I are no longer alone. There's a compact car parked on the highway a short walk away, a white hatchback. Once again, my heart leaps in the direction of hope. *There might be just enough room in the back seat and trunk for a bicycle and gear!* Inside, I can see a man and a woman talking, and at first, they seem oblivious to everything outside the vehicle. So, I pick up the sign again in both hands, face it in their direction, tilting the corners up and down. Nothing happens.

The car windows are shut tight, but the body language of the two occupants keeps my attention. The man in the passenger seat does the talking while the driver gazes out the windshield toward a distant horizon only she can see. Both hands hold onto the wheel. Next, he gestures and talks into his cell phone, the hands moving frenetically. He holds the screen towards her. But I can't tell if she even responds. The passenger turns back around in his seat and gives me a thumbs up. The slender man exits the car and starts walking towards me down the entrance ramp moving at a brisk pace. He waves one hand in greeting. In the other, he holds his cell phone, like there is something quite important on the screen if only I will look.

"I'm Dave," he shouts, extending his hand from a few strides away and sounding like we're getting close to a business deal right here next to the interstate. I hear the words, "I've got the answer to your chain problem right here."

"Good to hear. Because I sure could use a new chain right about now." I reply, shaking his hand and looking into his eyes to get a read on how crazy he might be. "I'm Robert. Is there a bike shop nearby?"

"It's a virtual one," Dave replies with a chuckle but keeps on talking, "right here in my hand. I could order you one right now from Jeff Bezos and friends, but it would take him several days to get his act together."

200

I start to nod, not in agreement necessarily, but to keep him going. *He wants to take his time getting to the point.*

"You don't want to wait that long."

"No, I don't."

"There is a brick-and-mortar bicycle shop over in Medora only a couple of exits down the highway. Here's their website," Dave says, showing me the screen. "I've been talking with Jennifer, the lady who runs it. Told her about you, standing here so close to the state line, hitchhiking. She says that she has a chain that will fit your bike."

"That's wonderful news!" I answer. "But, how do I get over there?" Because the only visible vehicle in sight is the white compact they're driving. I don't want to put a damper on the discussion, but in terms of volume, the car is about the size of a box of pop tarts on wheels. Medora is probably thirty miles away. It's not far, but only by automobile, not in terms of bicycle miles.

"And we are still working on that part," Dave admits with a smile.

I can feel myself being persuaded that there is a way for these disparate pieces to start coming together. I want to encourage the discussion. "Please tell Jennifer that I'll gladly pay for a new chain and once I get to Medora, a tune-up for the bike, too."

"Yeah," Dave agrees. "I'll do that."

"Can you take me there?"

"No," he answers, "Not possible. My friend can't leave. She's running late as it is." He sweeps his arm back towards the car. Inside the driver's long dark hair drapes across her shoulders as she stares straight ahead. Dave waves in her direction.

I'm unsure about the next step in this conversation and the lawyer in me wants more information. "So, you're trying to help out by giving me directions to the closest repair shop. Is that it?"

"That depends on you and whether or not you're dead set on hitchhiking over there by yourself," Dave answers. "Jennifer can bring the new chain and some tools and meet us somewhere in the middle. But she can't leave her shop right now. So, we can complete this transaction by hanging out around in Glendive until the store closes in a couple of hours. Or you can keep on doing the hitchhiking thing with your sign. It's totally up to you."

201

*That sign worked like magic!* I've been out here for hours, but only a couple of vehicles have passed me, none of them pickups. "And when does she close?" I ask Dave.

"Six."

"That's not too bad," I reply, still noncommittal. "And you've got a place in mind where we can pass the time that's out of the sun?" I ask, feeling the irony that only two days ago, I was touting the self-sufficiency of the bicycle, overflowing with the freedom and independence of riding one across the land, and pretending that kindness and compassion are not part of the equation. Today has been a quick study in how dependent I am on the numerous communities that populate this route and the people who inhabit them, a transformation from fiercely independent cyclist into a solitary man with a broken bike, miles from home; one who is watching a new friend develop a rather inviting offer. "Is there someplace we can go to wait?"

"Well, yes, there is," Dave declares with a grin that reflects the happiness he's feeling because this deal of his, this offering of kindness, is coming together. "Dave's Bicycle & Golf Emporium operates out of a storage unit right over there," he tells me, pointing towards the general direction of the city.

With that explanation, it occurs to me that, *Dave doesn't actually live here. He's storing his possessions here and maybe even living out of his storage unit. And the car on the roadside is hers, not his. But so far the impassive owner is coming along, interested just enough to provide the wheels and her time.* These two generous people may not have much in terms of wealth, but that does not get in the way of their giving what they can to help out a needy stranger on a broken bike. Much later in the day, Dave will have the chance to demonstrate his prowess in bicycle mechanics.

He is also a talker. As we walk back towards Daedalus, he describes some of the places and things I can look forward to in my upcoming ride across the state. He describes himself as an avid cyclist from a small town in central North Dakota, one who attributes his success in racing to a personal preference for leading from the back of the pack.

"Is it close enough to walk?" I ask him, "your storage unit?"

"It's too far when you're out in the sun with all this gear, and a perfectly good car is waiting," my newfound friend advises with a confident grin. "Let's see if we can break all this down and fit everything into the Cruze."

We can't forget the sign. It slides in last, resting on top of the frame and wheels and all the gear already filling the back. I slip into the back seat, holding a couple of saddlebags on my lap. But instead of thanking them as the door closes shut, I blurt out, "There's nothing in here that's worth much, just some well-used clothes and camping stuff." Locked inside a compact car, even with two ostensibly gentle strangers, I can feel the hard edge of uncertainty—yet again—that comes from living for years in the shadow of that massive breach of trust, the big lie. Philip Duran and Mark Manes were not the only ones with knowledge of the pending slaughter. The pretty young prom date and class valedictorian played a role in the betrayal. But even more egregious are the ones with actual knowledge of the destructive capability of their products who continue to poison with impunity the commercial marketplaces of our great nation with weapons intended for the battlefield.

For this solitary touring cyclist and to better honor Kyle and all the other victims, I cannot allow my fears to dominate over every step of the chain replacement process. The need for control is in my head. The heart understands that a higher good will come from allowing the bicycle to be transformed with a new chain. *The outcome can only improve with my trust in these two kind people. The heart understands that a higher good will flow from allowing my own transformation into a better man, a writer, and a grandparent with a fascinating story to tell.* Generous people have been lining up all day long to deliver their gifts, each one offering their time and effort. The scenes in which they play a role line up like breadcrumbs in the fairy tale, each one showing me the way to the next. My latest benefactors are Dave Unkenholz, fifth-generation North Dakotan and proud of it, and his peaceful friend.

"Not to worry," Dave replies. "We like tourists on bicycles around here. When you pass through town, you give us something to talk about. You spend money. Those are good things. If you posed a threat or were about stealing things, you'd have a fast car

203

and a gun, right? That bike of yours is personalized for slow travel. And you look like you've come a long way. Those things give you instant credibility around here; because of it, we're going to help you get your chain fixed and back on the road."

I don't know how to respond to them in words. But I can feel the connection that comes with just listening, and maybe even allowing a little faith to fill in the cracks of my defensiveness. Dave is too cheerful to be interested in mugging me, or anyone else for that matter. As for his patient friend, she seems content to be in control of the car. Dave doesn't introduce us. I don't ask. It feels like that information might be too intrusive, a risk I don't need to take. They are together in giving of their time and effort, in making this day stand out like no other. I'll choose to remember her as the mystery woman behind the wheel of the white sports car.

She steers us into a warren of storage units on the outskirts of town. We stop long enough to unload all the parts and pieces and gear. Then, she's gone without getting out of the car, but not without a look in Dave's direction. *What's not to trust?* I have no idea where they came from before finding Daedalus and me, or what they were up to, but they are both here now, moving the story forward as only trail angels can.

I have been living outdoors long enough that if the sun is visible, I can guesstimate the time and from there, get a sense of east versus west. It's a skill that brings the peace of knowing on any given day, which direction points towards home. But in Dave's hands, there is no need for undue concern over basic survival. Besides, the luxuries of the storage unit include a refrigerator. He reaches in and brings out a bottle of cold beer from a NoDak microbrewery. Dave opens the only bottle and hands it to me. I try to share it with him.

"No thanks," he replies. "But I would like to take your picture drinking it," which he does and makes a promise to post it on the internet. I ask him about good places to ride along the road up ahead. We talk about bikes and the places we've ridden them. We talk about family and home.

That's when inspiration hits. "Hold my beer!" I say out loud, remembering the sketches of a country-western comic, and set the bottle down on the cold concrete floor. I reach for my cell phone inside the pocket of my bicycle shirt, find a picture of my daughter Lee and show it to him. "I've got to send her a text. Let her know that I'm OK."

"Go for it," he says.

Before pushing the icon that lets me back into her most recent text, I visualize Lee safe and sound at home and type enough words to give her an update without giving too much of the detail away. "Safe and sound in Glendive. TWO DAYS EARLY! About to cross into No Dak. Love, Da."

*　　*　　*　　*　　*

The next four boot camp letters arrived in October. The first two opened with "Da," Lee's nickname for me when she was a small child. There is great power in nicknames. Her first sentences dripped with disappointment at not having received any correspondence from home, yet. But after getting over that regret and in the one dated October 7th, 2001, she included interesting details about this new way of life in the military and during that first month away.

> Wow—I need to slow down. Today is Sunday and we have 5 hours of free time to do a million things. I just got out of a twenty-minute shower. It was great. Sundays are the only days we get to shower at our leisure. Now I have to iron four sets of clothes and write too many letters. And I have like 2 hours left…Things here are beginning to shift here into a routine, and that makes it easy. The days go by slow but the weeks fly by. We all cram so much into one day, but it's always the same thing…We have PT every morning—which is nothing more than a series of push-ups and sit-ups, stretching and running—but it's at 3 a.m. No one functions well at that hour. Then we march around all day in these boots that are tearing my feet up.

The letter dated October 14$^{th}$, 2001, described the inevitable conflicts that were showing up within her division and between the sexes. It began with:

> Well hello—I know that there is a good reason you haven't written back yet—maybe there are simply no stamps left in the whole of Colorado, or you keep forgetting to mail. Whatever the case may be—get on it!
>
> But seriously—how are you doing? Things around here are completely out of control. There is a massive pink eye outbreak, everyone is sick and the rivalries between the guys and the girls are out of control. The guys are all dumbasses and talk when we shouldn't, spit all over the marching grounds and don't listen to details. So we get beat all the time. The females are the ones who carry the division—the Petty Officers tell us all the time. Yesterday we had an inspection and the females were on spot score, but when he inspected the guys, 5 failed and the rest came too close...
>
> Hey—you know I graduate November 29$^{th}$ you know! Only 5 people can come to graduation— but I'll double-check on that.

She ended with: "Keep in touch—We don't get much news in here—So let me know what's going on—on the 'outside.' Love, Lee."

In the next one she reverted to calling me "Dad" and quickly acknowledged that my cards and letters had finally arrived. She also confided that:

> In your letter you asked if I am happy. Absolutely not, but you're not supposed to enjoy yourself at bootcamp. It's all a mind game. It's like being a rat in a cage w/various traps and triggers. You learn the safest routes and you eventually learn

how to work your way around your maze. I just want to get out of here and fast!

Thanks for the letter——you people don't know how comforting mail can be. Write back soon——I understand the mail is running a bit slow——all things considered——take care——I love and miss you, Lee.

Her fourth letter, which arrived just in time for my early November birthday, began with the greeting "Bobby Bobby Bobby." That's what I mean about the power of nicknames. She wrote about her plans for Thanksgiving, the graduation that would follow, and her observations about the approach of winter from her vantage point on the south shore of Lake Michigan:

So things here are freezing. It tries to snow here every day, but so far the wind just blows like mad. All we do is rush from one point to the next. I only have 4 more weeks and we have to learn the graduation march and take all these tests. I can't believe how busy we always are——but it does make the days go much faster.

But then, she ends the letter with:

Man—I want to go home. I want to go home. I want to go home—now! I don't know how long I get to see you after graduation and that is driving me nuts—but I'll let you know as soon as I find out. I'll call next time I get a chance—hope you enjoyed reading all this chicken scratch—sorry if it runs all over the place—I'm operating on too little sleep if you ask me. Last night I was so cold I slept in my raincoat! Ha! I mean it—I'm done now—I love and miss you, Lee.

\*   \*   \*   \*   \*

With the sun much lower in the sky, the Cruze returns. Dave and I break down the bicycle, load it back into the car, and with the front wheel in my lap this time, we turn towards the entrance ramp where it all began several hours before. We drive for half an hour and cross the state line into North Dakota, but that doesn't slow us down one bit. We keep going until the next exit, the town of Beach. I have no idea what inspired the name. I'm certain that it wasn't the oceanfront view. What I can see is a large Walmart superstore right off the interstate with an immense parking lot.

We wait in a remote section of the lined parking spaces, away from the congestion of the people and cars close to the main entrance. I can't help but feel disappointed. There's no sign of Jennifer. I don't mind waiting on her. But, I was hoping that it would all come together before sundown. Instead, the lights of the parking lot are starting to come on; not all at once like the response to a single master switch, just one at a time, each one responding to an inner sensor, announcing to the world that it is time to dispel the darkness.

"She's on her way," says Dave, looking down at his last text. *It's sundown. The chain is still broken.* I can feel the impending disappointment. But then, a full-sized unblemished pickup truck streaks across the painted asphalt. It cuts through row after row of empty parking spaces, the driver bearing down on us, making a beeline for the remote corner of the lot where the three of us wait by the small but mighty Chevy Cruze, listless and bored with the slow pace of events, standing close together around an upturned bicycle. Daedalus is balanced on his seat and handlebars, the tires reaching up into the air, like the posture of a turtle stuck on its back. The truck heads straight for us. This can only be Jennifer of Dakota Cyclery, driving to the rescue in her white GMC half-ton pickup, the same one Dakota Cyclery probably uses to shuttle clients, customers, and their gear to the nine distant campgrounds that line the Maah Daah Hey trail.

After the introductions are done, Jennifer explains that it has been a long day and she would like to get home. "Can somebody pay for this so I can take off?" Without hesitation, I hand her

208

my credit card. She carries it back to the cab of the truck. I follow behind. Also, without hesitation, Dave opens the cardboard box and plastic of a new bicycle chain and busies himself with threading the chain through the sprockets of the chainring and derailleur.

A couple of days ago I was on course to pass through this expansive and foreboding stretch of prairie without ever connecting with the land or the people who make their homes here. But then, the bicycle broke and that unexpected circumstance kicked off an incredible series of memorable events. The breakdown came out of nowhere. It knocked me out of the saddle and into this psychological place where I had no choice but to be dependent on others, and be open to receive, to trust in the kindness of a series of helpful strangers, trail angels I would never have met under other circumstances.

I watch Jennifer of Dakota Cyclery slide the plastic through a remote credit card reader attached to her cell phone. Her movements are relaxed and sure, the hands of a practiced merchant and mechanic who has been to this rodeo many times before. Close by and with the bike still on its saddle, the traveling bike mechanic cranks the pedals through a couple of turns. He runs through the gears and smiles at his handiwork. Dave lifts Daedalus and flips the bike over again, rubber side down.

And all around us, night falls.

# CHAPTER: 14
## MOVING THROUGH MANDAN

*July 27, 2017*
*Mandan, North Dakota*

The Walmart parking lot with its easy interstate access proves to be an auspicious beginning for the North Dakota segment of the ride. *Trail angel Dave from Back of the Pack Racing, you are right about this camping spot.* He recommended this placid pond by the tall grove of cottonwoods as we said goodbye in the Walmart parking lot back in Beach, and just before he and his silent friend climbed back into the car to go home. "Just follow the interstate to the next exit," he said. "You'll be fine on your bike. The shoulders are wide. Drivers are used to seeing cyclists along this stretch of highway. But don't try passing any of them," Dave warned, ending his farewell in the same way he had said hello—with a light touch of humor.

I laughed at his joke, feeling a pleasant blending of gratitude and urgency, inspired by the strong desire to reboot my ride. I invited Dave to look me up in Denver the next time he passed through on his way to anywhere. I owed him at least that much, a warm shower and a place to spend the night. I was happy to have the chain fixed, ecstatic to be back on the saddle again after a day and a half of being unable to ride; such a worthwhile and redemptive window of time it was, filled to overflowing with random acts of kindness by extraordinary people, all of them conspiring to restore Daedalus and me, to purposeful mobility by sundown.

I sleep in the next morning and don't awaken until birdsong fills the nearby cottonwoods. As usual, an empty well-used coffee cup waits outside on the picnic table, ready for another round of the hot invigorating liquid. Inside the tent, the walls glow with low-angle sunlight, plenty of illumination for finding my clothes while looking for the cellphone. Outside, sunlight cascades through the leaves and shimmers off the lake. Traces of dew glimmer on the rainfly. *How perfect it is, this peaceful here and now.* I put the morning's water on to boil, turn on the cellphone, and anticipate the connection from scrolling through a precious string of texts with Lee. *Anything new from the apple of my eye?* Bare hands wrap around the warm metal of the three-cup percolator. Not because they are cold, but because warming them this way stretches inside to touch the soul. *Here it is, just me and the bike—alone again—sitting on the hard wooden bench of a picnic table listening to the bloop, bloop, bloop of the coffee pot coming to a boil. I have another day to fill…with pedaling and wonder!*

I must be getting closer to a deeper truth among my reasons for leaving on this quest, to bear witness to a symphony of light and sound, the latest in this long series of remarkable gifts from an almighty source, to come to grips with my own long-avoided belief in a higher power. *Thank God with a capital G that I rediscovered the bicycle late in life!* As a younger man, I had my share of difficulties with the hardwiring of my human brain with its five senses, but having a heart of infinite complexity. Yet it was through those same senses that I witnessed the changing of a broken bicycle chain within the narrow window of time foretold by Kyle's guiding spirit. Until that moment, I did not believe in miracles, especially ones bearing fruit on the painted lines of a Walmart parking lot. Today, the presence of an ineffable power at work in my life, like a soul compass guiding the way, and perhaps even for others to notice and follow along, for a while, is irrefutable. I'm even ready to concede that Isaiah had it right all those thousands of years ago when he opined, "The earth has no sorrow that heaven cannot heal."

In the wake of Columbine, many spoke of unity, hoping to engender some. Others offered thoughts and prayers. Instead, the months would turn into years, investigations and trials dragging on without much in terms of relief, accountability, or resolution. Obvious gains were notable, instead, in the increasing number of mass casualty events caused by gunfire in the public places along

211

Colorado's Front Range. Behind the scenes, parents whose family members had been wounded or killed by gun violence would revisit those memories, but never see their beloveds again. And, I watched as the spirit of Columbine lingered for a while, withered, and then faded into some inaccessible place, like the memory of a prodigal child, distant and remote, but never forgotten.

Shall I continue to describe Columbine as a massacre or sanitize the language by switching over to the phrase "mass casualty event?" Either way, seeds were strewn in its aftermath and especially by the presenters at the Memorial Service, in words both said and unsaid. Some landed on hard asphalt and became food for the birds. Others landed on the thorny ground of closed-off hearts and minds. Sprouts might appear, but nothing would thrive there. One seed, however, landed in the heart of this parent, a father with two teenagers still in the home. It took years for the seed to sprout into the deep and fertile soil. But once the roots were secure, the plant grew through adaptability and persistence into a mature human male and aspiring writer, one that flowered first into a bicycle warrior, and then, this book.

Without persistence, what remains is an enthusiasm of the moment. Without adaptability, what remains can be channeled into destructive fanaticism (Butler). Columbine and all its progeny testify to just how horrific this destructive fanaticism can get. Our planet would not be complete without natural disasters. Ubiquitous television screens and cellphones provide us with the latest dramatic details of every earthquake and hurricane, wreaking havoc and disrupting lives in faraway places, but without emotional involvement by the viewing audience. Twenty-four-seven journalism is conditioning us to the chaos and grief inherent in tragedy. I have learned to lump such events together into the larger category of accidental misfortune: I wasn't involved or hurt. Nor was there malevolent intent.

But Columbine was man-made, the product of two teenage boys ensconced within the material wealth of their community and seduced by a primitive belief that the power of the gods might be theirs to wield; that with guns and homemade bombs constructed in a basement workshop, they would become imbued with the ability to change something, anything. Like all teens, their prefrontal lobes were still in rudimentary stages of development (van der Kolk). Worse than that, the killers had placed what little faith they had in the power of vengeance. The choice cost them their lives. And, there were far too many other victims.

Except for the passage of the background check requirement and the lapsing of the assault weapons ban, little has changed in Littleton since Klebold and Harris demonstrated that being under the supervision of a criminal justice system is not an effective deterrent to assembling a private arsenal. As a father and parent, I cannot ignore this danger. I feel a primordial need to protect my home and family. It is a burden that cannot be shed. When my children were small and utterly dependent, it was possible for me and even logical to look at an assault rifle and see the weapon as one more way to protect my home and family. But our precious children must turn into teenagers. Along the way they learn to judge us as parents. Next, they resist, eschew, and even mock our natural desires to protect them by controlling their lives. By intention, quirk of fate, and natural process, most teens accept the challenge of emancipating into adulthood. In my experience as a parent and a child protection attorney, it is all too common for teenagers to push back against their communities, sometimes in jest, other times in anger. But there is no good reason for allowing them access to an AR-15 as they act out the anger.

Closing the gun show loophole, nationwide, is one proven way of preventing our precious children from arming themselves with weapons of war. Colorado's background check requirement now prevents juveniles from purchasing these weapons within its borders. But the gun show loophole is wide open throughout vast regions across this country. Another more pragmatic step is to impose heavy sales and property taxes at the state and local levels of government on both bullets, and the extended ammunition magazines that feed them into gun chambers. Never forget that all the bullets, weapons, and bombs that destroyed Columbine high school in 1999, were stored in the basement workshops of affluent neighboring parents. Anyone wanting to create and maintain that kind of private arsenal should be taxed heavily for the privilege, and second, for the enormous burden it imposes on their communities once the bullets start to fly. When ammunition costs a thousand dollars, there will be a lot fewer innocent bystanders.

*　　*　　*　　*　　*

I am fortunate to own a cellphone with its multiple modes of communication. But a lengthy string of texts, even in a virtual world populated with florid emoticons, cannot compete with a four-page letter constructed out of words and sentences and packing together a pleasing balance of ideas and emotion. In her October 31st, 2001 letter, Lee wove together needed detail about her pending boot camp graduation, with her hopes for the next stage in her training:

> I can't wait for you all to come out for graduation. So far this is what I know—I graduate on the 29th and can leave the base w/you guys until 9 p.m. that night. I am supposed to go to A-school the next day I guess, but it's only across the street, so I can still see you people. What's more, A-school is more like college, so family can come and see where I live, and I can be gone longer.

It was clear from her words that Lee had no idea that right after boot camp she would become a crewmember on a warship bound for the Persian Gulf. Without that knowledge, she closed her letter with innocence, affection, and even a sprinkling of hope for the future:

> I love you and can't wait to see you—Happy Birthday—hope you get my card in time—I'll take you out to dinner the next time I'm in town! You should stock up on candy for me when I get home—I am craving loads of it—gotta go—I love you, Lee.

Meanwhile back in Littleton, Colorado, her younger brother had begun his senior year in high school. In a perfect world, I would have been reading the handwriting on the wall: that once Ben went away to college, he would take with him all of my logical reasons for practicing law in order to pay the mortgage on a house in suburban Colorado, a home that no one wanted to live in except me and the pets. But instead of worrying about the changes that might accompany his coming-of-age, I was feeling the eagerness of a small child with hyperbolic hopes for the holidays, excited to be planning a trip to Lake Michigan for Lee's recruit training graduation. This major family event was becoming my only priority for the upcoming season!

And although he was far too cool to say the words, I think seventeen-year-old Ben was well-pleased with the prospect of traveling to Chicago to hang out with his older sisters again, soon. (Christen was coming too.) Ben kept himself busy with all the angst that goes with being a high school senior. He was making plans for college, while enjoying the newfound status of being the only kid at home. Not only was he in full control over who would drive the much-traveled car, Ben wasted no time in moving out of his traditional upstairs bedroom, the one with the repaired and repainted wall, and into a larger renovated space in the basement.

*   *   *   *   *

During the early 1800s and in the territory now named North Dakota, Meriwether Lewis and William Clark were setting off on their historical quest to discover a route to the Pacific Ocean. We can assume that Lewis and Clark would arm themselves with the latest in high-tech weaponry of their day, single-shot muzzleloaders. Those rifles surely gave them an edge when it came to hunting the buffalo and other game that came to drink from the broad Missouri River as they paddled and poled their wooden boats upstream. But the technological edge provided by their guns and bullets lost its leverage when the free-flowing river froze over in October of 1804, locking those same boats in place, and isolating the entire expedition in the middle of a broad prairie now called North Dakota. The days of easy hunting were gone and the guns were useless against prolonged exposure to cold, wind, and snow. Survival depended, instead, upon the willingness of its leaders to communicate and trust, to ask for and receive the mutual aid that was available from the thousands of Native Americans who lived in agrarian tribal communities along the Missouri and its tributaries.

The Native Americans were the people of the Mandan, Hidatsa, and Arikara tribes ("Mandan"). They built villages and lived in permanent dwellings called earth lodges on fertile lands close to their cultivated fields and with growing seasons lasting long enough to produce one good crop of food ("Earth Lodges: Homes of the Native Americans of the Great Plains Built with a Technique 6,000 Years Old"). It was a Mandan village that allowed the men of the Lewis & Clark Expedition—and it was all men at that point—to build their winter shelters on the opposite side of the river from their village. This prime location would become known as Fort Mandan. And it was prime in terms of real estate, because when fall arrived a diverse blend of neighboring tribes and European trappers would descend on the village, bringing a rich and varied assortment of goods to trade, including guns and knives, bison meat and fat, horses, and the occasional musical instrument, in exchange for corn, beans, or tobacco ("Lewis and Clark. Native Americans. Mandan Indians" | PBS).

It is also a fact of history that the Lewis & Clark Expedition remained in place until after the breakup of the winter ice and survived because of the comity and generosity of the Native American communities that opened their doors, rather than locking the explorers out. Another irrefutable fact is that in midwinter, a baby was born inside the newly constructed Fort Mandan, to a young Hidatsa woman and a French-Canadian trapper named Toussaint Charbonneau. Their child was a healthy baby boy named after his father. All three would join the expedition. William Clark in his journal entries would nickname the infant, "Little Pomp" or "Pompy." His seventeen-year-old mother, Sacagawea, was a valuable addition to the team as she spoke not only Mandan, Hidatsa, and smatterings of English and French, but she was proficient in the Shoshone tongue, a skill that would prove invaluable in securing a safe passage during their travel through Idaho.

But, the textbooks and movies of my youth had provided me with different lessons. I was taught that the expansion and development of the American West were a series of military battles, in which white men with guns prevailed, except for one glaring exception at the Little Big Horn. But living for years in the shadow of Columbine has honed my willingness to look beyond the constraints and prejudices of my youth and even beyond the most insistent voices for the presence of other perspectives, including the marginalized voice of someone like Kyle Velasquez. Traveling across those same broad plains on a bicycle two hundred years after Lewis & Clark has reinforced the decision made early in the planning stages of this trip, that a gun would only be an extra and unnecessary weight on my journey. Communication skills and a good sense of humor would be my chosen guides for this journey, providing the safest tools and techniques for traveling through distant lands far from home, especially when combined with the willingness of others to help a stranger in need.

\*     \*     \*     \*     \*

The next day's North Dakota sunrise is cool and cloudy. The skies even rain a bit while I am packing up. But the bigger challenge is the headwind. It first appeared yesterday afternoon, coming out of the east. This morning, it is back with a vengeance and for the first time since the beginning of this long trip, I dig into the depths of the drawstring bag full of raingear and pull out the water-resistant anorak, a windbreaker by any other name. Without it, the day's ride might be miserable. Instead, my chest and arms can stay warm and dry on the day's slow pedal.

By early afternoon, I am hungry, tired, and worn out, already dreaming about stopping for the day, but still pedaling the bike with all the gear down the main street of a sizable North Dakota city named Mandan. This is the third day of travel on my spiffy new bicycle chain. I have been buffeted by the wind all morning, at least until reaching the windbreak of these commercial buildings and storefronts.

The main street has a prosperous feel with a fine selection of possibilities for a much-needed meal. I stop at a locally owned coffee and sandwich shop, one that looks like the perfect place for updating the journal and staying warm. I consult the maps and ask some of the locals about camping options. They recommend a state park on the other side of the Missouri River and just a few miles ahead in Bismarck. Even if the wind picks back up, it would be no more than an hour's ride away.

Fortified by the pleasant combination of good food and a respite from the wind, I take a walk through the business district, past the storefronts, and the pickup trucks with their bumper stickers and rear window art proudly displaying tribal affiliations or US flags or both. The rain has stopped. I feel that lightness of being and renewed energy that comes from watching dark clouds break apart to reveal the sun's radiance. I walk through the door of one of several retail stores owned or operated by a cooperative of Native American artists. There's time today for being a tourist, but leave the store empty-handed.

I pedal the length of a long city block and then another, solo and self-sufficient, and realize that Daedalus and I are being followed. The bike has a small side-view mirror attached to the left handlebar. The shiny hood of a vehicle more than fills it. *There's plenty of room to pass here.* With a quick turn of the head, I can see the front grill of a black sedan. *This has got to stop! The street here is four lanes wide, most of them empty, except for me and this dark shadow trying to attach itself to my rear wheel.* I slow down. So does the car. I twist around again to take another look. Reflected light from a recent car wash sparkles in my peripheral vision. *The driver of that car doesn't care if other vehicles have to slow down or move around him.* The Mercedez pulls up alongside and we move down the street in tandem. The passenger window glides down. I can feel the driver's eyes looking Daedalus and me, over. The man behind the wheel leans over and asks, "Where you headed?" in a tone suggesting genuine interest.

But in the medium-cool voice of a self-propelled cyclist with a full belly, a destination in mind, and over a thousand miles in the rearview mirror, I reply, "East coast."

"That's gonna take some time," he replies, accenting the last word in the same way that comics do when they're expecting to get a laugh. "Got any plans for tonight?" He asks, holding a cellphone in one hand, the steering wheel of an immaculate car in the other.

"I'm pretty flexible," I respond.

"Good," the middle-aged driver responds. "Then why don't you take a break and stop for a minute? So, we can talk."

I ease Daedalus toward the curb, twist my foot out of the pedal clamp, and stop.

"I'd really like to hear some more about this trip of yours. Do you have the time to tell me about it? My office isn't far. You can take a nice break. We can talk. I'd like to hear your story."

"Is it close?"

"It's not out of your way. And if this conversation goes the way I think it will—and my wife doesn't object—I'm going to invite you to my house for dinner and a shower."

"Got any coffee at your office?"

"Sure do."

"Then, let's go," I reply. "Lead the way." The powerful car accelerates without a sound and turns into the next block. Pedaling the bike with all my gear, I follow the car's North Dakota license plates through a treeless warren of pavement and commercial buildings, finally stopping at one that advertises storage units for rent. Inside the open garage door of an obscure parking lot sits the black Mercedes, occupying a spotless expanse of epoxy-covered concrete. I pedal the bike across the parking lot but stop outside the open door.

*     *     *     *     *

In her exhilarating letter dated November 11th, 2001, Lee added bravado to the recurring themes of food, planning, and what the Greek culture describes as "agape" or familial love. (I wish that the English language had a wider range of synonyms for this complex four-letter word. The scarcity of synonyms for love makes it difficult for us speakers of American English, to distinguish between "love of family" and "love of country" and the eros of sexual desire. All too often, it falls on us parents to explain or at least demonstrate by our conduct the significant differences between these profound feelings.) It's my opinion that American culture is stuck fast on the notion that parenting has something to do with building nest eggs for our children, and its corollary, defending it with the most lethal weapon available. My children had no interest in waiting around for

219

anything like an "obscure promise of future wealth" to develop. So, I offer this improved vision for other parents and teachers; to give our children two things: roots, so that each child has the competence to find their own voice and the confidence to use it for communicating with others in the larger world, and wings.

> I'm jealous…You and Ben are going to have an amazing meal…Right now, I'd be cool with 7-Eleven. I'm craving crap food—you know chips, chocolate, the works. You would be a god if you could track down a couple boxes of those phenomenal girl scout cookies—the chocolate & coconut wonders! Oh man!

Then, Lee described what it's like to be a member of her division, halfway into the recruit training program:

> The mood around here is generally tight. People attack each other over nothing. I admit—I, too, jump out a bit too rashly myself—but we all knew that was going to happen. Just this morning I caught myself when this girl pushed me in line at chow. I just can't take all this togetherness anymore!
>
> My division got into a good-old fashioned mess hall brawl last night. One of our rival divisions was at the table next to us & people started to say little comments and one thing led to another and then everyone exploded. People were running around the tables grabbing people and such. The best part, is that the other division is an all-male division. And all these females jumped in. It was a mess and luckily the Petty Officers on duty were relatively cool about it & didn't ream us all. Everyone's kind of nervous though. We are all supposed to get a serious beating soon—but for now we are all standing by. Good stuff.

This was followed with more detail about daily life in the military and in particular, recruit training:

> Man—I'm watching my friend Walker put makeup on her face—she needs to stop. If she gets caught there'll be trouble. Why would you want to wear makeup in boot camp anyway? It's not like you have to look good—whenever a female walks by an all-male division all the guys make noises and little comments. The guys around here are crazy. You wouldn't believe the things that the RDC's tell their people—females are evil and such. All the males are afraid to talk to females because they all think that they might get set back in training. A legitimate fear if you ask me—it happens all the time.

She then chose a subject often mentioned and worried about at the dinner table and while Lee was still living at home:

> You are/were right—I have made a lot of friends here that I'm sure will be lasting. Poole, the girl who ran the 1 ½ mile with me, w/pneumonia & bronchitis and in a 12:30 time, has invited me to her wedding in December next year. She's a doll. There are a bunch of girls in here that really surprised me by turning out to be good people—I'm slightly impressed…And all that worrying about racism coming out—not so. My division is about evenly split between three races…No one has had any issues race-related here—although rumor has it, that is not the case base-wide.

Before closing, Lee reminded me of the importance of receiving lots of mail and even asked: "So do you enjoy getting mail as much as I do? I gotta say—mail call defines my day, but you have got considerably more to do in an afternoon than I do." She finished the letter with:

So now I'm rambling—I'll let you go—but I wanted to let you know I got your letter the other night and appreciate the time you took to write it out. I look forward to your next letter. Take care of yourself…I miss you. I miss you. I miss you. I love you. I have a phone call soon and I'll do my best to get a hold of you—have to hit my rack now—I love you. See you soon. Lee.

It felt wonderful to read and absorb all that information and emotion. But the best part, the most powerful part of her 111101 letter was in the greeting. There, she offered the gift of a new nickname and a tag so distinctive that as far as I know, the nickname only made it into the world once. The November 11th letter was the one in which she knighted me with the handle "Bob-by-Da-Blob-Da-Sis." Sadly, back at work, in the neighborhood, and even with extended family I was still "Bob."

*　　*　　*　　*　　*

I walk the bike into a hybridized man cave and lean it against the nearest unobstructed wall. As promised, the drip coffee maker sits on a countertop next to the full-sized refrigerator standing against the far wall. With interest, I watch as the middle-aged host multitasks between making a fresh pot of coffee and carrying on a cellphone conversation. I'm inside a commercial unit dedicated more to conversation than storage, with a desk and office chair opposite a comfortable looking sofa and side table. This is a congenial space alive with the crosscurrents of football, conversation, and business. But from the purple and white of his Minnesota Viking football team paraphernalia, I understand that the overweight man won't be bringing up the Denver Broncos. Then, he sets the cell phone down on his desk and I call out in greeting, "Hey! I made it. My name's Robert."

From the other side of the room, the businessman smiles and waves me closer. "Well, make yourself at home then. I'm Rod," he says, walking towards me with a welcoming expression and an open hand. "Rod Skytland. Glad to meet you. Welcome to my place." And right on cue, the cellphone starts into another cycle of ringing sounds. He checks the face of the phone. "Thanks for coming by, Robert. I better see what this guy wants. Grab a seat," he says, pointing toward the couch.

I look around the room while he talks, something about a rental property. Everything about this man is gregarious. But even while he talks to someone else, I can feel him taking my temperature, sizing me up for signs of irritation or discomfort. I've got about ten years on him, judging from the pictures of his children. But after four weeks on the road, I am lean and not mean, and ready to guess that someone influential, maybe a family doctor, has been on my host's case about losing some weight. I'm guessing that he's worried enough about his health and vitality, to be curious about me. Rod puts down his phone again and says, "Thanks, Robert, for stopping by on the spur of the moment like that and coming over. I really appreciate it."

"No problem," I tell him. "I'm glad to be here."

"So, how long have you been on this ride?" Rod asks. "Where'd you get started?"

The story begins with one guy in a group of five back on the West Coast. But when I reach the part about one member, departing from the group, the ring of a second telephone interrupts. This one is hardwired, a desktop model with push buttons and a traditional handset.

"Excuse me," he says, turning away once more to look at the caller ID. Instead of answering, he turns towards me and asks, "How did you get separated?"

It is fascinating to watch a dedicated multitasker in operation, and not all that different from the frenetic ways in which I used to get through my days back at the county. I try to pick up the story where it left off, but another call comes in. Rod takes this one. While he talks business, I walk over to my bicycle and grab an energy bar out of the handlebar bag. The sight of my own silent cell phone makes me smile. I leave it undisturbed and return to the comfortable sofa, listening to Rod describe a rental property he is trying to lease. He puts the phone down and asks, "So where do you sleep at night?"

"Mostly out in the open in a tent and sleeping bag," I respond. "I'm not only used to it, but I think my back prefers it, sleeping on the ground with nothing but a pad. The first week was a big adjustment. But after that, I started looking forward to how good my back would feel, first thing in the morning."

"That's interesting. 'Cause mine has been giving me some trouble lately. And I used to be in great shape. Grew up on a farm. Played football in high school. All the right stuff."

From there, the conversation drifts into kids and family and why anybody would want to leave home to get on a bicycle and ride across the country. I explain that the answer is complicated. In my case, the crucial step was putting together enough motivation to rediscover the bicycle. The timing was an essential ingredient in making this change; the kids were out of the house and on their own. Another piece was psychological. I had reached a pivotal point in midlife in which I had more interest in studying creative writing, comedy improvisation, and taking roles in community theatre, than in working full-time. But another pressing point was issuing from my lower back. It was in full revolt from all the repetitive stress of jogging and trying to run marathons. I started cycling because I couldn't run anymore.

"Add to all that logic," I tell him, "The shock and sadness of watching a not-much-older colleague get wheeled out the office on a stretcher by paramedics. She had a stroke at the end of a long workday. The image of another attorney being wheeled into a waiting ambulance was more than enough to instill in me a vision of becoming a trophy husband." The words come out with a straight face, but I have to pause because Rod has started to laugh. "So I started looking for a life partner with good health care benefits." He's still chuckling when I finish the explanation with, "The trophy husband thing is probably not on your radar screen. You're still married, right?"

"Oh yeah," he declares, "But I know a bunch of divorced guys that are real tired of the single life."

"I got tired of it, too, but waited until the kids were both out of high school. The divorce was hard for both of them, especially my daughter Lee."

224

"I can't get over that trophy husband thing!" says Rod with a smile.

"I like that part of the story too. Maybe we can…"

"Wait a minute," he says, interrupting again. But this time, it's with a satisfied smile as he takes a phone call from his wife. "OK Honey, I can be there. But listen, I just met this guy riding a bicycle across the country. He's funny and he knows how to tell a good story. We've been at it most of the afternoon. So, what do you think about me making some barbeque for dinner tonight and asking him to join us? That's right. I'm cooking. We can let him take a shower at our place, right? Relax for an evening. He's an older guy…Yeah…grown kids…you'll like him."

Then Rod pauses, listens for a while, and asks, "Maybe we can ask him to stay over in one of the kid's rooms?" They talk for a while about food and drinks. I listen attentively, overhearing as much as possible and pleased.

When he finishes the phone call, my host turns to me and asks, "So you're coming, right? Dinner, my place? What do you like to drink with your barbeque?"

# CHAPTER 15
## FREEDOM IN FARGO

*August 1, 2017*
*Fargo, North Dakota*

On the morning after the boisterous welcome that became the evening spent in the Skytland's home, Rod and Lori fill my body's tank with eggs, pancakes and syrup, and of course, coffee. Rod and I take selfies together outside on the front lawn of their comfortable home. Daedalus spent a night safe and sound inside the locked garage. I encourage Rod to rediscover the bicycle for his health and vitality, and even the pursuit of happiness. He sends me on my way with good wishes and a couple of ideas for decent places to eat up ahead. I am so moved by their hospitality that while pedaling through Bismarck, I stop for another round of coffee and compose a journal entry inspired by having been an overnight guest in their home. The result is a jumble of ideas about writing as an act of service. My intention is to pay their kindness forward by creating a better travelogue about this particular ride, the broader benefits of adding cycling to one's life, and a touch of advocacy about how much safer our public places will be once we emancipate our children with bicycles and secure places to ride them, instead of weapons of war like the AR-15.

On my way out of the largest city in North Dakota, I follow a bikeway into the verdant band of green that follows the channel of the Missouri River. Brown hills in the distance define the limits of the moisture carried within the river. The bicycle route merges into highway and heads east into the contours of a long steep hill. These same undulating hills will continue for most of the day, with pedaling that alternates between glorious descents and slow-motion climbs. The land on both sides of the highway is green now. Fences appear as the wide-open vistas and dry air of the high plains disappear into the bike's rearview mirror.

Somewhere around midday, the Lewis and Clark bicycle trail—the one I've been following for the past month—turns to the southeast in an apparent effort to reconnect with the Missouri River. That route leads to St Louis. *Goodbye Lewis and Clark, and Sacagawea. Daedalus and I are heading east. Bar Harbor, Maine, is out there somewhere.* I continue east into a treeless expanse of windy plains. The afternoon brings a small rain shower and another headwind. I promise myself that I will rise earlier tomorrow and get a quicker start.

The remains of the day are spent pedaling into a country unbroken by landmarks. I scan the horizon on both sides of the road for anything to break the treeless plains, but the eyes inform me that the landscape has become a place without edges. The mind fixates on anything that interrupts the view. There are neither hills nor streams in sight; only an occasional road sign breaks the monotony. Approaching one at a nominal speed of ten miles per hour, I'm compelled to examine every detail, the height of the pole and its shadow, then the color and shape of the metal sign. It's difficult to look away from the combination of letters and numbers. Until I roll past, looking for the next vertical object to fixate on. This turns the appearance of a water tower into a dramatic event. Once I spot one, it's impossible to imagine anything else. The fabrications seem to reel me in like a fish on a line. And it may require as much as an hour to reach one, but with a clear and specific goal ahead, the time feels well-spent. The water tower takes shape in slow motion, but eventually, dominates the landscape. At the base of one, I find myself overcome by a patch of shade and a place to rest. There's even a scattering of sheds and remnants of buildings that might once have been dwellings perched on patches of hardy grass. The good news is that with each new water tower, I'm finding my way across this treeless land. Another tower is waiting for me just down the road and beyond the horizon. All I have to do to get there is pedal.

This pattern repeats itself in a continuous loop under the beat of the sun throughout the afternoon. Eventually, my stomach interrupts with a no-nonsense reminder that it is time to refuel. By this time, I am being reeled in by the day's final water tower. I've been watching it grow in meaning and stature for over an hour. But this time, I am down to the last couple of swallows of water. *Don't want to drink them. Not yet.* A green rectangular sign comes into view. *Can't see the words yet. Sure hope it's less than a mile into town.* Daedalus and I close in on the water tower. What a relief that this one is surrounded by shade trees and buildings. Streets with houses lining them come into view and I see a pale white building behind a windbreak of trees with a parking lot and sign that reads, "Cafe." Lights glow from inside the window. I grab one empty water bottle and with the other hand twist the doorknob. *Please be open!* A blast of excitement floods into my fingers. A smiling waiter/ cook/ bartender turns on his barstool and waves me into the room. He invites me to sit anywhere. I choose a table close to the kitchen. Tears come as I write the name of this place into today's journal, describing how fantastic it felt to park the bicycle and walk into a room without sunlight or wind. This particular oasis is named the Road Hawg Grill. The beer is cold. The burgers and fries, sublime. Daedalus and I have reached the town of Hazelton, North Dakota. I can go no further today. There is a safe campsite in the bicycle-friendly park on the edge of town. Exhausted, I set up Big Agnes—my tent—and fall asleep, too tired to think.

*   *   *   *   *

In her last letter from boot camp, Lee shared a few of the changes she was observing in herself and some thoughts about life in the military.

> You know what's strange? When people get lonely, they do the strangest things. Everyone here is cleaving on to other people, I mean it's getting pretty desperate! And for me, I realized what it is that's driving everyone to that point…I used to wonder why everyone gets married right out of bootcamp but now it's all so clear. Everyone is looking for a constant, and in the navy a spouse is the only concrete thing, as long as you can get the same port—which happens in a most cases!

228

Recently, the base got a couple hundred new recruits in. We see them marching around all the time and wow. You wouldn't believe the difference between civilians and military. Maybe it's just that they're all new, but even the civilian personnel are different. The military people just carry themselves differently. It always makes me wonder if I've changed...but you'll see when you get out here in 11 days.

Pride and confidence flowed from her opinions and words, but also regret:

I have never felt like I had less control over any given situation. I mean, the next 4 years of my life are being dictated to me! What I wear, the length of my fingernails, even the damn distance between the creases in my shirts!

So, with 11 days left—I'm definitely feeling that there is simply no end to the madness. So talk about the quickest route to complete depression, nothing like a melodramatic letter from a displaced kid to ruin an afternoon. I guess it's just one of those days, you know. I can't wait until you guys all get here...I get the entire weekend for leave. So I can sleep where you guys sleep!

I can't believe that I haven't spoken two words to you in two months. That's strange to me. What's even more absurd is the way I have redefined basically everything. For instance, who'd have guessed that I would write these long, completely and painfully unnecessary letters to you picking apart every aspect of my mental state! Do you know that I would love to do now more than anything: lay outside in the grass in the sun. That's it. Maybe hit Dairy Queen afterwards, but just to snooze in the sun... ah...that would be beautiful. The simplest things are the things I miss the most—that and my bed! Oh my god—a real bed w/real sheets and dark! Complete darkness! And no PA system to blast "Reveille, Reveille" every morning!

\*     \*     \*     \*     \*

Inside my tent the next morning, I check for the semblance of renewed energy within my legs, lungs, and heart. The prospect of feeling excited about another day on the bike, has faded like yesterday's news. Here, amid the fifth week, exuberance has given way to staid confidence that today I can add another fifty miles to the cumulative total. But according to the map, it is almost seventy miles to Gackle, a small town with a big reputation for its bicycle hostel. *Funny name, Gackle. I wonder what I'll find along the way? I could really use something of singular beauty to restore some enthusiasm for the trip!* I pack my things, get back on the bike, and ride into Hazelton in search of food.

After breakfast, the morning miles go by in sweet succession as the flat featureless topography gives way to vegetation, streams and lakes. Flying birds and insects and signs of wildlife are everywhere, in far greater abundance than cars or people. And the day is still young. On both sides of the highway, the land is covered with ponds, lakes, and sloughs. Daedalus and I ride State Highway 34 over a causeway and across a long expanse of water towards a crossroads named Napoleon. The map describes it as a village with fewer than one thousand residents. *This is too soon for stopping and I'm having too much fun. Gackle is the right destination…but there are miles to go before I sleep.* The sun is warm and bright. The views in each direction are so compelling that I want to stay on the bike and ride slowly, stopping often, and using the cell phone camera with abandon. Even the wind is down today.

This area of North Dakota is called the Drift Prairie, named after the glacial processes that created it. But the name does not do justice to its sweeping elemental beauty in high summer and this self-propelled, solitary style of experiencing it. On a day like today, this bike is the ideal way to travel. Bicycles invite all the senses to participate. Inside a car or an RV, the traveler is encased in plastic and glass. If I'm the one behind the wheel, I would be tempted to keep my foot on the gas and roll on through a place like the Drift Prairie, absorbed more by the result of reaching the next town than in the natural beauty of the area I'm traveling through. From the inside of a car or truck, the landscapes pass by like scenes in a movie. But on a bicycle seat, the rider is the movie. Today's calm air is filled with the sounds and sights of vibrant aquatic and airborne life and I am moved by its grandeur and vitality.

Bicycle touring offers a heady kind of freedom. It comes with an ability to venture down any road I please, to poke through any town, and only occasionally have to deal with a fence or a road-block. The self-propelled aspect brings along an inherent sense of adventure. Mine started with the front-end costs of having to purchase the bike, panniers, and related equipment. Then, there's the daily food requirement which supplies the fuel that feeds the body that burns the calories that propel the bike and the traveler down the blue highways. There are campsite costs and occasional motel rooms. Food and shelter always come at a price. Only on the rarest of days have I heard the sound of an angry shit-heel hurling insults from the passenger window of a pickup truck. It does happen. But in retrospect, angry horns and insulting gestures were just as common in Denver's traffic during my daily commutes to work.

Swamps, like the one I'm traveling through, do not get much respect when it comes to travel magazines or the bucket lists of individual vacationers, not unless there is also easy access to a nearby interstate. And therein lies the irrepressible appeal of blue highways. The traffic can be minuscule. There is no better method for summertime travel between Bismarck and Fargo, North Dakota—the two most populous cities in North Dakota—than on a bicycle.

At the end of a seventy-mile day, I ride into the town of Gackle, population three hundred and ten, knowing only that I am hot, tired, and finished for the day. Happy, too, because a well-placed sign indicates that an ice cream store, a Tastee Freeze, is close by. Once I find it, a handwritten sign taped to the window grabs my attention with a simple proclamation, "Without ice cream, there would be darkness and chaos!" To do my share in the struggle against the forces of evil, I order the largest cone possible. Just being here in downtown Gackle reminds me of HG Wells' tribute to bicycle travel, written or spoken at a time when he was dreaming about things other than time machines or an invasion from Mars: "Bicycle tracks will abound in Utopia."

According to the Adventure Cycling map, Gackle offers "Cyclist Only Lodging." The same map indicates that for the next seventy-eight miles, which is the rest of the way to Fargo, services are limited. I am done with pedaling for today. The youthful sculptress of cool delectables agrees. She knows all about the bicycle hostel and highly recommends it to everyone passing through on a bicycle.

"How many cyclists pass through here each summer?" I ask.

"Enough to make me want to try it someday," she replies, handing me the cone. "There's a sign right over there with directions and a telephone number. It's Jason and Ginny Miller's place. They also run the honey business here in town." Ice cream cone in hand, I walk over to read about the bike shop/hostel known across the internet and throughout this small community as the "Honey Hub of Gackle: A Cyclist's Respite."

When I left the Skytland's home in Mandan, I was convinced that their place had to be the most hospitable home in this northern state, only to discover that the Honey Hub of Gackle could be a serious contender for the crown. It is so peaceful and restful here. I feel like I could stay for the rest of the summer. The Millers' neighborhood is unassuming. The website explains that in 2012, they converted their walk-out basement into an apartment, and then dedicated its use to the dozens of cross-country cyclists that ride through during the summer. The Millers are fifth-generation beekeepers. They operate a honey farm and processing plant in North Dakota for three months out of the year, and winter in northern California for the other nine, moving their bees and business in between on large tractor-trailer rigs.

The hostel comes with twin beds, a shower, a washing machine, WIFI, and a pleasant green and spacious backyard. Jason, the host, says that I am lucky to have the place all to myself. "It's unusual for this time of year." He shows me the spiral notebook sitting on a table, filled with the names of several hundred cyclists who have passed through and stayed this touring season. He describes with an enthusiastic smile how the yard can fill up with colorful tents when a large supported group passes through. "It gets crowded here from the end of June and through the 4th of July." Jason takes pride in the international mix of his guests. And, of course, Jason and Ginny accept donations, but they require no fee. For the Millers, sharing the basement of their home with the cycling community is an act of love and service. For explanation, Jason points to the guidance found in Matthew 25:35-40.

After Jason leaves, the room is empty except for me and my bags. I look around and decide that as glorious as today's ride was, without question, this humble home and bicycle hostel are the objects of singular beauty that I asked for as the day began.

I return to the Tastee Freez, the only restaurant in town, for a heartland dinner of meatloaf, mashed potatoes, and additional ice cream, leaving the cell phone and all of its functionality back at the room to recharge. I return to the hostel with a full belly and find my way into a backyard lawn chair cast in the glow of an evening sun descending into the treeline. It's not a stirring sunset. But it is the second drumbeat, a benediction for today's ride. When it's done, I retrieve the cell phone and check for messages. To my delight, there is a new text from Lee, a significant one, "Hey, Dad! How's the trip? Call me."

Tears fill my eyes, and I wonder. *Lee never calls. She's too independent for that.* I call her number right back. She picks up. "Hey, Lee. How are you doing?"

"Real good," she replies. "How is that bicycle trip of yours?"

"The trip is amazing, and it's wearing me out. So good to hear your voice" I say. "What's happening? Are you in Denver?"

"Oh, not that much…except that Fritz and I are getting married." Lee sounds confident, pleased, and happy.

"That's so exciting. Congratulations! Best news I've heard all day! All week! When's the date?"

"It's Sunday, the 26th."

"What month?"

"Dad," she replies with mock impatience, "This month!" Her words flow in a rush now. "We decided it was time. Most of the planning's already been done. We want to get it done this summer."

"Oh…" I say, wanting to confirm the date but deciding to let it go.

"Christen and I are making real invitations. But they are not ready yet. The ceremony is going to be up in the mountains."

"This is wonderful," I say, starting to laugh. "Lucky for me, my calendar is wide open that day."

"Where the heck are you, anyway? Lee asks.

"Gac-kle," I reply, feeling the word crackle on my tongue. "It's in eastern North Dakota, and saying Gackle has a way of making me smile…kinda like these wedding plans of yours. The people around here and the countryside are incredible."

"Never heard of it."

"It's small. The few hundred people who live here all year round, are tuned into the cycling community. I am actually staying in the walkout basement of a family's home tonight. There's a hot water shower and a washing machine. Nice chairs with reading lamps. I could easily stay over another night. It's that comfortable!"

"Sounds like you are really chewing up the miles," Lee comments. "So what happened back there in Montana? And what about those other guys? It doesn't sound like you've been hanging out waiting for anyone to catch up."

"You're right, Lee. It is a solo ride from here on out. And the short answer goes something like: after my chain broke in the middle of Montana, those three guys kept going. I put my thumb out, hoping for a kind rancher with a badass pickup truck to save the day."

"That must have sucked for a while."

"It did," I agree. "Until that guy with the truck did show up. He even took me into Glendive the next day. That's how I got ahead of the other three guys. And that's just the Cliffs Notes version. Let's have a beer together when I get back and I'll tell you the rest of the story."

"Yeah, sure," she replies.

"If I wanted to take a break and let them catch up, the hostel here in Gackle would be the perfect place for it. But groups are funny, you know? During those first couple of weeks on the trip, it felt like I was part of something bigger. But after the original group whittled itself down to four, it was never quite the same. It would take a lot of effort to try and rejoin. And why mess with it? Especially if I need to get busy making the arrangements to return to Denver for the wedding."

"True, true," she replied. "But they would make room. You know that, right?"

"No doubt." I agreed. "It is more secure to do this cycling thing in a group, but I am drinking a lot less beer this way. To their credit, I learned a lot from riding with those guys. But most of the decisions had to be made by committee, and that got way too complicated for me."

"Well, Da. You sound happy."

"Thank you, Lee, for noticing. You could add lean and healthy to that, too. This ride has been good for me, but it's wearing me down too. Thirty days on a bicycle seat could be my natural limit. I can come back anytime and restart this thing, maybe next summer. Do you have any idea how good it is to hear your voice?"

"I do most of my communicating by text these days. So enjoy it while it lasts. Don't have much use for email either. But I wanted you to know about the timing for the wedding."

"This is not your garden variety wedding announcement."

"Printed invitations are so predictable."

"The text and the phone call are perfect."

"So you can be there?"

"Absolutely. Wild horses couldn't keep me away," I promise.

"I've heard that before."

"So it's Sunday, the 26th. Do you have a location in mind?"

"Heck, yes. Everything is all planned out. You just have to get here."

"Where?"

"Nature is providing us the perfect location. It's a spot I picked out in the mountains above Idaho Springs, one of my favorites. We'll make it easy for you to find."

"Lee, this is wonderful. I wouldn't miss this for the world."

We say goodnight and I sit back in the chair in total contentment, unwilling to move. Today's ride was incredible. The generosity of the Millers here at the bicycle hostile is sublime. But neither one can compare with how good that phone call just made me feel. Good news from family can trump everything. And the phone call with Lee wins today's remarkable race for that singular event of unmistakable beauty.

It feels sad the next morning to leave behind the serenity of Gackle and the compassionate enterprise of the Honey Hub that lies at its beating heart. This town ranks high on my list of secret places well worth returning to someday, but only if I can make the approach on a bicycle or some other means of self-propulsion. The beauty of this place is palpable because of the vastness of the land, the abundance of birds and wildlife, and the minimum number of fences. Someone conditioned to traveling fast and arriving in the nick of time to claim a reservation might have difficulty appreciating its merits.

These are the words and the feelings I intend to express in describing the small town I have just left to another cross-country cyclist, this one headed to San Francisco and following the east to west trajectory called the Northern Tier ("Adventure Cycling Route Network"). Our paths are crossing on a remote highway in a land so flat that it has taken me a few minutes of watching to determine from the distinctive profile that it is coming toward me rather than moving in the same direction. It can only be another cyclist. Today, the visual recognition comes with a rush of adrenaline and the excitement of a chance to talk with someone about the resting place that lies up ahead. My legs have already picked up the pace.

But in this land of distant horizons, it takes a long while to close the distance. There's plenty of time to consider a range of possible subjects and narrow the field down to a couple of cogent talking points. Pavement flows by underneath the pedals. The approaching bike has a solitary rider and four panniers, probably unsupported, like me. There isn't another vehicle in sight or sound. And then, once we are about thirty yards apart, I point my finger towards the middle of the pavement. Most of the other cyclists I have encountered in this fashion enjoy the opportunity to take a break and talk. But it is not universal, and I respect the solitary ones bent on keeping it that way. Today, though, the rider responds by flashing the same sign and I can feel the smile lighting up my mustachioed face as I move the handlebars enough to cross over the two-lane highway so that we can talk face to face, front wheel to front wheel. Daedalus comes to a full stop, well into the shoulder on the other side of the road. The other cyclist pulls right up. "Hello, my name's Donna."

"Hi, I'm Robert, traveling from the West Coast," already guessing that we are at similar ages and stages of life.

"There's a coincidence," she replies. "Because I live in California. I'm on my way home. I started this in June from a friend's place in Boston." Donna goes on to describe the French woman who started the ride with her but quit on the third day. Her story reminds me of Ben Franklin's sage advice, "Guests, like fish, begin to smell after three days." Donna had the pluck to keep going, alone. She tells me with a confident smile that the city of Fargo is not far, but strongly recommends a pie and coffee break in Kindred before proceeding the rest of the way. She also recommends stopping at the bicycle shop in Fargo for a tune-up, the one inside the old trolley station in the middle of town, followed by pizza and beer at any one of the local microbreweries. It is a college town, after all. There are plenty to choose from.

I respond with, "I started on July 1st in Astoria, Oregon, planning to go all the way to Bar Harbor." And without going into a lengthy digression about the upcoming wedding, I simply say, "But after thirty days or so, I'm ready to call it quits and return home to Denver."

"You can always come back and finish next summer," she observes in a calm voice.

"Did you come through Minneapolis?" I ask. "It should be easy enough to pack everything up and catch a plane from there."

Donna lights up at the mention of the city, recommending another hostel named the Bicycle Bunkhouse, just in case I need a place to hang out that's close to the airport. "It's an amazing place. The best hostel so far on the Northern Tier. If you stay on this trail, you'll go right past the farm and the Bunkhouse."

Her descriptions sound so similar to my experience in Gackle that I have to recommend the Honey Hub as a kind of Disneyland experience for cyclists. We talk for a long time this way, exchanging suggestions without ever getting off our bicycles, standing in the sunshine on the shoulder of the road, remembering fondly the places we have been and the memories made there. When the conversation begins to wane, I ask to take her picture with my cellphone. She says sure. "Would you like me to text you a copy?" I ask.

"Probably not," Donna answers. "But thanks for the chat, thanks for stopping."

"Yeah! I enjoyed our talk," I say. "Stay safe and enjoy the rest of your journey."

"You too, Robert. Travel well," Donna replies, placing her foot into the cup of the pedal and pushing off toward what will be in a few more hours the sunset.

As I return to my side of the highway, I begin salivating over pie and coffee somewhere up ahead. I'm curious. *How far is it to a fork in the road named Kindred?*


I spend the night in a well-appointed public campground and park that parallels the Red River in Fargo. Large trees abound and a smooth bike path runs through it. Everything Donna said about Fargo has materialized, right down to the tune-up at the Great Northern Bicycle Company. Daedalus gets a lube and a clean bill of health. The shop doesn't charge for it. So, I buy a spare inner tube and a handful of energy bars in return.

I place the tent that night on an incline covered in thick grass. There's a stillness in the air, but overhead a light show rages within towering cumulus clouds. The heat lightning warns us that a storm is brewing. I snug the rainfly down over the tent with all the available pegs, lift the gear off the bike frames, and arrange all of it underneath for shelter. The trees are leafy and tall here for good reason. Until the ride into Fargo, North Dakota has been a place of wide-open horizons. But my perspective is changing under the weight of the coming storm, a morbid kind of realization grounded in an old movie with the same name as the city, based on a realization that people and families in this corner of North Dakota would have a legitimate need at times, for a crew of pickup-driving tree trimmers towing a woodchipper. From my one-night stopover, I am also learning that Fargo is not the blue-collar experience portrayed in the movie. As Donna promised, Fargo is a prosperous college town. So, too, is Moorhead, Minnesota, a sister city occupying the other bank of the Red River. And she was right about the assortment of eateries and brewpubs, and the college students who frequent them. My stomach is complacently full of both pizza and beer as I take shelter inside the double zippers of my "Big Agnes" tent and fall into a deep and restful sleep.

*Kaboom!* A thunderclap shakes the vinyl walls of the tent. The sound waves lift me into instant wakefulness. Eyes wide open, I peer into the darkness, resisting the urge to sit up, and oh, so grateful for the solid earth under my back and shoulders, and the warmth of a dry sleeping bag. An iridescent glow fills the tent and for a split second every aspect of the interior walls becomes visible. Outside, steady rain drums on the rainfly, and darkness returns. *Kaboom!* Two scant layers of plastic are all that separate me from a cold wet night. I try to close my eyes. *What's the point? This thunderstorm is going to last for a while. The tent has never felt more comfortable.* I pull the top of the bag up close and around my head. Sleep is impossible. Getting soaked is not.

Another bolt flashes and I feel soft earth beneath the cushion of the sleeping pad. It's not much wider than my shoulder blades and I am grateful for every square inch. Purchasing one in preparation for this trip was a good idea. So too, the decision to camp outside, on a night when storm clouds were gathering. I accepted the risk in exchange for the chance to see and feel the power of the storm, and to save the expense of a motel room; another example of the ease in making choices when moving through the world alone. Back at Fort Stevens, Oregon, I was happy to be included in the mix and well-aware of how free it felt, and how proud I was to be part of a group of five guys pedaling across the country.

Weeks later and on the day that I chose to split away from the remaining members, my beliefs in the nature of freedom would morph and change. Up until the day that Kyle's spirit took form and spoke to me by the side of the road, I believed that I could sleep that night whenever I grew tired, or wherever a better windbreak appeared. As long as I kept refilling the water bottles and refueling my body, there were no limits, nothing to hold me back, and no more decisions to be made by committee. Like Icarus of old, freedom was a roll of the dice, and I was making plans to whistle or weep with the outcome.

The gods of chance let me pedal on that way, acting like there was some kind of race to be won or events and circumstances controlled to my advantage. On that day in eastern Montana, I was sure that life was like a wild card game; right up until the moment when the hubris of my unbridled choices met the mechanical limits of a bicycle chain, head-on. Once again, Icarus had flown too close to the sun. It took two days and one night and a steady stream of trail angels to deliver me from my foolishness, and, to work through the details of my reinvention. I had no choice but to slow down and appreciate the kindness in their efforts, no choice but to feel immersed in gratitude with the chance to recreate myself and the bicycle, and to continue on my way, this journey. Tonight, as lightning illuminates the interior of the tent, I know in my bones that there are higher, brighter, more sublime expressions of freedom than having choices at the grocery store. I'm talking about the means and the ability to change, whenever calamity shows up at your door. *And bravo to anyone who can make the change before the actual need arises.* For my money, the politicians and pundits, the advertisers who make careers out of trying to persuade us that freedom means having choices, those gentle persuaders already have one hand into your pocket. For the remainder of this ride across the country—no matter how long that takes—my journey is an ascending spiral, and freedom, nothing more than my willingness to transform myself as needed, to keep going, and in the good company of family, friends, and community.

Big Agne rides out the storm, with me sawing logs inside her vinyl walls. Daedalus waits outside watching over the camp, a steady rain washing the road grime and dirt away. In the morning I wake up believing, *I can go anywhere, as long as it's east toward Minneapolis and the airport.*

*August 8, 2017*
*Dalbo, Minnesota*

Deep in the woods of central Minnesota, a modest black and white sign stands alongside the Northern Tier bicycle route, pointing the way to the Adventure Cycling Bunkhouse. From its orientation, the sign seems to be pointing at a well-kept barn and farmhouse adjacent to Highway 47 near Dalbo. Of equal significance, this is the place that competes with the Honey Hub of Gackle for excellence in cyclist-friendly hospitality.

The hostel is a renovated barn that can sleep close to fifty cyclists in a variety of bunkrooms and sleeping arrangements. Inside the main entrance, the words "Bicycle Bunk House" chiseled by hand into the main supporting beam welcome each visitor. A well-appointed kitchen occupies an adjacent room with both hot and cold taps for running water. The cupboards and refrigerator are filled with easily prepared meals and snacks. Resealable plastic tubs line the shelf space, each one labeled and well-stocked with coffee and teas, energy bars, and powdered drinks. There's a doorway leading into the silo, empty now, but still useful for displaying the pictures of the thousands of cyclists who have stayed here—or maybe they were just passing through—during the fifteen years of its existence. The walls of the main room are lined with well-stocked bookshelves, armchairs, and comfortable nooks for reading. A sturdy octagonal table and chairs occupy its center, perfect for cards or board games, or for laying out a folded paper map to full size and planning the next stage of the ride. Solar-powered showers are waiting outside. The bathrooms are outside too, old-fashioned, private, and clean. Daedalus and I arrive late in the afternoon on Tuesday, the eighth of August. We have less than fifty miles to go, as the crow flies. There's an airline reservation for Friday morning and the flight home. *Thank-you, Marceil, helpful partner and friend, for making the arrangements.*

I've got two days to take care of the business of finding a bicycle shop that will box up Daedalus and ship him back to Denver, and then find a motel room closer to the airport. It could, and even should be that simple and straightforward. But the Minnesota skies have opened up and rained on us every afternoon since entering the state. Farm dogs have taken issue with us pedaling down the country roads next to their fence lines. Apparently, there is an ongoing competition among them for the best menacing growl. Most go for a series of sharp intense barks delivered from a reclining position. A few though, have charged along the inside of the fence, only to slide into a controlled stop as the property line assumes control over the competition.

But three days ago, a well-fed, deep-chested Chow/Lab mix slipped under the fence and kept coming, charging down the highway, teeth bared and snarling, instructing me with the ominous sound that their toenails make, scraping across the asphalt as a large dog, upset at being disturbed from afternoon slumber, accelerates to full speed. He showed me the look in his wild eyes. And I responded by pushing those pedals hard, like we were all part of the Tour de France, up inclines and down, long past the fence line of his barnyard, and until the fully winded canine decided to break off the chase. Daedalus and I sent him home panting hard, and with a good story to tell his doggy friends about the huge rolling monster that threatened his property. For myself, I took a much-needed water break. But after a few breaths, went diving deep into the gear for the bear spray. As we close in on Dalbo, I find myself wondering, *The gods of travel are expressing their resistance to our leaving the trail without a tussle.* The aerosol can of pepper spray rests in its dedicated spot, tucked into the webbing of my handlebar bag right next to the brake lever. There it will stay for every last stroke of the pedals.

We reach the highly recommended hostel under cloudy skies but dry pavement. The odometer reads 2,046 miles. I am grateful to be on this side of a two-thousand-mile summer; because rain is in the forecast, not just an afternoon shower, but thunderstorms, several days worth. All I want is a dry place to rest and wait for a three or four-hour-long block of time to pedal down a Minnesota highway in traffic, connect with a new bicycle trail, and then follow the signs toward the busy airport. But with this weather, it looks like Daedalus and I are in for a fifty-mile slog to the finish line.

Wednesday dawns, dark and dreary. I listen to the rhythm of the falling rain from a sleeping bunk inside one of rustic bedrooms on the main floor, a room that offers a wooden door that can close and lock from the inside. But the privacy is wasted on me. There's no one else in the hostel. I can feel the warm drops on my baseball cap and shoulders as I walk outside to luxuriate in a private, hot-water shower. I make breakfast, brew some coffee, and pick out a copy of *Roughing It* from the bookshelf, a memoir/ travelogue written by Mark Twain in the aftermath of the Civil War. Young Samuel Clemens details and describes "several years of variegated vagabondizing," including a stagecoach ride across the heart of the western US, his time well-spent in Nevada during the silver boom as a reporter and occasional miner, and his subsequent relocation to California to return to the newspaper business. I have always been both a reader and a fan of Twain. This book has been on the to-do list for a long time.

There is an array of comfortable armchairs to choose from. Outside, it's still raining. Inside the Bicycle Bunk House, I am enjoying the book's introductory pages when a tall man with a patient smile enters the main room from the kitchen and says, "I just heard that we have another guest in the bunkhouse. I'm Donn Olsen. I always enjoy coming over to say hello and introduce myself."

I stand up to shake his hand and return the smile. Donn has a clean-shaven, prominent jaw, and he's standing next to one of several rough-hewn, squared-off vertical beams that support the ceiling inside this welcoming and renovated space. We talk about the weather. He asks me where I've been, and I explain that I may be staying for another day or two.

"Robert, you can stay as long as you like. We've got a register over there for you to sign. There's no charge for staying, but we do accept donations. Feel free to stick a pin in the map over there on the wall to show us where you're from." He points to the display with both pleasure and pride. It's a world map filled colorful pinheads defining more countries than I can name. "This is where my dad used to keep his dairy cows," Donn continues without missing a beat. "Before the bunkhouse, I was a helicopter pilot, retired military. When I got out of the army, I came right back home: and now, I don't like to leave."

"Donn, you've got a wonderful place here. It's filled with anything and everything a tired cyclist could want."

"We try," he responds, with the soft touch of understatement.

"I've been riding that bike over there since the first of July...all the way from the west coast," I try to explain. "This place is perfect for holing up for a while."

"Interesting to hear you say that," and pauses to catch my eye. "Because the weather people are forecasting that the storm is going to last for a while. You're welcome to stay right here until it passes." Then, he reaches for a Minnesota highway map from a small pile on the bookshelf, sits down at the table, and starts unfolding the map.

I pull out a chair and sit down alongside him, leaving lots of room for whatever he's about to show me.

"I started this hostel back around 2005 when the state was rebuilding that highway over there, says Donn. "Saw a couple of cyclists pushing their heavy bikes through construction sand. So, I called them over. Let 'em know that they were welcome to take a break on my front lawn; pitch a tent even and stay the night if they wanted. That's how I learned about Adventure Cycling. And that was the summer I got the idea for turning the old barn into a hostel for bicyclists. The Adventure Cycling people know all about this place. But their map only shows the safest route into Minneapolis. This one from the highway department shows you the quickest."

"OK then, let's see your route," I say, wanting to sound encouraging.

He picks out Dalbo with a thick forefinger. "And there's the airport. Straight down that highway. You can have that map if you want it." Donn takes out his cell phone and rechecks the weather report. He shakes his head. "I've been doing this thing—giving touring cyclists a safe and dry place to rest—ever since."

To keep up my side of the conversation, I introduce him to the family back home. Next, I try to explain daughter Lee's decision to enlist in the navy right after high school. I remember for him the fun we had reuniting as family for her graduation from recruit training in Michigan, and how, after being transferred to Norfolk, Lee became a specialist in computers and network communications. It was there on the east coast that she was assigned to the crew of an amphibious assault ship, the *USS Saipan*. She was on multiple cruises into the Persian Gulf as a crewmember during the Iraq War. And I admit that in the years since her discharge from the Navy, it has just been easier for us to stay within our separate orbits. Until this bicycle journey happened. I decided it was past time to reconnect with her via text messages and using all these unfamiliar places and interesting people as leverage, or at least something new to talk about. "And you know what?" I ask. "Now she's the one with the unique and unusual circumstances. She's getting married in Denver on the 26th."

Donn responds by pushing down on the table with large hands and rising up out of his chair. He agrees that Minneapolis, with its large airport and bicycle-friendly ways, is the right city along this northern tier for closing down my ride. "I have to go check on a few things," he says, walking toward the door. "You're going to spend the night here, right?"

"Oh yeah," I assure him.

"Good," he says. "Just don't leave before I get back."

No one else enters the bunkhouse for what's left of a gloomy day. Daedalus sits in a corner, mechanically sound but with nowhere to go. I spend it curled up in a well-padded armchair reading, trying to generate contentment with regular infusions of hot chocolate and a chaser of warm tea. But it's not working. I'm restless and bored with just sitting here, and feeling anxious because within two days, I'll be without a bicycle for orientation, trying to manage in a world populated with eye-contact avoidant people. *I'm going to miss all that pedaling and constant motion.*

In the midst of my discontent, a curious sensation starts working its way up my spine, warning me that I am not alone. I look up from the book and see a silent television screen staring back at me from the opposite wall. So, I scan the rest of the room, taking my time. *Of course, there's no one in sight. There's nothing in here but a sea of clutter. These walls are lined with shelves full of box games, knick-knacks, and books. Armchairs and furniture are everywhere, but half of those chairs are facing the other way. Could one of them have somehow acquired an occupant?*

I drop the book to the floor, suddenly interested in checking out a few mystery chairs when a familiar voice breaks through the tension, *Hey Boss! Look what I found?*

"It's Kyle!" I say, relaxed and happy once again, and glad to have someone to talk to. I can hear the words. But I don't see him, not yet; except for a deck of cards sitting on the conference table. It wasn't there during the conversation with Donn. *Or was it?* Then the shadows converge around the chair behind the playing cards into a traditional V-neck sweater and that face with its calming smile. He's just sitting there like he's waiting for a meeting to start, or for me to join him in a card game, or at least some conversation. He looks so young in those wire rims.

*Lookin' good, Robert, almost to Minneapolis/St. Paul.*

"Knockin' on the door," I reply. "And I'm goin' home... really look forward to getting back."

*Yeah,* he says without emotion. *Must be nice.*

"Thanks, Kyle. It *is* nice, even momentous," and I almost break into tears finishing the sentence. I let the words linger for a few moments, let the breath return to its normal range. "I was wondering if you were going to make a comeback appearance."

*Oh yeah, I'm over here at the table like I wanted to write something, looking at you propped up in that cushy chair.*

"And I like having you around."

*That's a good thing,* Kyle continues. *Because we're a team, Robert. I'll never forget what it was like to be trapped inside that school building. But you're the one that got stuck inside the community afterwards, and with that media lens thing going on and on.*

With my head slowly nodding, I say the words, "It took me a while to figure out where I wanted to go: what I wanted to do… what to hope for."

*But the best way to figure those things out,* says Kyle, his voice ringing with emotion, *is to be writing! You gotta start hanging out with other writers too.*

"Huh?" I reply, "I've been keeping up with the journal the whole time."

*Right now, today, you should be writing about how lonely it can get, trying to be the self-sufficient hero all the time,* says Kyle. *Isn't that the piece you have been missing for so long?*

"What are you talkin' about?"

*The guy who pedaled through Missoula and Great Falls, all alone and proud of it.*

"Ohhh yeah," I say, laughing with the memory. "Remember him well."

*Then you should also remember the not so independent cyclist that emerged in Glendive,* he says.

And this is the aha moment, the instant when I begin to see that I have, not just a message, but a story meant for telling. "How about this one?" I propose. "Even in the hour of spectacular failure—like a broken bicycle chain in the middle of nowhere Montana—faith can enter into our lives." And we stare across the room at each other, nodding.

Until Kyle breaks the silence with: *And it really does make a difference that this cyclist we're talking about has dedicated so much of his adult life to showing everyone how proficient he can be at being alone, at not needing help from anyone.*

"Because there are lots of lonely people in America right now," I say, picking up the pace. "And lots of them have purchased guns and ammunition, believing that having a loaded assault rifle to defend their stuff with is some kind of rite of passage, or at least a legal imperative."

*Whatever that means,* says Kyle with a laugh. *Maybe you were trying to describe how hard it is to see the trail angels, when you're looking out your windows through a gunsight.*

"Can I use that line in the book?"

*You better,* says Kyle, *And we're talkin' about* books *here.*

"More than one?" I grimace, responding to a private need to resist, for taking control of a situation that might get out of hand, and a sudden accumulation of fatigue into my legs and feet.

*Oh yeah, Robert. The journey is far from over.*

"Hold on," I say with a little whine creeping into the tone. "I'm on my way home."

*And I'm talkin' about another quest, Robert, a bicycle tour to the east coast.*

"Then let me finish with this part," I insist, but feeling an upswing in my mood, "You've helped me understand what it means to have a message. I won't forget this, Kyle. I can't."

*The trail angels are out there, ready and waiting. And you can always ask for help.*

"Like Donn," I say.

*Yeah, just look at how happy Donn Olsen is because he's part of the growth in this cycling community,* Kyle responds. *It would never occur to him to look down at someone because they wanted or needed some help.*

"Don't worry Kyle, I'll start writing. There are people in Denver that can help with this book, and a quiet place in the extra bedroom for me to write. Once I get settled in again, get past the wedding, I'll find the time for writing. I'm gonna do this."

*No worries, Robert. I've got your back...And keep the rubber side down.*


Late that afternoon, Donn returns. The smile on his face is infectious. He asks me to spend a second night there at the bunkhouse. Because instead of pedaling Daedalus through the rain, alone, he wants me to ride into the city with his assistant, Alisha, in the big GMC Suburban, to the bike shop of my choice. "Think of it, as a wedding gift for your daughter," Donn explains, a patient look on his face and tears welling up in his eyes. Mine too.

WORKS CITED

"Adventure Cycling About." *Adventure Cycling Association*, 20 Dec. 2018, www.adventurecycling.org/about/. Accessed 15 Nov. 2021.

"Adventure Cycling Route Network." *Adventure Cycling Association*, 10 Nov. 2015, www.adventurecycling.org/routes-and-maps/adventure-cycling-route-network/. Accessed 20 Nov. 2021.

"April 20, 1999." *Www.acolumbinesite.com*, 21 Apr. 1999, www.acolumbinesite.com/event/summary.php.

Butler, Octavia E. *Parable of the Sower*. New York, Four Walls Eight Windows, 1993.

Canipe, Chris, and Travis Hartman. "A Timeline of Mass Shootings in the U.S." *Reuters*, 31 May 2021, graphics.reuters.com/USA-GUNS/MASS-SHOOTING/nmovardgrpa/.

"Columbine High School Memorial Service | C-SPAN.org." *Www.c-Span.org*, 1999, www.c-span.org/video/?122805-1/columbine-high-school-memorial-service. Accessed 19 Nov. 2021.

"Congressional Record, Volume 146 Issue 11 (Wednesday, February 9, 2000)." *Www.govinfo.gov*, www.govinfo.gov/content/pkg/CREC-2000-02-09/html/CREC-2000-02-09-pt1-PgS555-2.htm. Accessed 15 Nov. 2021.

Cullen, Dave. *Columbine*. New York, Twelve-Hachette Book Group, 2009.

"Earth Lodges: Homes of the Native Americans of the Great Plains Built with a Technique 6,000 Years Old." *Walls with Stories*, Timera Media, 7 Aug. 2017, www.wallswithstories.com/architecture/native-americans.html. Accessed 20 Nov. 2021.

Erickson, Wm. H. "The Report of Governor Bill Owens' Columbine Review Commission." May 2001.

Frisk, Howard. "Channeled Scablands." *The Seven Wonders of Washington State*, 2015, www.sevenwondersofwashington-state.com/the-channeled-scablands.html.

"Great Plains Trail Alliance." *Great Plains Trail Alliance*, www.greatplainstrail.org/. Accessed 19 Nov. 2021.

Guy, Andrew. "The Denver Post Online - Columbine - Tragedy and Recovery." *Extras.denverpost.com*, 30 Apr. 1999, extras.denverpost.com/news/shot0430d.htm. Accessed 16 Nov. 2021.

Haney, Chuck. "The Maturing of the Mah Daah Hey." *Adventure Cyclist*, Dec. 2019, www.adventurecycling.org/sites/default/assets/resources/20191201_MaahDaahHey_Haney.pdf. Accessed 19 Nov. 2021.

"Historical Museum at Fort Missoula." *Fortmissoulamuseum.org*, fortmissoulamuseum.org/exhibit/fort-missoula-alien-detention-center/. Accessed 21 Nov. 2021.

"Https://Ballotpedia.org/Colorado_Gun_Shows_Background_Checks,_Initiative_22_(2000)." *Ballotpedia.org*, Lucy Burns Institute, 2000. Accessed 17 Nov. 2021.

"Japanese Submarine I-25." *Wikipedia*, 3 Nov. 2021, en.wikipedia.org/wiki/Japanese_submarine_I-25. Accessed 21 Nov. 2021.

Lamb, David. *Over the Hills : A Midlife Escape across America by Bicycle*. New York, Times Books, 1996.

"Letter from John Adams to Abigail Adams, Post 12 May 1780." *Masshist.org*, 2021, www.masshist.org/digitaladams/archive/doc?id=L17800512jasecond. Accessed 15 Nov. 2021.

"Lewis and Clark . Native Americans. Mandan Indians | PBS." *Www.pbs.org*, www.pbs.org/lewisandclark/native/man.html.

Lichtman, Allan J. *Repeal the Second Amendment: The Case for a Safer America*. New York, St. Martin's Press, 2020.

"Mandan." *Wikipedia*, 24 Oct. 2020, en.wikipedia.org/wiki/Mandan,_Hidatsa,_and_Arikara_Nation. Accessed 20 Nov. 2021.

"National Rifle Association Convention | C-SPAN.org." *Www.c-Span.org*, 1 May 1999, www.c-span.org/video/?122961-1/national-rifle-association-convention. Accessed 16 Nov. 2021.

"Online Speech Bank: Al Gore - Speech at the Columbine Memorial Service." *Americanrhetoric.com*, 2008, www.americanrhetoric.com/speeches/algorecolumbine.htm. Accessed 19 Nov. 2021.

Penn, Robert. *It's All about the Bike: The Pursuit of Happiness on Two Wheels*. New York/London, Bloomsbury, 2012.

RIDDER/TRIBUNE, KNIGHT. "Still-Grieving Colorado Turns out to Protest NRA Meeting; Gun Group Remains Defiant as 8,000 Oppose Presence in Light of Columbine Tragedy." *Baltimoresun.com*, 5 May 1999, www.baltimoresun.com/news/bs-xpm-1999-05-02-9905020166-story.html.

"Robyn Anderson on Good Morning America (June 4, 1999)." *www.youtube.com*, www.youtube.com/watch?v=zSe7UV8DfJY. Accessed 15 Nov. 2021.

Shepard, C. "1999: Aftermath of the Columbine High Shootings." *Acolumbinesite.com*, 21 Apr. 1999, www.acolumbinesite.com/after/1999.php. Accessed 19 Nov. 2021.

Soraghen, Mike. "Voices of Columbine: The Denver Post Online." *Extras.denverpost.com*, 16 Apr. 2000, extras.denverpost.com/news/chs0416w.htm.

Tapper, Jake. "Coming out Shooting." *Salon*, 2 May 1999, www.salon.com/1999/05/02/nra/. Accessed 16 Nov. 2021.

"U.S. Army's 25th Infantry Bicycle Corps: Wheels of War." *HistoryNet*, 12 June 2006, www.historynet.com/us-armys-25th-infantry-bicycle-corps-wheels-of-war.htm. Accessed 15 Nov. 2021.

*US Bureau of Alcohol, Tobacco, Firearms, and Explosives, "Firearms Commerce in the United States: Annual Statistical Update 2020.*

van der Kolk, Bessel. *The Body Keeps the Score: Mind, Brain and Body in the Transformation of Trauma*. London, Penguin Books, 2014.

"Vietnam Lotteries." *Selective Service System*, www.sss.gov/history-and-records/vietnam-lotteries/.

Wikipedia Contributors. "Sacagawea." *Wikipedia*, Wikimedia
    Foundation, 4 Mar. 2019, en.wikipedia.org/wiki/Sa-
    cagawea. Accessed 20 Nov. 2021.
Wikipedia contributors. "103rd United States Congress." *Wiki-
    pedia*, 14 Nov. 2021, en.wikipedia.org/wiki/103rd_Unit-
    ed_States_Congress. Accessed 15 Nov. 2021.

## ACKNOWLEDGMENTS

Thank you, Marceil, my intuitive and loving wife, for living in partnership during all these transformative years. We met in 2003 during the aftermath of Columbine. The pandemic of COVID-19 has only made us stronger. Thank you, my love, for your continuing support during the writing of this manuscript.

Thank you, Lee, Ben, and Christen, for your willingness to appear as characters in this book; to be frozen in time during the turning of the last century. I am ever grateful for your trust.

Thank you, Kyle Velasquez for the enormity of your sacrifice. I have endeavored throughout the book to show compassion and respect in your memory. I am grateful to the surviving families of Columbine.

Thank you, my friends and colleagues who worked so tirelessly in both the County Attorney's Office and at Jeffco Human Services during all our years together: especially to Dorothy Threlkeld, Marilyn Ransdell, and Patricia Harpt for your continuing friendship, insights, and research assistance. Thanks too, to Jeffco Human Services' current leader, Mary Berg, with whom I shared many moments both during Columbine and after; and Lynnae Flora, for her willingness to consider this manuscript in terms of confidentiality issues and other feedback.

Thank you, beta readers Brent Green, Carol Orsborn, Mark Gilbert, Rene Feil, and Richard and Karen Parker, for your insights and thoughtful recommendations.

Thank you, writing friends and colleagues at Lighthouse Writers of Denver: Anne van Etten, Leslie Jamison, Courtney Morgan, John Arthur Neal, Kay Tolchin, Lynn Wagner, Mary Estill Buchanan, and Rachel Weaver, for your guidance with earlier versions of the manuscript. Special thanks to Emily Black, for her editing services during an important stage in the book's development, and for sharing her memories of living in Denver during and after Columbine.

After the supportive environment of Lighthouse, it felt like I was losing ground entering into the uncertain publishing world of query letters and online submissions. Until I found myself ensconced within another group of creative thinkers and writers at the Youngstown Lit Fest at Youngstown University during October 2021.

Thank you, Larry Smith, editor and publisher of Bottom Dog Press and Susanna Sharp-Schwacke for your interest in the manuscript and your dedicated support for it and the art of writing.

## ABOUT THE AUTHOR

JRW (Robert) Case is a Buckeye by birth, born and raised in Akron, Ohio. He now lives in Denver, Colorado, with his wife and partner, Marceil, and their mischievous Boston Terrier. Robert is also a life-long reader. When his bicycling journey across the USA began during the summer of 2017, the author did not yet realize that its path closely followed in reverse, a road trip taken by another author/father with his teenage son to inspire a 1974 best-seller, *Zen and The Art of Motorcycle Maintenance*, though Robert M. Piersig's earlier work glosses over its coming-of-age implications, describing its theme as an inquiry into values.

Decades later came the tragedy of Columbine with its profound and pervasive implications for us as persons and as a country. Case writes, "It felt like a heavy stone striking the placid waters of a quiet pond, sending out waves in all directions; all of them modulating in terms of size and energy, but impacting everything in their paths." The author and his family lived close by, and their lives would forever change. Robert worked then as a child protection attorney with a personal connection with one of the Columbine victims and deep ties to a community.

Once his children were grown and gone into their own lives, he began to make room for an hour or two of journaling each day before going to work. He was also drawn to acting and improv shows, culminating in the role of Morrie Schwartz in the community theater production of *Tuesdays with Morrie*. One by one, the stories and essays began to emerge from the author's pen, several of them good enough to share with his men's group or at church retreats. These seeds would grow into essays and into books. And now, this latest book, *Cycling Through Columbine*, establishes JRW Case as a bicycle poet-warrior of the literary world.

# BOOKS BY BOTTOM DOG PRESS

## HARMONY SERIES

Bottom Dog Press, Inc.
P.O. Box 425 /Huron, Ohio 44839
http://smithdocs.net

Printed in the USA
CPSIA information can be obtained
at www.ICGtesting.com
LVHW092314060924
790162LV00001B/26